It's About
Time

Kabbalistic Insights for Taking Charge of Your Life

ROSH CHODESH
society

Course Authors
Rabbi and Mrs. Zalman Moshe
and Leah Abraham

Curriculum Development Team
Rabbi Naftali Silberberg
Rabbi Mordechai Dinerman
Mrs. Chava Shapiro
Mrs. Shaindy Jacobson

Printed in U.S.A.

© Published and Copyrighted 2012 by
The Rohr Jewish Learning Institute
822 Eastern Parkway • Brooklyn, NY 11213
All rights reserved.

No part of the contents of this book
may be reproduced or transmitted in any form or by any means
without the written permission of the publisher.

(888) YOUR-JLI • 718-221-6900
www.myJLI.com

The **ROHR JEWISH LEARNING INSTITUTE**
gratefully acknowledges
the pioneering support of

GEORGE AND PAMELA ROHR

Since its inception
the Rohr JLI has been
a beneficiary of the vision,
generosity, care, and concern
of the Rohr family.

In the merit of the tens of thousands
of hours of Torah study
by JLI students worldwide,
may they be blessed with health,
Yiddishe nachas from all their loved ones,
and extraordinary success
in all their endeavors.

וַיִּקְרָא ה׳ אֶל שְׁמוּאֵל וַיֹּאמֶר הִנֵּנִי

— שמואל א ג:ד —

God called out to Shmuel,
and he responded,
"Here I am (*Hineni*)!"
—I Samuel 3:4

"Hineni!"
"This is how the pious respond to God's calling,
with humility and readiness."
—Rashi, Genesis 22:1

IN THE WAKE OF THE HOLOCAUST,
AS THE JEWISH PEOPLE ROSE FROM THE RUINS AND THE ASHES,

Mr. Shmuel (Sami) Rohr, of blessed memory,

heard God's calling. His response was a resounding *"Hineni!"*
With humility, selflessness, determination, and peerless commitment,
he established a family and served as a leading protagonist
in the renaissance of *Klal Yisrael* around the world.

THIS COURSE IS LOVINGLY DEDICATED
TO THE MEMORY OF

Mr. Shmuel (Sami) Rohr

ר׳ שמואל ב״ר יהושע אליהו ז״ל

PATRON AND BENEFACTOR OF MULTITUDES
OF TORAH INSTITUTIONS THE WORLD OVER
WHO PASSED AWAY ON

י״ז מנחם אב, ה׳תשע״ב

August 5, 2012

May the Torah study undertaken in his memory
by many thousands of JLI students worldwide,
whose study is inspired by his vision and generosity,
grant much nachas and menuchah to his neshamah
and be a source of comfort and inspiration to his esteemed family
who carry on his legacy with gezunt and menuchah.

לזכרון ולעילוי נשמת

ר׳ שמואל ב״ר יהושע אליהו ז״ל
רוהר

תנצב״ה

Table of Contents

It's About

Time

The Kabbalah of Sleep
How to Reenergize and Prioritize Your Life

ROSHCHODESH
society

Introduction

We all know how it feels after not getting a good night of sleep. We may snap at our spouse for something trivial, like not putting away the cereal box. We are less focused and motivated at work, and take far less pleasure in activities we normally enjoy. Indeed, several studies have linked sleep deprivation to poor work performance, driving accidents, relationship problems, and mood problems such as anger and depression. Unfortunately, there are nearly one hundred sleep disorders affecting millions of Americans. We might wonder: Wouldn't life be so much better if we didn't need sleep?

In this lesson, We will learn why we really do need sleep: not only to sustain our physical and emotional health, but the health of our souls as well. By the end of this lesson, it will be clear that this mysterious phenomenon of sleep is packed with spiritual meaning and has much to teach us about life—about the opportunities G-d gives us, our potential for growth, and our purpose in this world.

I. Why Do We Sleep?

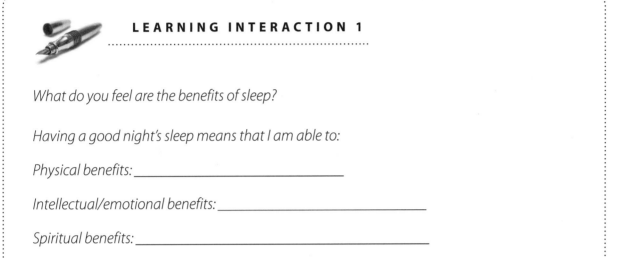

LEARNING INTERACTION 1

What do you feel are the benefits of sleep?

Having a good night's sleep means that I am able to:

Physical benefits: _____

Intellectual/emotional benefits: _____

Spiritual benefits: _____

Text 1

We don't really know why we need to sleep in the first place. We know we miss it if we don't have it. And we know that no matter how much we try to resist it, sleep conquers us in the end. We know that seven to nine hours after giving in to sleep, most of us are ready to get up again, and 15 to 17 hours after that we are tired once more. . . .

All this downtime comes at a price. An animal must lie still for a great stretch of time, during which it is easy prey for predators. What can possibly be the payback for such risk? "If sleep doesn't serve an absolutely vital function," the renowned sleep researcher Allan Rechtschaffen once said, "it is the greatest mistake evolution ever made." . . .

At Stanford University, I visited William Dement, the retired dean of sleep studies, a codiscoverer of REM sleep, and cofounder of the Stanford Sleep Medicine Center. I asked him to tell me what he knew, after 50 years of research, about the reason we sleep. "As far as I know," he answered, "the only reason we need to sleep that is really, really solid is because we get sleepy."

D.T. Max, "The Secrets of Sleep," *National Geographic Magazine,* May 2010

Text 2

אָדָם לְעָמָל יוּלָד.

איוב ה,ז

Human beings are born to toil.

Iyov/Job 5:7

II. The Excitement of Renewal

Question for Discussion

For a moment, imagine that you did not need any sleep to function—that you could live your entire life awake and never get tired. How might you describe a life with no sleep?

Text 3

יִתְגַּבֵּר כָּאֲרִי לַעֲמוֹד בַּבֹּקֶר לַעֲבוֹדַת בּוֹרְאוֹ,
שֶׁיְהֵא הוּא מְעוֹרֵר הַשָּׁחַר.

שולחן ערוך, אורח חיים א,א

Strengthen yourself like a lion to rise in the morning to serve your Creator. You should awaken the morning.

Rabbi Yosef Caro, *Shulchan Aruch, Orach Chayim* 1:1

III. Letting Go of Yesterday

Text 4

The sun'll come out tomorrow.
Bet your bottom dollar that tomorrow, there'll be sun.
Just thinkin' about tomorrow
Clears away the cobwebs and the sorrow till there's none.

When I'm stuck with a day that's gray and lonely,
I just stick out my chin, and grin and say:

The sun'll come out tomorrow.
So you've got to hang on till tomorrow, come what may.
Tomorrow! Tomorrow! I love you, tomorrow!
You're always a day away.

"Tomorrow," *Annie*, lyrics by Martin Charnin, 1976

Text 5a

בָּרוּךְ אַתָּה ה', אֱלֹקֵינוּ מֶלֶךְ הָעוֹלָם, אֲשֶׁר יָצַר אֶת הָאָדָם בְּחָכְמָה, וּבָרָא בוֹ נְקָבִים נְקָבִים, חֲלוּלִים חֲלוּלִים. גָּלוּי וְיָדוּעַ לִפְנֵי כִסֵּא כְבוֹדֶךָ, שֶׁאִם יִפָּתֵם אֶחָד מֵהֶם, אוֹ אִם יִפָּתֵחַ אֶחָד מֵהֶם, אִי אֶפְשָׁר לְהִתְקַיֵּם אֲפִלּוּ שָׁעָה אֶחָת. בָּרוּךְ אַתָּה ה', רוֹפֵא כָל בָּשָׂר וּמַפְלִיא לַעֲשׂוֹת.

ברכת השחר, סדור תהלת ה'

Blessed are You, Lord our God, King of the universe, who has formed the human being with wisdom, and created within the human being numerous orifices and cavities. It is revealed and known before the throne of Your glory that if but one of them were to be blocked, or if one of them were to be opened, it would be impossible to exist, even for a short while. Blessed are You, Lord, who heals all flesh and performs wonders.

Siddur Tehilat Hashem, Morning Blessings

Question for Discussion

Why do you think it is necessary to repeat *Asher Yatzar* blessing every day?

Text 5b

נָהֲגוּ הָעוֹלָם לְבָרֵךְ בְּכָל שַׁחֲרִית . . . בִּרְכַּת אֲשֶׁר יָצַר, לְפִי שֶׁבְּכָל יוֹם נַעֲשָׂה הָאָדָם בְּרִיָּה חֲדָשָׁה, לָכֵן שַׁיָּךְ לְבָרֵךְ בְּכָל יוֹם וָיוֹם, "אֲשֶׁר יָצַר אֶת הָאָדָם בְּחָכְמָה".

שולחן ערוך הרב, אורח חיים ו,א

It is customary to recite every morning . . . the asher yatzar blessing. Every day, a person becomes a new creation. Therefore, it is appropriate to recite daily the blessing, "Who has formed the human being with wisdom."

Rabbi Shne'ur Zalman of Liadi, *Shulchan Aruch HaRav, Orach Chayim* 6:1

Text 6

בָּשָׂר וָדָם, מַפְקִידִים בְּיָדוֹ חֲדָשִׁים, וְהוּא מַחֲזִירָן בְּלוּיִים וּשְׁחָקִים. אֲבָל הַקָּבָּ"ה, מַפְקִידִים בְּיָדוֹ בְּלוּיִים וּשְׁחוּקִים, וְהוּא מַחֲזִירָן חֲדָשִׁים..

מדרש תהלים כה

When one deposits a new item with another person for safekeeping, the person returns it worn and old. But with regard to God, we deposit our soul worn and torn, and He returns it to us new.

Midrash Tehilim 25

Text 7

דְּבְכָל לֵילְיָא וְלֵילְיָא, עַד לֹא יִשְׁכַּב וְעַד לֹא נָאִים, בָּעֵי בַּר נָשׁ לְמֶעְבַּד חוּשְׁבְּנָא מֵעוֹבָדוֹי דְּעָבַד כָּל הַהוּא יוֹמָא, וִיתוּב מִנַּיְהוּ, וְיִבְעֵי עֲלֵיהוּ רַחֲמֵי.

זוהר ג קעח,א

Each and every night before one goes to sleep, one should make an accounting of all the deeds they did that day. One should repent and ask for mercy.

Zohar 3:178a

Text 8

רִבּוֹנוֹ שֶׁל עוֹלָם: הֲרֵינִי מוֹחֵל לְכָל מִי שֶׁהִכְעִים וְהִקְנִיט אוֹתִי אוֹ שֶׁחָטָא כְּנֶגְדִּי, בֵּין בְּגוּפִי, בֵּין בְּמָמוֹנִי, בֵּין בִּכְבוֹדִי, בֵּין בְּכָל אֲשֶׁר לִי, בֵּין בְּאֹנֶס, בֵּין בְּרָצוֹן, בֵּין בְּשׁוֹגֵג, בֵּין בְּמֵזִיד, בֵּין בְּדִבּוּר, בֵּין בְּמַעֲשֶׂה . . .

יְהִי רָצוֹן מִלְּפָנֶיךָ, ה' אֱלֹקַי וֵאלֹקֵי אֲבוֹתַי, שֶׁלֹּא אֶחֱטָא עוֹד, וְלֹא אֶחֱזוֹר בָּהֶם, וְלֹא אָשׁוּב עוֹד לְהַכְעִיסֶךָ, וְלֹא אֶעֱשֶׂה הָרַע בְּעֵינֶיךָ, וּמַה שֶּׁחָטָאתִי מְחֹק בְּרַחֲמֶיךָ הָרַבִּים, וְלֹא עַל יְדֵי יִסּוּרִים וַחֲלָיִים רָעִים.

קריאת שמע על המטה, סידור תהלת ה'

Master of the universe! I hereby forgive anyone who has angered or vexed me, or sinned against me, either physically or financially, against my honor or against anything else that belongs to me, whether accidentally or intentionally, inadvertently or deliberately, by speech or by deed. . . .

May it be Your will, Lord my God and God of my fathers, that I shall transgress no more nor repeat my wrongdoing, that I shall never again anger You, nor do what is wrong in Your eyes. In Your abounding mercies, erase my iniquities, but not through suffering or severe illnesses.

May the words of my mouth and the meditation of my heart be acceptable before You, Lord, my Strength and my Redeemer.

Siddur Tehilat Hashem, Prayer Before Retiring at Night

 Question for Discussion

In this prayer, we abandon any resentment toward others who wronged us. Why is it important to forgive before going to sleep?

IV. You Grow in Your Sleep

Text 9

יָדוּעַ הַהֶפְרֵשׁ בֵּין מַלְאָכִים וּנְשָׁמוֹת, שֶׁמַּלְאָכִים נִקְרָאִים עוֹמְדִים, וּנְשָׁמוֹת נִקְרָאִים מְהַלְכִים . . .

וְהַיְינוּ שֶׁאַף עַל פִּי שֶׁגַּם עֲבוֹדַת הַמַּלְאָכִים הִיא בְּאוֹפָן שֶׁל עֲלִיָּה לְדַרְגָּא בְּהַשָּׂגַת אֱלֹקוּת וּבְהִתְפַּעֲלוּת הָאַהֲבָה וְיִרְאָה, מִכָּל מָקוֹם, עֲלִיָּה זוֹ הִיא בְּסֵדֶר וְהַדְרָגָה. וְהַיְינוּ שֶׁגַּם בַּעֲלִיָּיתָם לְמַדְרֵיגָה נַעֲלֵית יוֹתֵר יֵשׁ לָהֶם שַׁיְיכוּת לְמַדְרֵיגָה הַקוֹדֶמֶת. וְלָכֵן נִקְרָאִים בְּשֵׁם עוֹמְדִים, כִּי הָעֲלִיָּה שֶׁלָהֶם הִיא בִּבְחִינַת גְּבוּל. וְרַק הַנְשָׁמוֹת נִקְרָאִים מְהַלְכִים שֶׁעֲלִיָּיתָם הִיא בִּבְחִינַת בְּלִי גְבוּל.

ספר המאמרים תשכ"ז, ע' רפז

The difference between angels and people is as follows: Angels are called "standers," whereas people are called "walkers."...

Angels constantly grow in their service of God. They are constantly enhancing their comprehension of God and their love and awe of Him. Nevertheless, their manner of growth is incremental. When they reach a higher rung, they are still connected to the previous one. Thus, they are called "standers." Only human beings can experience radical, even infinite growth. Therefore, they are called "walkers."

Rabbi Menachem Mendel Schneerson, *Sefer Hama'amarim* 5727, p. 287

Text 10

שֶׁלְּאַחֲרֵי שֶׁמַרְגִּיל אֶת עַצְמוֹ בַּעֲבוֹדָה מְסוּיֶּימֶת עַד שֶׁנַּעֲשֵׂית אֶצְלוֹ כְּמוֹ טֶבַע, צָרִיךְ לְהוֹסִיף חִידוּשׁ בַּעֲבוֹדָתוֹ בְּאוֹפָן שֶׁלְּמַעֲלָה מֵרְגִילוּתוֹ . . .

כַּאֲשֶׁר עֲבוֹדַת הָאָדָם בְּהַשִּׁימוּשׁ לְקוֹנוֹ עַל יְדֵי לִימוּד הַתּוֹרָה וְקִיוּם הַמִּצְווֹת הִיא לְלֹא הֶפְסֵק הַמּוּכְרָח מִצַּד טֶבַע הַבְּרִיאָה (כְּמוֹ הַהֶפְסֵק דְּשֵׁינָה), לֹא נִיכָּר בְּהַנְגָּשָׁה כָּל כָּךְ הַחִידוּשׁ בַּעֲבוֹדָתוֹ, לִהְיוֹתָהּ בְּאוֹפָן תְּמִידִי . . . וְעַל פִּי זֶה יֵשׁ לְבָאֵר טַעַם לִבְרִיאַת הָאָדָם בְּאוֹפָן שֶׁבְּכָל יוֹם וָיוֹם צָרִיךְ לִישׁוֹן וּלְמָחֳרַת נַעֲשֶׂה "בְּרִיָה חֲדָשָׁה"—כְּדֵי לְהַדְגִּישׁ הַחִידוּשׁ שֶׁבַּעֲבוֹדָתוֹ.

תורת מנחם תש"נ, ח"ד, ע' 92

> > >

Once a person has become accustomed to a specific pattern of behavior, one must strive to reach a new and higher peak. . . .

This new dimension of service is reflected in the fact that each day, one's activity is interrupted through sleeping, and one awakens the next morning as a new creation. . . . Were a person to continue the study of Torah and fulfillment of mitzvot without interruption, this newness would not be perceived. Because one's service would be constant, any increase would follow as a natural and gradual progression, rather than as a radical change.

Torat Menachem 5750, 4:92

LEARNING INTERACTION 2

In what areas of my life can I grow incrementally? What areas of my life could use a paradigm shift, or "quantum" growth?

_____

_____

_____

V. Why Is This Day Different? (Optional Section)

Question for Discussion

Why is it necessary for G-d to constantly renew the work of creation?

> ### Text 11
>
> הַמְחַדֵּשׁ בְּטוּבוֹ בְּכָל יוֹם תָּמִיד מַעֲשֵׂה בְרֵאשִׁית.
>
> ברכת קריאת שמע, סידור תהלת ה'
>
> *He renews the work of creation in His goodness constantly, every day.*
>
> *Siddur Tehilat Hashem*, Blessings preceding the *Shema* prayer

Question for Discussion

How might you act/live differently, knowig that each day is sustained by a unique Divine energy?

> ### Text 12
>
> וּבְכָל שָׁנָה וְשָׁנָה יוֹרֵד וּמֵאִיר . . . אוֹר חָדָשׁ וּמְחוּדָשׁ שֶׁלֹּא הָיָה מֵאִיר עֲדַיִין מֵעוֹלָם . . . וּבִפְרָטֵי פְרָטִיּוֹת כֵּן הוּא בְּכָל יוֹם וָיוֹם.
>
> תניא, אגרת הקודש יד
>
> *Each year, a new and renewed light . . . that has never yet shone descends and shines. . . . In fact, this takes place every single day.*
>
> Rabbi Shne'ur Zalman of Liadi, *Tanya, Igeret Hakodesh* 14

VI. Revitalizing the Soul

Text 13

הַנְּשָׁמָה הַזּוֹ מְמַלְּאָה אֶת כָּל הַגּוּף, וּבְשָׁעָה שֶׁאָדָם יָשֵׁן, הִיא עוֹלָה וְשׁוֹאֶבֶת לוֹ חַיִּים מִלְמַעֲלָה.

מדרש, בראשית רבה יד,ט

The soul fills the body, and when a person sleeps, it ascends and draws life from above.

Midrash, *Bereishit Rabah* 14:9

VII. Lesson Conclusion

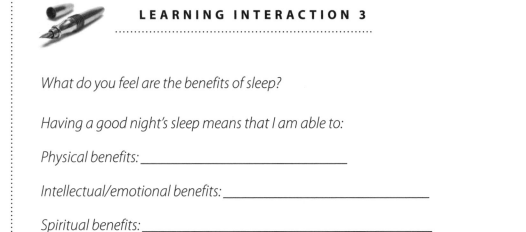

LEARNING INTERACTION 3

What do you feel are the benefits of sleep?

Having a good night's sleep means that I am able to:

Physical benefits: _____

Intellectual/emotional benefits: _____

Spiritual benefits: _____

Key Points

1 Having a break in consciousness to sleep affords us the opportunity to feel renewed excitement for life with each new day. To fully reap this benefit, we must consciously strive to wake up purposefully, like a lion, eager and ready to face a new day.

2 As human beings, we have our failings and regrets. The new beginning that sleep affords us is the opportunity let go of the past and obtain a fresh start. Thus, we repent and forgive other human beings before retiring.

3 A person ought to strive for tremendous spiritual growth. Sleep underscores the concept that today's accomplishments should be novel and monumental compared to those of yesterday.

4 According to Kabbalah, each day brings forth a unique spiritual energy. Each day is inherently new, and sleep allows us to tap into this.

5 Sleep is more a means to these ends. Sleep has an essential spiritual value for the soul. The soul returns to its source during sleep, to revitalize and refocus on its mission. In a similar vein, reciting the bedtime *Shema* helps us prioritize what is important to us, and helps us reconnect with our life's mission.

6 During this time of exile, when G-dliness is not revealed, we are said to be spiritually "sleeping." Just as physical sleep allows us to live more meaningful and productive lives, so too, this time of exile inspires us to be spiritually "awake" and in tune with our Divine mission.

Bibliography

Text 3 – Rabbi Yosef Caro (1488–1575). Born in Spain, fled the country with his family during the expulsion in 1492, and eventually settled in Safed, Israel. Also known as "the Beit Yosef," after the title of his commentary on the *Arba'ah Turim*, and Maran ("our master") for his status as a preeminent authority on Jewish law. Author of 10 works on Jewish law and the Torah, including the *Beit Yosef*, *Kesef Mishneh*, and a mystical work, *Magid Meisharim*. Rabbi Caro's magnum opus, the *Shulchan Aruch* (Code of Jewish Law), has been universally accepted as the basis for modern Jewish law.

Text 5b – Rabbi Shne'ur Zalman of Liadi (1745–1812). Chasidic rebbe and founder of the Chabad movement, also known as "the Alter Rebbe" and "the Rav." Born in Liozna, Belarus, he was among the principal students of the Magid of Mezeritch. His numerous works include the *Tanya*, an early classic containing the fundamentals of Chasidism; *Torah Or; Likutei Torah*; and *Shulchan Aruch HaRav*, a reworked and expanded code of Jewish law. He is interred in Hadiach, Ukraine, and was succeeded by his son, Rabbi Dovber of Lubavitch.

Text 7 - Zohar. The most seminal work of Kabbalah, Jewish mysticism. It is a mystical commentary on the Torah, written in Aramaic and Hebrew. According to Arizal, the Zohar consists of the teachings of Rabbi Shimon bar Yocha'i who lived in the Land of Israel during the 2nd century. The Zohar has become one of the indispensable texts of traditional Judaism, alongside and nearly equal in stature to the Mishnah and Talmud.

Text 9 – Rabbi Menachem Mendel Schneerson (1902–1994). Known as 'the Lubavitcher Rebbe," or simply as "the Rebbe." Born in southern Ukraine. Rabbi Schneerson escaped from the Nazis, arriving in the U.S. in June 1941. The towering Jewish leader of the 20th century, the Rebbe inspired and guided the revival of traditional Judaism after the European devastation, and often emphasized that the performance of just one additional good deed could usher in the era of Mashiach.

Text 13 – Midrash Bereishit Rabah is an early rabbinic commentary on the Book of Genesis, bearing the name of Rabbi Oshiya Rabah (Rabbi Oshiya "the Great") whose teaching opens this work. This *midrash* provides textual exegeses and stories, expounds upon the biblical narrative, and develops and illustrates moral principles. Thought to be the earliest non-halachic *midrash* extant, it was produced by the sages of the Talmud in the Land of Israel, its Aramaic closely resembling that of the Jerusalem Talmud. It was first published in Constantinople in 1512 together with four other midrashic works on the other four books of the Pentateuch.

Additional Readings

A Refreshing Death

Every day, some 43,200,000,000 man-hours are slept down the drain.

That's 6 billion individuals, each sleeping an average of 7.2 hours every calendar day. One might argue that slumbered time is our most wasted resource.

Indeed, why spend 25 to 30 percent of our lives doing nothing? Why sleep?

To many of the planet's sleepers, this may seem a pointless question. Why sleep? Because our body demands it of us. Because that is how we are physiologically constructed---that we require so many hours of rest each day in order to function. But to the Jew, there are no pointless questions. If G-d created us a certain way, there is a reason. He could just as easily have created us without the need for sleep, so that every moment of our lives could be put to constructive use. If our active hours must always be preceded by the minor death of sleep, there is a lesson here, a truth that is fundamental to the nature of human achievement.

Growing By Leaps

Another intrinsic fact of life is growth. In the first two decades of life, our growth is at its most real and tangible. We daily gain knowledge and experience. We can even gage our growth by inches of height gained per year or by the steady maturing of our bodies. But growth is a lifetime endeavor. Indeed, it can be said that there is no stasis in life: that the mind that ceases to learn, forgets what it has learned in the past; that the heart that ceases to develop new feelings, atro-

phies emotionally. That in every area of life, one who ceases to progress, regresses.

However, there are two types of growing. One growth is a progressional growth, a growth in which each gain is based upon, and is proportional to, our past achievements. Here the past develops into the future, improving and perfecting itself in the process.

But there also exists another type of growth--a growth that is a complete departure from the past. A growth that is a leap upward for something that is beyond relation to all that has been previously achieved. For we have the capacity to not only improve but also transcend ourselves. To open a new chapter in life that is neither predicted nor enabled by what we did and were up until now. To free ourselves of yesterday's constraints and build a new, recreated self.

This is what the void of sleep contributes to our lives. If we didn't sleep, there would be no tomorrow--life would be a single, seamless "today." If we didn't sleep, our every thought and deed would be an outgrowth of all our previous thoughts and deeds. There would be no new beginnings in our lives, for the very concept of a "new beginning" would be utterly alien to us. If we did not experience the obliterating passivity of sleep, we could not possibly conceive of a break from the past.

Because we sleep, we are accorded what is perhaps the greatest gift of life: morning.

Based on an address by the Rebbe, Av 6, 5750 (July 28, 1990. Sefer Hasichot pp. 596-599) and on other ocassions.

Reprinted with permission from meaningfullife.com

Waking Moment

I offer thanks to You, O living and everlasting king, for having restored my soul within me; great is Your faithfulness

Our first conscious act of the day is to avow our indebtedness and gratitude to our Creator. As soon as we wake from sleep, before getting out of bed or even washing our hands,[1] we recite the above-quoted lines of the *Modeh Ani* prayer, acknowledging that it is He who grants us life and being every moment of our existence.

The ideas contained in the ostensibly simple lines of *Modeh Ani* fill many a profound chapter in the legal, philosophical and mystical works of Torah. They touch upon the omnipresence and all-pervasiveness of G-d; on the principle of "perpetual creation" (G-d's constant infusion of vitality and existence into the world, without which it would revert to utter nothingness); on the laws governing the return of a *pikadon* (an object entrusted to one's care) and on the Kabbalistic concept of *Sefirat HaMalchut* (the divine attribute of Sovereignty).[2] So why is the *Modeh Ani* said immediately upon waking, with a mind still groggy from sleep? Would it not have been more appropriate to precede it with a period of study and contemplation of these concepts?

Night and Day

The physiology of our bodies and the rhythm of the astral clocks partition our lives into conscious and supra-conscious domains. During our waking hours, our mind assumes control of our thoughts and actions, screening, filtering and interpreting the stimuli that flow to it, and issuing commands and instructions to the body. But at night, when we sleep, the "command-center" shifts to a deeper, darker place within our psyche—a place where fantasy supersedes logic, sense supplants thought, and awareness is replaced by a more elemental form of knowing. Hard facts become pliant, absurdities become tenable, in this nocturnal world.

There are certain truths, however, that are unaffected by these fluctuations of knowledge and awareness. Our faith in G-d, His centrality to our existence, the depth of our commitment to Him—we know these things utterly and absolutely, and we know them at all times and in all states of consciousness.[3]

Wakefulness and sleep affect only the external activity of the intellect; what we know with the very essence of our being, we know no less when plunged into the deepest recesses of slumber. On the contrary: when awake, we must wade through the presuppositions and polemics of an intellect shackled to the "realities" of the physical state in order to arrive at these truths; asleep, our mind loosened from its subjective moorings, we enjoy a closer and deeper (albeit less conscious) awareness of our innermost convictions.

The *Modeh Ani* prayer exploits a most unique moment of our day—the moment that lies at the threshold of wakefulness, the moment that straddles the conscious and supra-conscious domains of our day. There are other moments, other prayers, in the course of our day which take full advantage of our powers of intellect and reasoning—prayers that follow lengthy and profound meditations upon their content and significance. But each morning, as we move from the liberating hours of sleep to a day of conscious thought, a most unique opportunity presents itself: the opportunity to express to ourselves a truth that inhabits our deepest selves, to declare what we already know to the awaiting day.

----

1) The *Modeh Ani* prayer does not contain any of the names of G-d, referring to Him instead as the "living and everlasting king." It is for this reason that we may recite it before washing our hands in the morning, when it is forbidden to say any "words of holiness." Chassidic teaching explains that this does not mean that *Modeh Ani* is less a communication with G-d than the other, "holier" prayers. On the contrary: it addresses the very essence of G-d, which transcends all divine "names" and descriptions—including the concept of, and the conditions required for, "holiness."

2) See the Rebbe's essay, *On The Essence of Chassidus* (Kehot, 1978).

3) Maimonides makes this the basis for a *halachic* ruling in the section on the Laws of Divorce of his codification of Torah law, the Mishneh Torah. At issue is the seemingly oxymoronic question of whether a person can be forced to perform a certain action "willingly." According to Torah law, the marriage bond is created by an act of the husband; consequently, in the case of divorce it is he who dissolves the marriage by handing a writ of divorce (*get*) to his wife. If the woman petitions for divorce, the court is authorized to obligate the man to grant her a *get*. Should he refuse to comply, the court is empowered to coerce him to do so. But since a *get* is valid only when granted willingly, the court must also force him to say, "I am willing." Yet what significance can his declaration possibly have? If the court is authorized to enforce the divorce, why demand the statement? And if his consent is truly needed, can words so obviously mouthed under duress be regarded as "consent" on his part?

Maimonides explains: As a Jew, this person "wishes to be of Israel, wishes to observe all the commandments and avoid all of the transgressions of the Torah; only his evil inclination has overpowered him. So if he is beaten so that his evil inclination is weakened, and he says, 'I am willing,' he is considered to have divorced willingly" as his declaration is consistent with his true, inner will (Mishneh Torah, *Laws of Divorce* 2:20).

Reprinted with permission from meaningfullife.com

The Philosophy of Sleep

By Nechoma Greisman; edited by Rabbi Moshe Miller

Many have the custom to stay up late on Shavuot night and read the *Tikkun LeilShavuot*, selections from the entire Torah, including the Five Books of Moses, the Prophets and Writings,*Mishnah* , Talmud, *Zohar*, and so on. Some people do not recite the *Tikkun* but simply study the entire night, until morning.

What is the reason for this custom that *we* stay up very late on Shavuot, or don't sleep at all? The *Midrash*states that the night before the Giving of the Torah, the Jewish people went to sleep. Why did they go to sleep the night before getting the Torah? "Because sleeping on Shavuot night is sweet, and the night is short!" The *Midrash* goes on to say that during that night a miracle occurred and mosquitoes did not bite them.

I don't know where you live, but where I live, in Kfar Chabad, we have a mosquito plague, and very often you wake up in the middle of the night — eeeee… You try and find that mosquito that's not letting you sleep. This can go on for hours. But that night, the mosquitoes didn't bother anybody. It was a very sweet and peaceful sleep.

When G-d came in the morning to give them the Torah, the *Midrash*continues, they were still sleeping. G-d says, "I came and there was no one; I called and there was no answer." G-d is ready to give them this great gift and everybody's asleep. G-d has to wake them up and he says,*Nu*, it's time to get the Torah.

This is what the *Midrash* states. But what does it mean? There's obviously more to it than meets the eye. The Rebbe points out that the Torah is always very, very careful about not saying a bad word. In other words, the Torah in general is very clear to do things in a positive way. When the Torah says something negative, such as calling an animal spiritually impure (*tameh*), this is only for the purpose of practical instruction. Where no practical instruction is intended, the Torah will go out of its way to use positive words.

The Torah describes impure animals as those "which are not pure," rather than as impure. But when it comes to matters pertaining to Kosher, when one has to know the law clearly, the Torah does use negative expressions. Normally, negative words do not have to cross your lips; use a euphemism, unless you have a specific reason to be blunt and explicit. For example, there is a very serious disease, a malignant disease, that one shouldn't call by its name, for that adds to its power. Or when you're talking about certain parts of life that are very intimate, you can talk about them in a way that people know what you mean, without being explicit.

Accordingly, why does the *Midrash* speak so disparagingly about the Jews before the receiving of the Torah? Let's say they didn't do such a good thing — is there any reason to publicize it so that all future generations will know how bad they were, that instead of waiting up eagerly for the Torah they went to sleep? That's not such a nice thing to say. The Torah could have overlooked it. What kind of teaching is it for us to know that our forefathers did something that isn't so great? After all, ever since then we're doing a *Tikkun* for it, we're trying to repair it, which means that it wasn't a good thing. So let's just say simply that they overslept a little, and we say *Tikkun*. But the *Midrash* goes into great detail.

Our sages go into all of the details for there are several lessons that can be learnt.

It just doesn't make sense that they went to sleep and overslept on that night, because we know that from the very day they came out of Egypt they started counting the days until Sinai. They started counting because of the excitement of looking forward to the Torah. It was a natural when one wants something one counts the days until it arrives. Our sages say that during each day of the seven weeks of the counting, the Jews in the desert, rose to a higher spiritual level. So you can imagine that by the time they reached the 49th day of counting and the 49th level of holiness, they were on a much higher level than they were the day they began the counting. On the night before they received the Torah, having reached a higher level of understanding and sensitivity — precisely now they went to sleep, and overslept?! It just doesn't make sense.

The Chassidic masters explain that G-d gave us a soul and he clothed the soul in a body. We are fully aware of the fact that our body is what we see and experience. When the soul leaves the body, the body remains a corpse, like a doll; there's nothing there. The body is essentially subservient to the soul. Now, even though there's a great purpose in living in this world in a body, for if there wasn't, G-d would not have created a world and would not have put us in the world, nevertheless, it is clear that the soul is in a sense confined within the body. There is a certain restraint that the soul must undergo because it is in a body. If the soul was not in a body it wouldn't have to stop serving G-d in order to eat and sleep and wash the dishes. There are certain needs that the body has that put a damper on what the soul would want to do twenty-four hours a day. So the body, in a sense, prevents the soul from expressing itself fully, and from serving G-d constantly. A person gets tired. A soul doesn't get tired. After a while you get bored.

You lose your train of thought. You can't concentrate any more. You need to sleep, you need to rest, you need to have your coffee. We're just human beings. So the body slows the soul down.

However, when a person sleeps, a totally different thing happens. During the time of sleep, even though the person is obviously still alive, the heart still beats and the person still breathes, nevertheless, a segment of the soul leaves the body during the time of sleep.

During sleep there is a loss of consciousness. One does not fully hear, nor speak, nor see. There is an idea of death, a whisper of death — the Talmud calls sleep one sixtieth of death. Many people die in their sleep. Because during sleep everything slows down. The heart, the respiration, everything functions at a much slower pace than when the person is awake. During sleep the soul that was inside the body rises to its source above.

During sleep, when the soul is free of the body, it can in a sense go higher and reach revelations that cannot happen during the day, when a person is awake. At Sinai, this was the intention of the Jews in going to sleep. They knew that they had been working for seven weeks to elevate themselves to be ready to receive the Torah. But all of their preparations had been done, in a sense, during the day when they were awake and conscious. And they felt that now that they had reached such a high level, maybe now, if we go to sleep, our souls will reach such a high level that we can get the Torah while asleep. For we will be on a much higher level than we can attain through our own efforts. This was the true intention. They were hoping that through their sleep they would be able to reach a level of holiness that would be much greater than they could reach on their own accord during the day.

This is what the *Midrash* explains: Their sleep on Shavuot night was very sweet. Sleep can only be great and holy and special if you are on the level of Shavuot, if you have done all the necessary preparations. Then you can go to sleep with the hope that great things will happen, that you will see great revelations during your sleep.

"The night was short." Here "night" alludes to concealment. We know that darkness, night, hides things. Have you ever tried looking for your glasses in the middle of the night and then in the morning, there they are just by your night table, two inches away from your hand? At night you just grope and you can't find your slippers or anything. So what does the night do? The night doesn't change anything. It just hides things. You cannot see. In the day you see it all, it's so simple.

The Jews had reached a level where the concealment was minimal. They had almost overcome most of the night. There was still a bit of a night left but it was much shorter than it was when they started. So they felt, now we have done what we can do with daytime, let's see what sleeping can do for us.

G-d, in recognition of their good intentions said, "You know what? They're really so sincere that I will help them along by preventing the mosquitoes from biting." Had G-d been opposed to their sleeping He wouldn't have made this tremendous miracle that the mosquitoes which bit last night and the next night, all of a sudden this night didn't bite.

Why, then, do we recite the *Tikkun* year after year? Because G-d says, "I know what your idea was, but you made a little mistake. That's all. It was an innocent error. I'm not punishing." We don't see that there was any punishment. We don't see in the *Midrash* or in the Torah that there was ever any reprimand or any punishment meted out to them. The only thing G-d said is, "I want you to make a *Tikkun*. Don't do it again, and to remember that you shouldn't do it again, every year I want you to stay up."

What was their mistake? It was a very innocent error that many people still make today — that the ultimate purpose is the spiritual world, rather than the physical world. G-d , however, wanted a dwelling place in the lowest world, as the *Midrash* states. Actually, to make a dwelling place for G-d in this world was not possible until we received the Torah, and G-d annulled the decree separating spirituality and physicality, so that now even the physical can become spiritual through the service of Jews. Thus, their error was entirely understandable, for it took place before the Torah was given.

Prepare for Takeoff

How to go to sleep to be awake

By Tzvi Freeman

Skill testing question:

Which of these two will be better able to focus on *tefillah* - prayer
and thereby have a great day:

Activity	Goldstein	Goldberg
Retiring to bed	Falls asleep watching a rerun of *Brain Dead* while washing down pizza with cola on the couch.	Mentally reviews the day, says the Shema Yisrael, falls asleep in bed reading Baal Shem Tovstories.
Waking up	Rudely awakened by e-mail alert. Checks more e-mail and stock report before falling back asleep. Repeats until resigning himself to getting off the couch.	Wakes up by circadian rhythm. Says Modeh Ani as approaching consciousness. Smiles when recalling Baal Shem Tov dreams.
Washing up	Jumps off the couch in frenzied panic. Grabs mug, car keys and cellphone charger. Runs frantically to the car.	Gently slides out of bed to greet the sunrise. Washes, takes care of bodily necessities and gets dressed. Washes hands and says morning blessings.
Breakfast	Stumbles into Starbucks on the way to shul to grab a hyper-caffeinated brew. Gets into a yelling match with the attendant over the bill / change / brew / temperature / politics / whatever.	Sips a hot drink while engaged in a half-hour Tanya class with the rabbi.

Meditation	Listens to news and traffic report on car radio while sipping coffee, texting clients and hurling imprecations at fellow drivers.	Sits quietly, pondering the morning lesson. Visualizes the continuous act of creation unfolding about us.
Prayers	Takes care of some business decisions by cellphone while the *minyan* "warms up." Jumps in late but catches up in no time. Sticks around to chat, then runs out in yet another mad rush.	Phone is on buzz. Starts with the *minyan*, saying each word out loud. Ignores the buzzes.

Where Is Your Launching Pad?

In the last installment, we spoke about the order of prayer as a four-runged ladder. We know where the top of our ladder leans: on a state of awe, joy and reverence, a place where a sharing of innermost desire with the Infinite can occur. Simple enough. Now, where do we plant the bottom of the ladder? In other words, what are the first humble steps that lead to the ultimate high? Where is our launching pad and what does it look like?

Well, here it is: A Bed!

Why a bed? Because everything that happens during your today relies on two crucial factors: how you get into that bed, and how you get out of it.

When you open your eyes and get out of that bed, you are making your grand entry onto the stage of life. If you stumble out into the bright lights, not really sure whether you are still dreaming or whether this is really real, what lines are supposed to come next or what on earth you are doing here, you've bombed before you've started. Like an actor, you want to spend those precious, backstage moments priming yourself, getting into character, immersing yourself in the sum total of everything that will come next.

Problem is, you're entering your stage out of an unconscious state known as sleep—not a con-

ducive posture for deliberate preparation. Your only choice, then, is to do the pre-stage warmup before you retire. Most significantly, the last hour before bed, and especially the last five minutes. Wherever you put your head in those precious moments is where you're going to find it when you wake up.

The Caesar once summoned RabbiYehoshua ben Chanina, and said, "They say that you are very wise. Tell me what I will see in my dreams tonight!"

The rabbi said to him, "You will see that the Persians will enslave and plunder your kingdom. They will carry you off to their land in chains of gold!"

The Caesar thought about this the entire day, and at night that is what he dreamt.

King Shavor of Persia once summoned Shmuel—a wise rabbi who lived in Mesopotamia—and said, "They say you are very wise. Tell me what I will dream tonight!"

Shmuel replied, "You will see that the Romans come and they will take you captive. They will make you grind date pits in a golden mill."

The king thought about this the entire day, and at night that is what he dreamt.[1]

Aiming For Wakefulness

Where do you want your head to be when you wake up? Basically, you want it to be clear. You want it to be actually awake.

King David said, "I will wake the morning"—not that the morning woke him, but he woke the morning. Meaning that he was the proactive party who decided it was morning, rather than the morning dictating to him that he must be awake. You see, if you are only awake because it is morning, you are not really awake—you are sleepwalking. If it is morning because you are awake, however, then you are awake and in control.

Most people, you see, are not awake. They are simply not asleep. Not asleep is not the same as being awake. If you're not awake, you're not holding the steering wheel. You're not driving your world, your world is driving you. When you're awake, you have direction, purpose and meaning. When you're awake, there's an awareness, a knowledge that you are here, a character playing his part in a world much bigger than yourself that you did not make. When you're awake, in all that you do, you are aware that the Director/Producer of this drama is taking an intense interest in how you play out your part—and you act accordingly. And you find yourself speaking to Him, as well—in other words, you find you can pray.

The question then is, how do you go to sleep in order to be awake?

Reprinted with permission from the author and Chabad.org

It's About

Time

Rising Above
A Practical Guide to Emotional Mastery

ROSH**CHODESH**
society

Introduction

Our emotions flavor every scene, color, and interaction. They pull and prod us through life. On the wings of emotion, we soar rapidly to a degree that is the greatest envy of cold, methodical intellect. Emotions influence our reality: A friendly encounter in the morning cheers our day, attracts success, and breeds contagious enthusiasm that brightens our environment.

However, emotions do not only travel Heavenward. Left to their own devices, these expressions of our spirit can also become its fetters. Hatred claims to be as equally passionate as love, but love and hatred journey to utterly opposite destinations. Envy arrives all too naturally, but it damages our relationships. A sad news item in the morning can dampen our enthusiasm and slow us down considerably.

We are the mothers of our many emotions, but like children, our feelings require constant guidance as they develop. In this lesson, we will focus on an emotion that seems to exist primarily for us to tame: anger. If emotions in general have an inbuilt tendency to escalate out of control like a colt bolting through a stable-door left ajar, then anger is an expert racehorse. The faster and more furiously it charges, the more unpredictable and unstable the situation becomes.

What we will not deal with here is the kind of overwhelming rage that sometimes accompanies severe tragedy and injustice. Rather, we will focus on the small things in life that get under our skin and cause us to lose control momentarily—those things that, a few years (or even just minutes) later, seem miniscule and irrelevant.

Studying about anger management can teach us a lot about patience, about our potential, and about the mysterious ways in which the Creator masterfully guides the myriad happenings in our lives.

I. The Human Struggle

Text 1

עִקַּר מְצִיאַת הָאָדָם הוּא מִבְּחִינַת נֶפֶשׁ הַבַּהֲמִית וְהַמְּדַבֶּרֶת.

עץ חיים נ,ב

The human being is primarily comprised of the impulsive drive and the trait of rationality.

Rabbi Chaim Vital, *Etz Chayim* 50:2

Text 2

הַמֹּחַ שַׁלִּיט עַל הַלֵּב בְּתוֹלַדְתּוֹ וְטֶבַע יְצִירָתוֹ. שֶׁכָּךְ נוֹצַר הָאָדָם בְּתוֹלַדְתּוֹ, שֶׁכָּל אָדָם יָכֹל בִּרְצוֹנוֹ שֶׁבְּמוֹחוֹ לְהִתְאַפֵּק וְלִמְשׁוֹל בְּרוּחַ תַּאֲוָתוֹ שֶׁבְּלִבּוֹ, שֶׁלֹּא לְמַלֹּאת מִשְׁאֲלוֹת לִבּוֹ בְּמַעֲשֶׂה דִּבּוּר וּמַחֲשָׁבָה.

תניא, פרק יב

The mind rules over impulse by virtue of a human's inborn nature. Employing the mind's power of will, people can restrain themselves and control their emotional drives, preventing the heart's desires from manifesting in action, word, and thought.

Rabbi Shne'ur Zalman of Liadi, *Tanya*, ch. 12

LEARNING INTERACTION 1

Here are some common scenarios. First, picture what your instinctive reaction to each scenario might look like. Next, determine the best way to deal with each situation, given the luxury of forethought.

Scenario	How do you feel like reacting?	How should you respond?
Your boss loudly demeans you at work.		
You witness your child being bullied on the playground.		
You are being tailgated on the highway by an aggressive driver.		

Text 3

Emotions more or less begin inside two almond-shaped structures in our brains which are called the amygdala. The amygdala is the part of the brain responsible for identifying threats to our well-being, and for sending out an alarm when threats are identified that results in us taking steps to protect ourselves. The amygdala is so efficient at warning us about threats, that it gets us reacting before the cortex (the part of the brain responsible for thought and judgment) is able to check on the reasonableness of our reaction. In other words, our brains are wired in such a way as to influence us to act before we can properly consider the consequences of our actions.

This is not an excuse for behaving badly—people can and do control their aggressive impulses. . . . The prefrontal cortex of your brain, which is located just behind your forehead, can keep your emotions in proportion. If the amygdala handles emotion, the prefrontal cortex handles judgment. The left prefrontal cortex can switch off your emotions. It serves in an executive role to keep things under control.

Harry Mills, Ph.D., "Physiology of Anger" *www.mentalhelp.net*

Text 4

A driver's education teacher resigned after he was accused of having a student driver chase down a motorist who had cut them off and then punching the man.

David Cline, 36, quit yesterday after being suspended over the incident. . . .

"Here's a guy who's a very good teacher, and he does something that's less than wise," said William Morris, attorney for [victim] Macklin, 23. "We're very concerned about the Durham County school system losing a good teacher. It's our prayer that they will forgive his trespass." . . .

Cline, who was arrested and released on $400 bail, was charged with simple assault, punishable by up to 60 days in jail. . . .

Macklin, who allegedly suffered a bloody nose, wouldn't discuss the details, saying only, "This is an unfortunate thing that happened to me."

The incident occurred September 19 in Chapel Hill, about 20 miles from the high school.

Cline was teaching two female students how to drive when the other car cut them off, according to police. Cline instructed the student driver to chase down the car; they caught up to Macklin, and Cline got out and punched him, police said.

Macklin then took off, and the instructor allegedly had the student chase after him again.

When Cline's car was pulled over for speeding, Macklin pulled up to tell the officer what had happened, police said.

Estes Thompson, "Driver's Ed Teacher Quits After 'Road Rage' Incident," *Associated Press*, Oct. 16, 1997

II. The Pitfalls of Anger

Text 5a

אַל תְּבַהֵל בְּרוּחֲךָ לִכְעוֹס, כִּי כַעַס בְּחֵיק כְּסִילִים יָנוּחַ.

קהלת ז,ט

Be not hasty with your spirit to become wrathful, for wrath lies in the bosom of fools.

Kohelet/Ecclesiastes 7:9

Text 5b

רַגְזָן לֹא עָלְתָה בְּיָדוֹ אֶלָּא רַגְזָנוּתָא.

תלמוד בבלי, קידושין מ,ב–מא,א

An angry person is left with nothing but anger.

Talmud, Kidushin 40b-41a

Text 5c

הַכַּעַס מִדָּה רָעָה הִיא עַד לִמְאֹד, וְרָאוּי לְאָדָם שֶׁיִּתְרַחֵק מִמֶּנָּה עַד הַקָּצֶה הָאַחֵר, וְיִלְמַד עַצְמוֹ שֶׁלֹּא יִכְעַס וַאֲפִלּוּ עַל דָּבָר שֶׁרָאוּי לִכְעֹס עָלָיו . . .

וְאָמְרוּ, שֶׁכָּל הַכּוֹעֵס אִם חָכָם הוּא חָכְמָתוֹ מִסְתַּלֶּקֶת מִמֶּנּוּ, וְאִם נָבִיא הוּא נְבוּאָתוֹ מִסְתַּלֶּקֶת מִמֶּנּוּ, וּבַעֲלֵי כַעַס אֵין חַיֵּיהֶם חַיִּים.

לְפִיכָךְ צִוּוּ לְהִתְרַחֵק מִן הַכַּעַס עַד שֶׁיַּנְהִיג עַצְמוֹ שֶׁלֹּא יַרְגִּישׁ אֲפִלּוּ לַדְּבָרִים הַמַּכְעִיסִים. וְזוֹ הִיא הַדֶּרֶךְ הַטּוֹבָה.

משנה תורה, הלכות דעות ב,ג

> > >

Anger is an exceptionally negative trait. It is appropriate to distance oneself from it to the furthest extreme; a person should train oneself not to become angry, even when anger seems appropriate. . . .

Our sages said, regarding anger, that it strips wisdom from the wise and prophecy from the prophet, and that the life of the irate is not considered life at all.

The sages therefore taught that one should train oneself to keep away from anger to the point of not reacting, even to a situation that would normally provoke anger. This is the finest approach.

Maimonides, *Mishneh Torah*, Laws of Temperaments 2:3

Text 5d

The sages would thoroughly have approved of the modern concept of anger management. They did not like anger at all, and they reserved some of their sharpest language to describe it. . . . The verdict of Judaism is simple: Either we defeat anger or anger will defeat us.

Chief Rabbi Lord Jonathan Sacks, "Anger Management," *United Synagogue Daf Hashavua* 22:22, Vayakhel-Pekudei 5770

III. A Biblical Paradigm

Text 6

וּבָא הַמֶּלֶךְ דָּוִד עַד בַּחוּרִים, וְהִנֵּה מִשָּׁם אִישׁ יוֹצֵא מִמִּשְׁפַּחַת בֵּית שָׁאוּל וּשְׁמוֹ שִׁמְעִי בֶן גֵּרָא יֹצֵא יָצוֹא וּמְקַלֵּל. וַיְסַקֵּל בָּאֲבָנִים אֶת דָּוִד וְאֶת כָּל עַבְדֵי הַמֶּלֶךְ דָּוִד וְכָל הָעָם וְכָל הַגִּבֹּרִים מִימִינוֹ וּמִשְּׂמֹאלוֹ.

וְכֹה אָמַר שִׁמְעִי בְּקַלְלוֹ, "צֵא צֵא אִישׁ הַדָּמִים וְאִישׁ הַבְּלִיָּעַל. הֵשִׁיב עָלֶיךָ ה' כֹּל דְּמֵי בֵית שָׁאוּל אֲשֶׁר מָלַכְתָּ תַּחְתָּיו, וַיִּתֵּן ה' אֶת הַמְּלוּכָה בְּיַד אַבְשָׁלוֹם בְּנֶךָ, וְהִנְּךָ בְּרָעָתֶךָ כִּי אִישׁ דָּמִים אָתָּה".

וַיֹּאמֶר אֲבִישַׁי בֶּן צְרוּיָה אֶל הַמֶּלֶךְ, "לָמָּה יְקַלֵּל הַכֶּלֶב הַמֵּת הַזֶּה אֶת אֲדֹנִי הַמֶּלֶךְ, אֶעְבְּרָה נָּא וְאָסִירָה אֶת רֹאשׁוֹ".

וַיֹּאמֶר הַמֶּלֶךְ "מַה לִּי וְלָכֶם בְּנֵי צְרֻיָה, כֹּה יְקַלֵּל כִּי ה' אָמַר לוֹ קַלֵּל אֶת דָּוִד, וּמִי יֹאמַר מַדּוּעַ עָשִׂיתָה כֵּן . . . הַנִּחוּ לוֹ וִיקַלֵּל כִּי אָמַר לוֹ ה'. אוּלַי יִרְאֶה ה' בְּעֵינִי, וְהֵשִׁיב ה' לִי טוֹבָה תַּחַת קִלְלָתוֹ הַיּוֹם הַזֶּה".

וַיֵּלֶךְ דָּוִד וַאֲנָשָׁיו בַּדָּרֶךְ, וְשִׁמְעִי הֹלֵךְ בְּצֵלַע הָהָר לְעֻמָּתוֹ הָלוֹךְ וַיְקַלֵּל וַיְסַקֵּל בָּאֲבָנִים לְעֻמָּתוֹ וְעִפַּר בֶּעָפָר.

שמואל ב, טז,ה–יג

When King David came to Bahurim, behold, there came out from there a man of the family of the house of Saul, whose name was Shimi, the son of Gera. He came out, and kept on cursing as he came. He cast stones at David, and at all the king's servants, and all the people and all the mighty men were on his right hand and on his left.

So said Shimi in his curse, "Go away, go away, you man of blood and wicked fellow. The Lord has returned upon you all the blood of the house of Saul, in whose stead you have reigned. And the Lord has given the kingdom into the hands of Absalom your son, and behold you are taken by your own evil, for you are a man of blood."

> > >

Question for Discussion

How was King David able to respond this way? What steps can we learn from King David, to transcend our emotions when necessary?

Abishai the son of Zeruiah said to the king, "Why should this dead dog curse my lord the king? Let me go over, I beg you, and remove his head."

The king said, "What have I to do with you, sons of Zeruiah? Let him curse, because the Lord has [surely] said to him, 'Curse David.' Who then shall say, 'Why have you done so?'... Let him alone, and let him curse, for the Lord has bidden him. Perhaps the Lord will see [the tears of] my eye and the Lord will requite me with good for his cursing me on this day."

David and his men went by the road. Shimi went along the hillside opposite him, going and cursing, and he threw stones and earth toward him.

Shmuel II/II Samuel 16:5–13

Text 7

אֵיזֶהוּ גִבּוֹר? הַכּוֹבֵשׁ אֶת יִצְרוֹ, שֶׁנֶּאֱמַר (משלי טז,לב), "טוֹב אֶרֶךְ אַפַּיִם מִגִּבּוֹר, וּמֹשֵׁל בְּרוּחוֹ מִלֹּכֵד עִיר"

משנה, אבות ד,א

Who is mighty? He who overcomes his impulse, as it is stated (Mishlei/Proverbs 15:32), "Better is one who is slow to anger than a mighty person, and one who controls his spirit than the conqueror of a city."

Mishnah, Avot 4:1

Question for Discussion

How does overcoming an inner urge make one mightier than a conqueror of cities?

FIGURE 2.1

It is difficult to determine how to escape heated feelings while the storm is raging. Plan ahead. Think now of possible buffer-zone activities. This will increase the likelihood that you will actually take the much needed breather—and will also make the pause more effective. We have listed some ideas below (borrowed from *Emotional Healing for Dummies*, pp. 55 and 160); you may have your own thoughts of what will work best for you.

- Go for a walk.

- Listen to an upbeat / calming piece of music.

- Talk to a friend.

- Take 5–10 minutes to practice a six-breaths-a-minute breathing exercise.

- Picture an uplifting image and focus on it, such as a calm lake, a mountain or a sunset, or a cherished moment. Choose an image that makes you feel good and capture it in your mind, or carry a postcard or photo in your wallet.

- Change your breathing: Notice when you are breathing in your upper chest. Focus your thoughts on moving your breath down towards your stomach area. As you breathe, let your abdomen expand outwards. With every in-breath, think, "I am breathing in refreshing calm. "With every out-breath, sigh and think, "I am breathing out disturbing emotions."

- Change your thoughts: Thoughts influence both your feelings and breathing. Thinking "I can't cope!" or "I can't stand it!" makes you more anxious and disrupts your breathing and ability to think clearly. Take time to think calm thoughts such as, "I can manage this situation. I can work out what I need to say and how best to say it."

- Change your posture: Remember how your body feels when you are calm and confident. Let go of tension in your jaw, shoulders, hands, and wrists. Straighten your spine, allowing space in your belly for your calming breath.

Text 8

A woman was waiting at an airport one night,
With several long hours before her flight.
She hunted for a book in the airport shop,
Bought a bag of cookies, and found a place to drop.

She was engrossed in her book, but happened to see
That the man sitting beside her, as bold as could be,
Grabbed a cookie or two from the bag between,
Which she tried to ignore, to avoid a scene.

She read, munched cookies, and watched the clock,
As the gutsy "cookie thief" diminished her stock.
She was getting more irritated as the minutes ticked by,
Thinking, "If I wasn't so nice, I'd blacken his eye."

With each cookie she took, he took one too.
When only one was left, she wondered what he'd do.
With a smile on his face and a nervous laugh,
He took the last cookie and broke it in half.

He offered her half, as he ate the other.
She snatched it from him and thought, "Oh, brother,
This guy has some nerve and he's also rude!
Why he didn't even show any gratitude!"

She had never known when she had been so galled,
And sighed with relief when her flight was called.
She gathered her belongings and headed for the gate,
Refusing to look back at the "thieving ingrate."

> > >

She boarded the plane and sank in her seat,
Then sought her book, which was almost complete.
As she reached in her baggage, she gasped with surprise:
There were her cookies in front of her eyes!

"If mine are here," she moaned with despair,
"Then the others were his and he tried to share!"
Too late to apologize, she realized with grief,
That she was the rude one, the ingrate, the thief!

Valerie Cox, "The Cookie Thief," in Jack Canfield and Mark Victor Hansen, *A 3rd Serving of Chicken Soup for the Soul,* pp. 199–200

Text 9

וְאַל תָּדִין אֶת חֲבֵרְךָ עַד שֶׁתַּגִּיעַ לִמְקוֹמוֹ.

משנה, אבות ב,ד

Do not judge another until you have stood in that person's place.

Mishnah, Avot (op. cit.), 2:4

Text 10a

אָמְרוּ חֲכָמִים הָרִאשׁוֹנִים, "כָּל הַכּוֹעֵס כְּאִלּוּ עוֹבֵד עֲבוֹדַת כּוֹכָבִים".

משנה תורה, הלכות דעות ב,ג

The ancient sages declared, "If one becomes angry, it is as if one has served idols."

Mishneh Torah, Laws of Temperaments, 2:3 (op. cit.)

Question for Discussion

What is the correlation between anger and idolatry?

Text 10b

שֶׁבְּעֵת כַּעֲסוֹ נִסְתַּלְקָה מִמֶּנּוּ הָאֱמוּנָה. כִּי אִלּוּ הָיָה מַאֲמִין שֶׁמֵּאֵת ה' הָיְתָה זֹּאת לוֹ, לֹא הָיָה בְּכַעַם כְּלָל. וְאַף שֶׁבֶּן אָדָם שֶׁהוּא בַּעַל בְּחִירָה מְקַלְלוֹ אוֹ מַכֵּהוּ אוֹ מַזִּיק מָמוֹנוֹ וּמִתְחַיֵּב בְּדִינֵי אָדָם וּבְדִינֵי שָׁמַיִם עַל רֹעַ בְּחִירָתוֹ, אַף עַל פִּי כֵן עַל הַנִּזָּק כְּבָר נִגְזַר מִן הַשָּׁמַיִם, וְהַרְבֵּה שְׁלוּחִים לַמָּקוֹם.

תניא, אגרת הקודש כה

When one grows angry, his faith departs. If he would believe that whatever happened to him was orchestrated by God, he would not become angry at all. True, he is suffering from the curses, blows, or damage to his property being inflicted by a human being who possesses freedom of choice. That person is therefore guilty by the laws of man and the laws of Heaven for the evil he has chosen to inflict. Nevertheless, as far as the victim is concerned, this incident was already decreed in Heaven, and God has many agents.

Tanya (op. cit.), *Igeret Hakodesh* 25

Text 11

כָּל מַה שֶּׁבָּרָא הַקָּדוֹשׁ בָּרוּךְ הוּא בְּעוֹלָמוֹ, לֹא בָּרָא דָּבָר אֶחָד לְבַטָּלָה.

תלמוד בבלי, שבת עז,ב

Of all that God created in His world, He did not create a single thing without a purpose.

Talmud, Shabbat 77b

Question for Discussion

Why would G-d put you in a situation where someone rejects or criticizes you? What kind of growth or purpose can there be in emotional distress?

Text 12

יַתִּיר הֲוָה מַה דְּעֲבַד לֵיהּ שִׁמְעִי בֶּן גֵּרָא מִכָּל עֲקָתִין דְּעֲבְרוּ עֲלֵיהּ עַד הַהוּא יוֹמָא, וְלָא אָתִיב דָּוִד
לְקָבְּלֵיהּ מִלָּה, דְּהָכִי הֲוָה יָאוּת לֵיהּ, וּכְדָא אִתְכַּפָּרוּ חוֹבוֹי.

הַשְׁתָּא אִית לְאִסְתַּכְּלָא, שִׁמְעִי תַּלְמִיד חָכָם הֲוָה, וְחָכְמְתָא סַגִּיאָה הֲוַת בֵּהּ, אַמַּאי נָפִיק לְגַבֵּי
דָּוִד וְעָבַד לֵיהּ כָּל מַה דְּעֲבַד? אֶלָּא מֵאֲתַר אַחֲרָא הֲוָה מִלָּה וְאָעֵיל לֵיהּ בְּלִבֵּיהּ מִלָּה דָא, וְכָל דָּא
לְתוֹעַלְתָּא דְּדָוִד, דְּהָא הַהוּא דְּעֲבַד לֵיהּ שִׁמְעִי גָּרְמָא לֵיהּ לְמֵיתַב בִּתְיוּבְתָּא שְׁלֵימָתָא, וְתָבַר לִבֵּהּ
בִּתְבִירוּ סַגִּי, וְאוֹשִׁיד דִּמְעִין סַגִּיאִין מִגוֹ לִבֵּהּ קֳדָם קוּדְשָׁא בְּרִיךְ הוּא. וְעַל דָּא אָמַר "כִּי ה' אָמַר
לוֹ קַלֵּל", יָדַע דְּהָא מֵאֲתַר עִלָּאָה אַחֲרָא נָחַת מִלָּה.

זוהר ב, קז,ב

The insulting behavior of Shimi ben Gera toward David was worse than anything he had hitherto experienced, yet David did not answer him a word, accepting the humiliation as deserved. His sins were therefore forgiven.

It is fitting to consider why Shimi, who was a scholar and a wise man, behaved to David as he did.

The truth is that the insults and curses that he uttered were not from his own initiative. God planted them in his heart for David's benefit, so that David would repent with a perfect repentance—with a broken heart and with many tears. David therefore said, "The Lord has [surely] said to him, 'Curse David.'" David knew that the cursing and words of insult were inspired from above.

Zohar 2:107b

Key Points

1 The greatest qualitative difference between humans and all other creatures is the capacity to control natural instincts and impulses.

2 Jewish sages have historically reserved some of their sharpest language to describe rage, and suggest that we avoid it at all costs, even when it is the logically appropriate reaction. This is because anger spawns many other faults and mistakes.

3 The first step to overcoming anger is to refuse to act when angry. Learn to recognize the physiological signs of an emotional hijack, and take time for a breather to avoid inappropriate impulsive responses.

4 A good second step is to try to see things from perspectives other than your own. It is possible that you are missing information. Maybe your anger is being provoked for an entirely different reason other than the actions of the other party in the situation.

5 The third step is to recognize the presence of God, and that everything that happens is meant to be. Instead of anger, we can come to see these incidents as moments for personal growth.

6 In order to recognize the opportunities that are opened for us with each event in our lives, we must internalize the notion of Divine providence. Prayer is the optimal way to draw on our belief in God's unifying presence in all events.

Bibliography

Text 1 – Rabbi Chaim Vital (1542–1620). Lurianic Kabbalist and author. Rabbi Vital was born in Israel, lived in Safed, Jerusalem, and later Damascus. He was the principal disciple of Arizal, Rabbi Yitschak Luria, though he studied under him for less than two years. Before Arizal's passing, he authorized Vital to record his teachings. Acting on this mandate, Vital began arranging his master's teachings in written form, and his many works constitute the foundation of the Lurianic school of Jewish mysticism, which was later universally adopted as the Kabbalistic standard. Among his most famous works are *Ets Chayim,* and *Sha'ar Hakavanot.*

Text 2 – Rabbi Shne'ur Zalman of Liadi (1745–1812). Chasidic rebbe and founder of the Chabad movement, also known as "the Alter Rebbe" and "the Rav." Born in Liozna, Belarus, he was among the principal students of the Magid of Mezeritch. His numerous works include the *Tanya,* an early classic containing the fundamentals of Chasidism; *Torah Or; Likutei Torah;* and *Shulchan Aruch HaRav,* a reworked and expanded code of Jewish law. He is interred in Hadiach, Ukraine, and was succeeded by his son, Rabbi Dovber of Lubavitch.

Text 5b – Babylonian Talmud. A literary work of monumental proportions that draws upon the legal, spiritual, intellectual, ethical, and historical traditions of Judaism, the thirty-eight tractate Babylonian Talmud contains the teachings of the Jewish sages from the period after the destruction of the Second Temple through the fifth century CE. It has served as the primary vehicle for the transmission of the Oral Law and the education of Jews over the centuries; it is the entry point for all subsequent legal, ethical, and theological Jewish scholarship.

Text 5c – Rabbi Moshe ben Maimon (1135–1204). Better known as Maimonides or by the acronym Rambam; born in Cordoba, Spain. After the conquest of Cordoba by the Almohads, he fled Spain and eventually settled in Cairo, Egypt. There, he became the leader of the Jewish community and served as court physician to the vizier of Egypt. His rulings on Jewish law are considered integral to the formation of halachic consensus. He is most noted for authoring the *Mishneh Torah,* an encyclopedic arrangement of Jewish law, and for his philosophical work, *Guide for the Perplexed.*

Text 5d – Rabbi Dr. Jonathan Sacks (1948–). Born in London, chief rabbi of the United Hebrew Congregations of the Commonwealth. Attended Cambridge University and received his doctorate from King's College, London. A prolific and influential author, his books include *Will We Have Jewish Grandchildren?* and *The Dignity of Difference.* Recipient of the Jerusalem Prize in 1995 for his contributions to enhancing Jewish life in the Diaspora. Knighted in 2005

Text 12 – Zohar. The most seminal work of Kabbalah, Jewish mysticism. It is a mystical commentary on the Torah, written in Aramaic and Hebrew. According to Arizal, the Zohar consists of the teachings of Rabbi Shimon bar Yocha'i who lived in the Land of Israel during the 2nd century. The Zohar has become one of the indispensable texts of traditional Judaism, alongside and nearly equal in stature to the Mishnah and Talmud.

Additional Readings

Anger

by Jay Litvin

You wanna know about anger? I'll tell you about anger. That's all I can do. I can tell you about it. And then you do what you want. Or what you can. Because anger will ruin your whole stinking life, if you let it. And maybe even if you don't. Anger, my friend, is one tough cookie. It grabs you. Twists you. Overcomes you. And then goes about destroying the things you love best in your whole life.

That's anger.

It grips you in the middle of your chest. Your chest feels tight. What you're feeling is the resistance of your flesh and muscle and bone against a pressure, an energy, an evil excitement that is bursting to get out. It's stronger than you, buddy. You have to know that. It's stronger and when it can't burst out of your chest or squeeze through the spaces of your rib cage or rip your heart into little pieces, it finds another route. It starts to flow out to your arms, up into your head. It hits the muscles in your shoulders and makes them tense and tight and ready to strike out. It makes your arms tingle and your tendons rigid. Your whole neck goes hard as the anger begins to flood your brain.

Sure you try to stop it. But this makes you even more tense, more frustrated, as you now begin to feel like the victim of this surge of fury. The anger's got you. You're angry that you're angry. You're feeling helpless against the uncontrollable urge. And as it fills your mind you're losing your

power to resist it. Because now it's got your rational self in its jaws and its making mincemeat out of your attempts at logic and understanding.

Now, my friend, watch as your thoughts turn black and accusing. Watch how the anger has not only conquered your mind but now has your mind colluding with the anger. Fueling it. Thoughts that won't go away. Accusations. Blame. Indignation. Guilt. Jealousy. Hurt feelings. Scars and old wounds enflamed and enflaming.

And now comes the test: Will you act or not? Will you speak or not? Will you yell and hurt, insult and accuse? Will you trash and destroy? Will you lie and manipulate?

Will you begin to destroy your life and all the things you hold so dear?

An exaggeration? Not by a long shot. Because anger can destroy in a flash or over time. Even after all the I'm-sorry's and forgive-me's, even after you've made up and are trying to put it back the way it was, even after the flood of warmth that often follows after you've cooled-down, the damage has been done. And the damage can be forever.

Year after year, outburst after outburst, chink by chink you are destroying something that you once cherished, and maybe still do. You'll notice, if you have that much awareness left, that there's not as much trust as you once enjoyed, not as much openness. Not as much love.

I'm an expert on anger. I've lived with it all my life.

My anger has caused me and others irrevocable harm. I've tried countless ways to get a hold on my anger, but nothing seemed to work. The strength of the emotion was such that no techniques could quell its outburst. And it seemed that no matter how hard I tried to understand the source of this anger—whether in the past or the present—and to erase or correct it—I could not stem its destructive outbreak.

Anger, despite its destructiveness, holds pleasure, a surge of energy that enlivens the life of one whose life has grown dull. There is the righteousness—the sense of justice and punishment. The victory—not allowing one's loss or defeat to go without response. The vengeance—for the wrongs of yesterday or today. The simple feeling of strength and power, the sense of control, the gratification of seeing fear in the eyes of another rather than feel it in oneself.

And, of course, there is the delight of release and the relaxation that comes after one's fury is spent. And often there is the softening, the opening of the heart that had been so imprisoned in bonds of frustration and hurt, old and current, real and imagined. There is the desire for forgiveness and reconciliation, even the pleasure of guilt and remorse that follows.

The pleasure inherent in anger is the source of its sin. The destructiveness becomes simply the price of the pleasure, and the pleasure—like an addiction—is craved after and uncontrollable. Like envy or jealousy or greed or gossip it is nearly impossible to control, so powerful is the satisfaction and fulfillment it brings.

But if one is very lucky—for in the end I think it is primarily good fortune and Divine grace that overcomes anger—one gets to see that there is a different kind of pleasure, one that comes from kindness and forbearance, understanding and forgiveness, and, in simple terms, the pleasure that comes from having peace in the home and between humans, especially humans that you love.

And once you have the good fortune to see or experience this, well, this pleasure so out-intensifies the pleasure from anger that you simply don't want to waste your time. Because, you see, anger is a luxury for those who believe they have time.

But time is an illusion. Time is here only now. And once you realize this, you get to make a decision about how you want to spend your now. Especially when you know that it is the only now you have and may ever have.

Do you really want to spend it in anger and create all that destruction?

Now, don't get me wrong. When I say that overcoming anger is primarily a matter of luck or good fortune, I am not saying that one who is afflicted with uncontrollable anger (is there any other kind?) shouldn't do, as I did, everything that he or she can to get it under control, whether that be therapy, meditation, jogging or whatever. Though it may be luck and Divine grace that finally brings the desired outcome, in the meantime the responsibility for anger and its consequences lies entirely with me and you.

And when I say that no techniques worked for me, I could just as easily say that all have worked for me, for I have literally spent decades working on this unfortunate part of myself in the hope of ending the spiral of destruction and loss of trust that anger brings in its wake. I look at this work as an investment, as seeding the field knowing that in the end it is only G-d that determines when and whether the crops will grow.

In the meantime it is up to us to plough, seed and pray, plough, seed and pray until the heavens open, the rains fall and the seeds begin to sprout and fruit.

But when finally I changed—and thank G-d changed I have—it seemed like a gift, one of the greatest gifts I have ever received, from G-d. I not only felt and feel grateful, but downright lucky.

My nows are filled with more good times, feelings of unity, pleasant vibes in the house, happier children, a better marriage, more compatible work relationships and even less frustration when driving on Israeli roads (perhaps the real test). Plus, I get to like myself more and walk the earth without the nagging feeling that I am a menace to myself and others.

Let me be clear. I still get angry. Anger, it seems to me, is just one of those emotions that people have, whether they should or not. Certainly the ideal may be that one would never get angry, but I haven't met those folks. Or, the ones I have met are in the category of *tzaddikim,* the righteous ones that walk the earth and heavens.

But I don't fit in that category, nor do the people I know and have known. So, for the vast majority of us, anger is a part of life, even though I believe, as our Sages teach, that anger is akin to idol worship, that it is a denial of G-d's providence, omnipotence and omniscience.

But overcoming that denial, or rather coming to see and accept G-d's hand in every aspect of life, is another of those things, like overcoming anger, that for most of us takes a life time, if it ever happens at all, if we're ever lucky enough.

Thus, anger remains.

The difference in my life now is that I just can't tolerate it or the destruction and hurt that it causes to others. I feel it, I recognize it, I accept it, and then, when I'm lucky, I let it go, along with all the obsessive thoughts that accompany it—the accusations and condemnations, the hurt and injustice, the jealousy, the desire for revenge.

I'd like to take credit for these changes, but in truth they feel as much the result of happenstance as effort, of G-d's intervention and providence.

First, the destructiveness of my behavior in all its terror became so vivid I could not tolerate it. I not only saw this in times of anger, but also in vision and memory of angry times past, visions that I think were gifts from Above. I became tormented by all that I was capable of destroying, and had. I saw and felt the hurt and damage I was causing others with my cruel words and actions. I saw and felt it as if I were the object of my own anger. And I cringed and cried as I felt the pain and damage I was causing to those I loved most. It was as if the anger was happening all over again, but now I could see it with distance and perspective, though the feelings were as intense as if it were happening now. Not feelings of anger, but feelings of revulsion for what I was watching, for what I had done.

Second, during some recent difficult times, I have been the object of love and concern, patience and dedication by some of those at whom I had been the angriest. In the face of their kindness and of my need, I could no longer muster the anger I once had. Now, I could only feel gratitude and love and perceived in these one-time objects of my anger such angelic souls that I felt searing shame at my past actions towards them.

That they were now so loving despite the anger that I'd spent at them over the years increased their virtue even further and where once I could, in moments of blind anger, see only their negativity, now any perceived hurt or disappointment I felt from them was balanced with my awareness of and appreciation for their goodness and kindness. And to them I ask and will continue to ask forgiveness.

I also began to more and more recognize G-d's hand in my life, and His goodness. The reality of G-d's participation in and control of the world, even in times that could be described as "bad," penetrated deeper and deeper into my psyche and soul. Thus, no matter what happened I began to see and truly believe that this, too, comes from G-d. The hurts or disappointments, the lacks and the frustrations—all come from G-d. There is no one to blame. Or if there is, it is only Him. Each obstacle, each frustration, each hurt, each fear, every childhood injury or lack comes ultimately from Him, for my benefit, as part of my life's journey—a journey tailored by Him only for me.

From this perspective I saw that anger is always wrong. It has no justification, no matter how righteous the justification feels. Acknowledging both the humanness of this emotion and its total wrongness gives me a place from which to relate to my anger. Knowing it is wrong, the mental obsessions are also wrong. There is nothing to do with my anger other than to acknowledge it and let it pass. And often, letting it pass requires that I ask, that I beg G-d to take it from me, to open my heart and my mind so that I can perceive what is taking place more compassionately, from a wider perspective, from outside myself and inside the other.

And luckily, this has taken place enough times that I am able to experience what life is like without my anger: what life in my home is like, what my relationship with my wife is like, what my relationship to myself is like, and what my relationship with G-d is like.

And, it is good. So much better than ever before. It is, without exaggeration, like a rebirth. And each moment, each day that I live without anger or even with less anger, I beg and pray that it not return. It is, in spite of its humanness, so very evil and destructive. And each day that it does not return, I thank G-d for His intervention, for the "luck" He provided and provides.

Please hear this: Even after your remorse, if you are fortunate enough to be forgiven by those you love, you will still not be able to recapture and relive all those days and nights you wasted in your anger, time that could have been spent in love and good feeling. Anger fills the irreplaceable now, disallowing the wonder that could be.

It destroys the goodness of life.

Jay Litvin was born in Chicago in 1944. He moved to Israel in 1993 to serve as medical liaison for Chabad's Children of Chernobyl program, and took a leading role in airlifting children from the areas contaminated by the Chernobyl nuclear disaster; he also founded and directed Chabad's Terror Victims program in Israel. Jay passed away in April of 2004 after a valiant four-year battle with non-Hodgkin's lymphoma, and is survived by his wife, Sharon, and their seven children. He was a frequent contributor to Chabad.org.

Reprinted with permission of The Judaism Website—Chabad.org

**Toward a Meaningful Life
with Simon Jacobson**

Radio Show Transcript - February 6, 2000

Rabbi Simon Jacobson: Good evening, this is Simon Jacobson, and it's a pleasure to be here with you again.

Last week's show, "Honoring Parents Who Don't Seem to Deserve Honor," addressed a topic that really seemed to hit home with the callers. The barrage of calls that came in were not just predominantly, but *exclusively*, from people who hadn't spoken to their mothers or fathers for years. I was desperately searching for somebody to call in and tell us that they do love their parents and that they have some type of healthy relationship with them, but to no avail.

Some people did email me about beautiful relationships that they had with their parents, but I was getting the sense that the only people who listen to the show hate their parents! Though I serve a role, then, to at least fill that niche, it's also important to know that the teachings that I'm trying to express on the show are not just to heal wounded hearts (even though all of us are wounded) but can also help us all grow and reach greater heights than we'd be able to reach on our own.

That has always been the theme and the most gratifying part of doing this show-along with hearing your responses and receiving your emails and different forms of communications-to look at ourselves as one collective family of souls who are trying to make sense out of life, trying to find deeper meaning, and who are cutting away the weeds so the flowers can emerge.

Unfortunately, we have to spend much of our lives and our time cutting away weeds, dealing with impediments, psychological scars and blockages that don't allow us to focus on the positive. But the belief that I try to espouse here is that we each have inside of us a flower, and the ultimate goal is not spending the rest of our lives in damage control, but allowing the beauty and inherent dignity of human beings to arise and surface.

In that spirit, I decided to do a topic which deals with another form of "weeds," and that is the issue of anger.

Who of us has never gotten angry and has not had some type of outburst and often, in retrospect, an unjustified outburst? Some of us are known to have short fuses. Anger is another one of those expressive emotions that are extremely difficult to master precisely because of its force and power. Interestingly, anger is compared in the Kabbalah and Jewish mysticism to fire.

We know that when a fire begins to rage (as in "raging anger"), once it's raging, it's very difficult to control. Perhaps at the outset, with that initial spark, you can nip it in the bud. But often, when anger becomes a full-blown expression of rage, whatever the cause may be, it burns and consumes both yourself and those around you.

The invisible damage that anger imposes upon ourselves and the people around us has been documented. You hear a lot about children who have grown up in homes where their parents, father or mother, will have uncontrollable fits of rage, and this does great damage, even if it doesn't express itself in some form of physical abusive or other overt type of harm.

The expression of anger itself is very negative energy, especially because it's expressed and not controlled. Of course, you always have to begin looking at yourself, the times when you have your own uncontrollable anger, but this is much easier to do when you're calm.

I'll begin from a Torah perspective. There's an interesting statement in the Talmud which states: "One who gets angry is compared to someone who has committed idolatry-an idol worshipper." Idol worship, of course, in the Bible, is considered to be a cardinal sin.

Now that's an interesting, seemingly strange parallel. Why would anger be compared to idol worship? Idol worship seems to be a defiance of G-d, whereas anger is clearly, at worst, a defiance of other human beings. Yet the Talmud does compare the two.

There are different explanations given for this, but I want to focus on one, which is actually cited in a classical work of Chassidic thought (another branch of Jewish mysticism) which says that the reason for that is that the person who gets angry, at least for that moment, has forgotten that there's a G-d in this world. They've forgotten that life is run by Divine Providence, not randomly, and therefore when something happens to you; when something provokes you to make you feel angry, you have to realize that even though the person who caused that behavior has free will and is accountable for his or her behavior, there is a reason why it happened to you.

Because there's a reason for it, by focusing on your reaction to it instead of focusing on the reason, it's like denying that G-d is the one who ultimately sets the stage and sets the tone.

I have to emphasize that this does not mean that G-d intervenes or in any way suspends our free will, yet, when you're on the receiving end of certain irritating actions, there is a certain message and a certain lesson to be learned from them.

This is why the Talmud calls anger a form of idol worship, as explained in Tanya, a classical work of Chassidic thought.

Now, this itself needs explanation. He does make some exceptions, for instance, when you get angry at something or someone because they did something wrong. If you see a criminal who has hurt a child or an innocent person, would anyone argue and say you have no right to get angry?

Obviously, there is a place for anger there. So he explains that the reason for anger in a situation like that is that if your anger or your being upset can in some way repair the situation, or can help it, then there is a place for it. However, if the anger is purely a selfish expression of your being hurt rather than bringing about any type of productive result, that's where it borders on a form of "idolatry."

It's a very profound way of looking at anger. It really makes us look at ourselves, because obviously we have to begin with a discussion of it on a somewhat more philosophical and psychological perspective before dealing with the actual issue.

What happens when you are in a fit of rage, what can you do? You can't say, "Okay, I'm going to open up a Talmud and when I read that it's idolatry, I'm suddenly going to calm down."

In a way, we have to train ourselves before we are actually in a situation like that to see how we can tame those fits of rage, tame our energies and channel them in the right direction.

So first I'll take a call. Angry callers or calm callers are all welcome this evening. We have Andrew on the line.

Caller: Thanks for taking my call. I have a slightly different problem and I'm wondering if you can give me some advice. I don't have fits of rage, but everything makes me angry, like a pot boiling. Can you address that?

Jacobson: Right now, Andrew?

Caller: No, just in my daily life. I could give you fifty examples, but just in living my life, people annoy me, situations make me angry. How do you deal with that?

Jacobson: Well, let's see if I can provoke you so we can have a live experiment right on air!

Caller: I'm much too nervous for that.

Jacobson: Well, first of all, I appreciate your call. I don't mean to be humorous at your expense. Obviously, my first question to you would be, are you aware of it causing direct damage in your life or to the people around you, or is it something that you just carry inside of you?

Caller: I would think that it hurts my relationships, particularly with my girlfriend.

Jacobson: Well, there are short-term solutions and long-term ones.

Caller: Give me a short-term one.

Jacobson: Okay, we'll start with a short-term one. Long-term ones can take weeks, months, years, millennia! First of all, the single most important thing is to make sure that there's no one in the line of fire. That when you recognize that you are about to get annoyed to the point of...

Caller: No, I'm not going to pop. Don't get me wrong. It's like a simmering thing.
Jacobson: So how does it express itself if you don't pop? Do you start yelling?

Caller: No. I'm just not nice to people. I'm sarcastic with people; bitter sounding. I become a grumpy old man.

Jacobson: And this is a consistent part of your life?

Caller: Right. Give me some advice.

Jacobson: Listen to me. Do you have any spirituality in your life? Do you have anything that you do that is not focused on your own needs?

Caller: Well, I'm not a super-spiritual person. I was hoping that you could give me some non-spiritual advice.

Jacobson: Okay, I see you really have a menu-you have very specific guidelines. Maybe you should tell me what type of advice I should give you! But I'll tell you, if you're not a particularly spiritual type of person, the first thing to focus on is not yourself, because as I pointed out here, anger is an expression of self-focus, which ultimately is a denial of G-d in your life.

Even if someone doesn't want to have G-d in their life, or they don't feel a need for it-and Andrew is perhaps testimony for someone who does have a need for it-you have to have something in your life that's outside of yourself. Because how then can you avoid the inevitable: that things will irritate you and you become so consumed with it that there's no relief?

Relief comes when you have a certain diversity. Even in investments they say you have to diversify because you may lose in one area. Don't put all your eggs in one basket. The same thing is true psychologically. If a person focuses entirely on himself and the way he does things, making sure "my needs are being met," inevitably there will be situations where a person will be irritated, where a person will be annoyed, because he or she has no relief and there's nowhere else to turn.

However, when our horizons are somewhat broader, and we can see life from a different perspective, we can say, "Okay, this may not have worked, I'm upset, but I have other eggs in my basket that I can depend on, that I can turn to." That someway diffuses it.

I often find that when people are really consumed with anger, it's usually one of two causes: either as children they've seen that as a coping mechanism of their parents-it became a "legitimate" way of venting, even though it's destructive; or, they're very self-focused, and if it doesn't work exactly their way, they get completely upset and can't handle it.

So whether you call it spirituality or whether you call it some form of transcendental experience that allows you to diversify, this allows you to see other horizons.

Look at little children. Little children are very emotional. You give them a toy, keep them distracted, and they can be completely delighted. When they get hurt, they start crying and screaming. They have fits of rage as well.

You can't compare it to adult rage but you can learn from that. What is causing the child to be so mercurial, so temperamental? Because a child doesn't yet have, what's called in Hebrew, "daas." Daas is not just a form of knowledge; it's a mature understanding of things, that life is not always black and white. It's not a matter of either you have it or you don't have it, sometimes you gain something and you lose. Often you have to give up something to get something.

Children have narrow perspectives. Their minds are not yet matured. Their horizons are narrow. So if they have what they want, they're happy. If they don't have what they want, they get upset.

As adults, we can grow chronologically into adulthood but still be children; still have those little toys. They may not be Lego's, or they may not be blocks that you sit on the floor with, but they're sophisticated toys, adult toys. So we play our games, and when that game is take away from us, we're left with nothing, so we get angry at ourselves, angry at others, angry at life itself, because we have no relief. There's nowhere to turn and there are no alternatives.

Okay, we have Billy on the line.

Caller: Hello Rabbi. Actually I'm just driving and I heard your program. It's very interesting. I agree with a lot of the things you're saying. I have just a few ideas to add to that. As far as being consumed with anger, it can be very difficult to get out of that at different points in your life. I think part of that probably has to do with coming to understand your past, like you said, the way your parents were or how the dysfunction of your family impacted you. Also, it helps to understand who you are as a person. You may be an intense person with a lot of intensity about how you react to things.

I do think that spirituality for me has been very important in my life to help me put it into perspective. I happen to be Christian, and I know that certain Bible verses and practicing my faith and religion helps me to cope and deal with my issues of anger, otherwise I would be like a loose, rabid dog, taking it out on everyone. So I think that that's a very important thing.

Also, coming from a physiological or psychological standpoint, I think one has to look at whether or not it's an illness in someone's situation. Someone might be depressed or chemically imbalanced, which might cause the person to be very angry about their situation, which then, in turn, physiologically might change the chemistry of the brain and then you might have this anger and constant depression which just keeps evoking itself.

Jacobson: I appreciate your identifying different forms of anger; it's great to have it clarified. Would you get angry right now, for example, if a cop pulled you over and gave you a ticket for speaking on your cell phone?

Caller: I don't think so. I think I'd have confidence because I have a retired chief of police and a few police officers in my family to help me with that situation, but I might become a little angry or scared.

Jacobson: I understand. I just mean that sometimes, certain little things happen in life, you're pulled over and…

Caller: You lose it.

Jacobson: Right. Some people are very good at tolerating big problems in life but when it comes to the little things, they go crazy.

Caller: But I think that that probably has to do, Rabbi, very much with the way you were brought up and your family (some people come from real easy-going situations and some people come from really dysfunctional, hard situations where they've seen a lot of anger between their parents and that's all they know).

Jacobson: Well, I appreciate your call Billy and please call again!

Yes, anger has many causes, and unfortunately it has a negative impact on us and on others around us. Now I think it's important to distinguish between the things that happen to you in your life and how you address them. Anger is not about whether you get angry, but, in general, it's about your attitude; your attitude and reactions to phenomena, to experiences in life, and how you see yourself in your community and the world around you.

Things happen to us that are often unpredictable. We can only write a script that goes so far, and even then, it rarely works. So things happen to us that provoke us, that elicit different reactions. When you get angry, it's also an opportunity to look at yourself and then review and say to yourself, "Why did I get angry?"

So the first thing to do is to look around and identify the causes. What makes you angry? How the government is behaving? How your co-workers are behaving? Family issues? Is it everything? Is it none of the above?

One of the expressions of anger in New York City, at least, is the honking of a horn. I don't know who created that, but I think many people tell me that it's very therapeutic for them, when they're traveling, especially when there's a lot of traffic, even if it doesn't help. It's just a way of expressing their anger through that horn-which, of course, is illegal-but on the other hand, it's just an interesting thing that automobiles have become this type of therapy for some.

However, I don't really believe it helps anybody; it's just a good way of physical expression-instead of punching someone you just keep your hands on that horn.

We have Liba on the line.

Caller: Hi Rabbi Jacobson. My situation is that I'm not sighted, and when I am somewhere

where things are not working out, I begin to feel abandoned and helpless, and then I panic. And then that panic leads to anger. What do you suggest?

Jacobson: Does that anger express itself internally or…

Caller: It starts internally, and unfortunately, sometimes it bubbles over.

Jacobson: Well, it's a difficult situation frankly, Liba, to answer, because the panic is often legitimate as a result of a feeling of helplessness, as you point out, a certain vulnerability. One can't criticize or in any way challenge that panic. I would say, first of all, it's important for you to create a support group that you can always reach to.

By building more security in your life, you will minimize and even avoid having too many panic attacks. So getting to the root of it, if you would have less panic, you would have less anger.

And sometimes you have to get to the root of something and just create alternative methods of security, that help preempt panic attacks and the resulting anger. Often anger can be reprogrammed through behavioral change or through change of circumstances to get out of the line of fire so to speak.

People often ask me about anger and I say, "If someone is provoking you again and again and again, maybe you shouldn't get back into that boxing ring. Find yourself another place to go to if possible."

Caller: I've tried.

Jacobson: Well, in this situation it's important as much as possible to find a friend who can help avoid or minimize the reasons to panic. That's

on a very technical level. On a more emotional level, I would suggest that you have someone to call at a point like that where you can just vent to them. There are some people who are very good to call when you're angry because either they're immune or they just have that type of what's called resilience.

Caller: That's an emotional answer. Now give me the spiritual answer.

Jacobson: On a spiritual level, no one is perfect in his or her faith. We all have fits of anger. We all have tantrums. We all have different ways we express anger. The fact is that the Talmud says it's a form of idolatry. And I think that if one is looking to grow towards spirituality, toward G-d, which is a journey, the more you have G-d in your life, the less a person should panic and the less a person should be angry.

The story that I'm very fond of repeating is a very powerful story about one of the Rebbes when he was arrested in the former Soviet Union; he was not willing to cooperate with the authorities and someone pointed a pistol to his head and said, "Rebbe, this pistol has changed many people's minds to corroborate with us." The Rebbe looked at them calmly, with almost no feelings, and said, "This little toy can frighten a person who has one world and many gods, but not someone who has One G-d and two worlds."

So in other words, the real embrace of G-d, and the test of G-d in your life, is not when things are going well but when things aren't; when we have that reason to panic, or when we have that reason to be upset at ourselves or at G-d or the universe.

Caller: It's when I feel abandoned.

Jacobson: Well, ultimately, it comes down to embracing G-d for all you're worth, for all your life itself at that time, because that's ultimately the only real source of solace when everything else seems to have abandoned you. But I do believe that you need to create a human support system as well.

Caller: That's a good idea. Thank you, Rabbi.

Jacobson: Okay, we have Susan on the line.

Caller: Hello, Rabbi. I just had to tune in tonight. I listen every once in a while, and the show and the discussions are phenomenal. It happens coincidentally that I was very, very angry yesterday. My mother is in a nursing home and she needed me to bring her a remote control, because the aides in the nursing home constantly just push it over and it falls on the floor. So I did bring it up but I'm not mechanical, and I didn't realize that I needed to do other things with it, like punching numbers, and I called my daughter but she couldn't help me over the phone.

It goes back further than that because my husband (who's deceased now) was in the line of radio equipment and he always knew how to handle these kinds of things, but the idea that I had to go back into the store where he worked and get the item and then bring it up… The anger was starting before I got to my mother-in-law, and I took it out on her and I took it out on the nurses by saying to them, "I didn't want to be here; I had other plans." I do have some psychological problems (I have a doctor that I see), and I apologized to my mother-in-law in the evening, but I have to talk to my doctor about how to control my anger. Perhaps you have an idea?

Jacobson: Thank you Susan for the call. I'll respond briefly. You yourself acknowledged that it's not always the circumstance that's causing you to be angry-it's yourself and how you react to it. Of course, we can justify many reasons for us to get angry, but there are many other ways to deal with it. I do think Susan, as I was suggesting to some of the other callers, each of us has our own case by case situation, yet each of us has to embrace some form of soul and spirituality, something that transcends our own immediate needs, our own space. And that's ultimately the place of relief, the place of rescue, an oasis, that becomes the place you can run to, or go to, when what is happening in your life is being taken away and you have every reason in your own mind to be angry.

That may mean going out for a walk, it may mean calling a friend as I mentioned. There are friends who are very good at this; they can absorb a lot, and it's important not to focus on the circumstances because then you consume yourself with all the external details ("This is making me angry, and this one did this to me"). You become a victim and trap yourself, and then your anger ultimately consumes you.

Okay, we have Rachel on the line.

Caller: When you say that anger is like idol worship because you're not seeing G-d in the situation … I wish it were that easy. I have deep faith that Hashem runs the world and is behind everything that happens, so when things happen to me I don't say, "How could this happen to me" as a form of idol worship, I say, "Why is *Hashem* doing this to me?"

So if the neighbors' kids are running around upstairs, I don't get angry with my neighbor, I say, "Hashem, why did you put me in the situation that I should be up all night with kids running over my head?"

If I could say anger is idol worship, then I would just have to realize that Hashem is behind everything and then my anger would go away. But that's not the case, because now I get angry at Hashem.

Jacobson: That's a very good question. I would say that in a situation like that, G-d ("Hashem" for those of our listeners who don't know that that's a Hebrew way of referring to G-d), in that case, often becomes a form of an idol as well, if anger is directed at Him, because the whole concept of G-d is not just a force that is causing things to happen, it's also a higher wisdom and a larger picture.

It's like getting really upset in the middle of watching a film and running out of the room, and someone tells you later that there was a happy ending. So basically, you got upset at a certain segment of it and didn't see the entire picture.

So there's definitely room for broadening our perspectives, which will help in lessening the anger we have. Now, I'm not putting myself in a position where I would like children running on top of my head, or some other provocative thing-I have my own fits of anger myself-yet, I think when you say " G-d," what you really want to say is not just another scapegoat to blame, but G-d meaning also that I've done what I could in a given situation, and there's nothing else that I can do.

Now in any other particular circumstance, where you have specific items that make you angry, there are always things you can do. Either you get yourself out of the situation, or tell the person that's causing you that pain, "Please, I can't handle it anymore."

If the circumstances are such that no matter what you've done, you can't get yourself out of the line of fire, then ultimately that *bitachon*, that faith, that trust in G-d, is not just another punching bag, but it leads you to understand that maybe there's some deeper thing going on here and you have to, I wouldn't say smile about it, but in some way learn what the message is.

Now it's a little difficult when you're talking about children running around on the floor upstairs, because I don't see what spiritual message is there-that's like a technical thing that I'd wrack my brain to find some solution to. On this show I'm trying to show different forms and different causes, and some of them are easier to solve and some are more difficult to solve. But I appreciate your call.

So we go to Norman on the line.

Caller: Good evening. I'm listening and agreeing with just about all that you're saying.
Jacobson: Well, what are you not agreeing with?…That's what I'd like to know!

Caller: I'm not even sure that there's anything that I disagree with…

Jacobson: Norman, you're making me angry now because radio means some type of tension.

Caller: Well, I don't see anything I disagree with; I'm going to retract that! I see everything being very valid, and I just devised something which I'm going to see if it helps me. It is true that the opposite of anger is love: suitable, correct love. So therefore, I'm going to try to say to myself and remember this: When I'm angry, I'm going to remember to say, "G-d's Love Always Delivers" which is G-L-A-D.

If I remember this, it may help, because I agree with you that anger is putting the other person at a lower rung and making myself more important. I need to remember that the other person's feelings are very important. If they did something wrong, they could be told correctly and suitably and politely. And that's our challenge.

By the way, I did have a situation where I had people over my head, and you know how I somehow placated myself? I said, "You know, it could be worse. They're my neighbors, they're upstairs, they're banging. I could be in a concentration camp. That's *really* a bad situation."

Jacobson: That's true. Maybe we should create some type of support group for people who get angry at upstairs neighbors who have children running around and maybe get some suggestions of how to pad the floors or some other type of solution.

Caller: That's a big challenge, but it is a challenge and it can be overcome. I always say to myself, "If this is so irritating, what am I supposed to learn from this?" And often I get some lesson.

Jacobson: Okay, Norman, thank you for your call, and your vote of confidence.

We have Leah on the air.

Caller: Hi Rabbi. I think I'm pretty well calm. I don't get angry with people, really, I have other mechanisms for dealing with that, including my faith. But I'm talking about anger against groups; for instance, I think there's a lot of hate and anger against minority groups, let's say, towards Jews, or I don't like the Arabs, I'm angry at what they're trying to do in Israel. I'm angry at what's going on in Austria right now. I'm angry at the causes for the Holocaust. I cannot forgive certain people.

So that's what I'm talking about: group anger. For instance, many, many people have this hate and anger even toward our President and our own government. And they are constantly talk-

ing hate on the other side of the dial with 24-hour diatribes against certain people running for office. There's real anger and hate there all the time, and I think this is what we listen to. My question is: how can I not be angry at things that really affect me in the world?

Jacobson: Well, it's legitimate to be angry at injustices and crimes that have been perpetrated on innocent people. There's legitimacy to that because it means we're not indifferent. However, I wouldn't call that anger, I would call it a healthy reaction to things that are inappropriate, particularly if that anger can help you avoid situations like that, or teach your children, or your community that there are certain things that shouldn't be tolerated. In those cases, anger has a role, but not as an expression or an indulgence of your own feelings, but rather a very deliberate and specific form of expression that's showing that things are not right; particularly in a case where anger can help correct the situation, repair it, and also learn for the future.

However, anger that is an expression of your own indulgent feelings and one that is directed at others-as a defense or a lashing out-that is destructive both to yourself and to others. That's how I would make the distinction. And how one travels from one type of anger to the other requires introspection, requires that spirituality we're talking about. It also requires having outlets and channeling that anger.

If something that is legitimately unjust is making you angry but you express it in a way that is destructive, then you have to have objectives friends who can help you channel it in a constructive way.

Now sometimes I'll get upset at something, and I'll call a friend and tell him what happened, and he'll say to me, "Well, why don't you try this and this." And in a way this can free us because it releases us; we feel we have another outlet.

Sometimes it is a form of panic as Liba said earlier, and you feel anger is your only recourse. When you find another way, when someone says, "Why don't you try this and that," you feel that there is an outlet, a solution, and the anger will dissipate because you have another way of dealing with the problem. And that's critical in channeling it.

I'd like to also address the issue, if time allows, of "Is it healthier to express your anger when you feel it simmering inside of you, and just get it out of your system, or is it healthier to repress it and try to keep it under control?"

But let's go back to the calls; maybe someone will have an answer. We have Leah on line 2.

Caller: Hello Rabbi. I think you may have answered this comment, but I'll go ahead with it anyway. How can you control anger that you feel was programmed into you from infancy, from childhood, in a volatile household (to put it mildly)? I think it's the cause of my free-floating anxiety, guilt, and hair-trigger responses which almost seem involuntary and immobilizing. I admire people who play it cool but I'm not one of them. I think it's because of that early exposure to anger.

And then when you talk about anger being like idol worship, it's hard to relate to that when you feel you had no input into this kind of feeling; it didn't develop by itself.

Jacobson: Right. That's an important aspect of the topic. I know many people have that unhealthy coping mechanism that they picked up early on, ingrained in them as you just put it. I think, first of all-and I must commend you on

this-that just having the awareness of the cause and not trying to justify it is an important step. It's like many people who have anger in their blood from their childhood. Instead of recognizing that, they just always blame others. They say, "It's not me. People are out to get me, etc."

So first of all, the fact that you're aware is already half a cure. The next step would be what you can do about it. Though I've said it several times on the air, I must reiterate that it's ultimately diversification. You have to find other outlets. You have to find other ways of communicating and when there's a real outburst, you should try to find a situation where there's no one around-let yourself go to the ocean, listen to some music-something that keeps you away from others when you're having that type of outburst.

Because this happens to all of us at some point or another, we can't always stop it. And any responsible adult can be accountable for and asked to vent his or her anger in private, where it will not hurt others.

When dealing with anger, it's important to find other outlets and know that just because this is the way your father and mother dealt with issues, you don't have to (or want to) be that way.

So when something causes you to be angry, you literally, constantly have to speak to someone and say, "What else can I do in this situation? What are my alternatives? I always have that outburst."

Now, are there any panaceas, are there any magic tricks? I can't state any on air here because I don't have them. However, I think it's a process of awareness, of constantly monitoring yourself, turning to others for help, not thinking you can solve it on your own, because anger is deep-rooted, and ultimately prayer, spiritual communion, study, anything that broadens your horizons, pulls you into another space that's outside of yourself, and can ultimately diffuse it. Much more can be said on the topic, but we then need to get into a lengthier discussion to address this particular case.

We go to David on line 3.

Caller: Hi Rabbi. You said so much. I was getting angry with you in the beginning, at the program, at the callers, angry at myself. I reserved time because I wanted to listen to you and then I wasn't getting any messages. And of course, then when you talked about anger being equal to fire, I remember you also said fire can be either self-consuming or it can be enlightening. And I said to myself, as you've been saying, we have to look at what anger is trying to teach us by what we're angry at: the bad programming that we've had from childhood that makes us act this way. And then you asked the question whether it's a good idea to repress your anger until maybe you can find a padded room to go into and knock your head against the wall when it's more appropriate instead of in public or someplace else.

In my case it was bad role modeling from my childhood. When I saw my son running around with a baseball bat expressing his anger, I said, he learned this from me being a rageaholic. But if I can use the anger as enlightenment, I guess it will help us to learn why we're acting that way, to enlighten us and learn how we can improve ourselves and turn to the power of *tefillah* (prayer).

I think it does help a lot. I want to thank you for that.

Jacobson: Thank you David. I'm glad…this was a perfect example. Someone who was angry at the show, at myself, at everyone, and it somehow

dissipated. Maybe if you're on hold long enough, anger does dissipate.

Okay, we have Elisha on the line.

Caller: No actually this is Danielle, his Mom. I'm calling for my son who happens to be six years old. He's a very good boy, in fact, tonight he reminded me, he said, "Mommy, Rabbi Jacobson is on, are we listening tonight?"

Jacobson: Six years old?

Caller: Yes, and he's very good, he listens very well. He goes to yeshivah and he's very good with his *middos*, but sometimes all of a sudden his mood will change and he'll say, "I'm angry. I'm angry with everybody. I'm angry with you. You're annoying me."

It happened actually this morning and I really didn't know what to do, and I'd like to have you give some input for a parent for a child.

Jacobson: I'm glad to hear we have audiences of different age groups! Briefly, children's anger is completely different from adult anger because, as I mentioned earlier, children have a propensity to be emotional. But if there is a continuing pattern of anger, not just sporadic instances, but a continued pattern, there may be other things bothering the child that we are not aware of, something in school, for example.

Children are often ashamed or bashful because they think they may be punished or hurt. Often they have a friend at school who's really badgering them and they may think that if that friend is a relative of or close to the principal or the teacher, they may not want to share it.

That's just an example. There are things that often bother children that express themselves in anger and I think it's important to look at what's going on in the child's life that you may not be aware of as a parent. That's if it's a continuing pattern.

If it isn't, then a child having an outburst or a tantrum is quite natural because it's the way the child learns to grow and learns to express itself. Then there's an issue of how the child sees the parents address that. Obviously, it should never be returned in kind. When children see how parents deal with a problem, it teaches them greatly how to approach a problem; that anger is not necessarily the only way to address a problem.

In a way, you're dealing with a blessing here. Many of the calls this evening came from adults who have already been shaped. But a child can be taught. There are many things you can do. You can say, "Elisha, there are many ways to express ourselves when we don't like something." You can first try pleasantly, and then be more firm. And I think by setting an example and communicating it, Elisha and any child can really learn from that.

So we go to Irving on line 1.

Caller: Yes, hello. I have to fix my hearing aid. I wanted to know about anger. You see, anger is something which is not premeditated. It's spontaneous. How do you cope with something that's spontaneous? You can't. I'm "pooh-pooh" 90 years old and I know for a lifetime that it's very hard because you don't know when to expect it-it's not something you think out logically, it's something that just pops out!

Jacobson: Irving, coming from an experienced person like you, I think we all can appreciate that. I would say very briefly that spontaneous reactions are influenced by how we prepare ourselves before we've begun to have those emotional feelings. Much of what I was saying this evening is how in general you can change your attitude-but not when the provocation is occurring, because that's very difficult. Once the storm strikes, you can't start building strong foundations.

So you have to wait and see how your attitude is in more peaceful times when you're not being provoked, and being aware that when you have angry expressions, you should just prepare the ground that you should have different outlets. It's like the rush of water in a river. If you have only one direction, when it really begins to explode, when it really begins to intensify, the water starts rushing to the point of complete eruption.

However, if you create different channels and the river can run off before you get angry, then when something will provoke you, you've prepared yourself. That is, I believe, the best type of solution in that area which is preventive medicine. It's not a guarantee, but it's a way of approaching life, of creating diversification by way of different options.

Thank you for the call, Irving, and I'm glad to hear that we have many different age groups listening to the show; it's really very encouraging. You've been listening to *Toward a Meaningful Life with Simon Jacobson*. We're on the air every Sunday from 6-7pm on WEVD 1050AM. This show is brought to you by the Meaningful Life Center which I have the honor to direct, an organization dedicated to bringing teachings that can empower us all with the tools that can help us live more meaningful lives: dealing with anger and other negative emotions, not annihilating yourself but channeling them into expressions and seeing your bouts of anger or different emotional expressions as signposts-you can even say "red flags"-that G-d puts in front of you to give you a way of looking at yourself. When things are just smooth, you often don't look at yourself. When you have strong reactions to things, including anger, it makes you look at yourself, your place in this world, and your attitude toward life in general. So if we see it that way, as a caller put it earlier, that anger can be a fire that illuminates instead of a fire that consumes, then it can be put to use, and channeled properly. It can be productive when it's directed and controlled and not focused as your own indulgent feelings, and at the same time, it can also teach us how to be more pleasant and more loving in areas of our lives.

So until next time, this has been *Toward a Meaningful Life*. Thank you very much.

Reprinted with permission from meaningfullifecenter.com

It's About Time
Time

Food in Focus
The Kabbalah of Spiritual Dieting

ROSH**CHODESH**
society

Introduction

The Jewish nation was born in a desert, a territory not exactly famous for granaries and vineyards. God lovingly swaddled His newborn in clouds of glory and weaned it on bread from Heaven—the manna that rained down afresh each morning and had to be collected in jars. This did not mean that early risers and nimble gatherers ate better than the elderly or laid back. Rather, God instructed that each person was to gather a specific measure of manna: one *omer* per day. The Torah relates that both the greedy who purposely overloaded their containers as well as the ascetics who made do with partially filled jars would miraculously find themselves with an exact *omer* upon returning to their tents.

Generally, the foods we eat are a blend of useful molecules that the body absorbs and thrives on, and unnecessary molecules that are expelled because the body does not require them. The Talmud (Yoma 75b) relates that unlike ordinary food, the manna was of perfect nutritional value. It was absorbed completely by the body, leaving no waste to be discarded.

When we were spoon-fed by God in the desert, we were given precisely the most beneficial portion sizes, food types, and state of freshness. Nor was there the concept of undereating or indulging. That ideal situation lasted forty years, after which God considered us mature enough to enter the Land of Israel, till the soil, and produce our own food. He also entrusted us with the menus and the choice of responsible eating. Needless to say, we have struggled with our plates and stomachs ever since. More than at any point in history, we are aware today of the risks of bad eating habits. Nevertheless, the struggle to stick with a healthy food plan persists. We also tend to crave precisely the foods that are not beneficial or perhaps are even detrimental to our ultimate well-being: a far cry from the lessons of the manna!

In this lesson for the month of Shevat on the Jewish calendar—a month possessing particular energies relating to food and sustenance—we will draw upon the insights of Judaism to help us develop both physically and spiritually healthy eating habits.

I. Food and Us

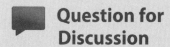

Question for Discussion

In your estimation, what are the key factors that contribute to the contemporary tendency of unhealthy eating habits?

FIGURE 3.1

Average Amount of Time Spent on Common Pursuits Over a Lifetime

Pursuit	Men	Women
Cooking	1½ years	3 years
Eating	4 years	4 years
Exercising	2 years	1 year
"Getting ready" (i.e., grooming and dressing)	6 months	2 years
Household chores	1½ years	2½ years
Restroom time	3 years	6 months
Shopping	1 year	2 years
Sleeping	25 years	27 years
Watching TV	10 years	13 years
Work	10½ years	8½ years

II.   A Mission of Sparks

Text 1a

כִּי זֶה טַעַם יְרִידַת הַנְשָׁמָה בָּעוֹלָם הַזֶּה, לְתַקֵּן
וּלְבָרֵר . . . נִיצוֹצִין.

עץ חיים כו,א

The purpose of the soul's descent into this world is to rectify and refine . . . [Divine] sparks.

Rabbi Chaim Vital, *Etz Chayim* 26:1

Text 1b

According to the Kabbalah, all of reality is studded with Divine "sparks." . . . The human mission in life is to redeem these Divine sparks . . . to free them from their imprisonment in this mundane world, and permit them to reunite with their Source. This is achieved through the fulfillment of Torah and Mitzvot. Each holy act, performed with materials of this world, releases their latent Divine sparks. The ultimate goal of humankind, which will be realized at the end of time, is to effect the release of all these sparks and their return to G-d.

Rabbi Feitel Levin, *Heaven on Earth* [Brooklyn, N.Y.: Kehot Publication Society, 2002], pp. 34–35

Text 2a

בְּכָל דְּרָכֶיךָ דָעֵהוּ.

משלי ג,ו

Know Him in all your ways.

Mishlei/Proverbs 3:6

Text 2b

וְכָל מַעֲשֶׂיךָ יִהְיוּ לְשֵׁם שָׁמָיִם.

אבות ב,יב

All of your deeds should be for the sake of Heaven.

Mishnah, Avot 2:12

Text 3a

לָמָה בָּרָא הַקָּבָּ"ה דְּבָרֵי מַאֲכָל וּמַשְׁקֶה שָׁאָדָם תָּאֵב לָהֶם [לֶאֱכוֹל וְלִשְׁתּוֹת]. וְהַטַּעַם שֶׁהֵם. . .
נִיצוֹצוֹת . . . שֶׁהֵם מִתְלַבְּשִׁים בְּדוֹמֵם, צוֹמֵחַ, חַי, מְדַבֵּר, וְיֵשׁ לָהֶם חֵשֶׁק לְהִדָּבֵק בִּקְדֻשָּׁה . . . וְכָל
אֲכִילָה [וּשְׁתִיָּה] שֶׁאָדָם אוֹכֵל וְשׁוֹתֶה הִיא מַמָּשׁ חֵלֶק נִיצוֹצוֹת שֶׁלּוֹ שֶׁהוּא צָרִיךְ לְתַקֵּן. וְזֶהוּ שֶׁכָּתוּב
"רְעֵבִים גַּם צְמֵאִים", כְּשֶׁאָדָם רָעֵב וְצָמֵא לָהֶם, לָמָה זֶה? "נַפְשָׁם בָּהֶם תִּתְעַטָּף".

כתר שם טוב, קצד

Why did God create people to crave food and drink? Because sparks [of holiness] . . . are embedded in the inanimate, in the vegetative, in the animal, and in the human, and they have a desire to cleave to holiness. . . . Each time a person eats or drinks, that person is interacting with Divine sparks that he or she is meant to rectify. This is the [deeper meaning of] the verse (Psalms 107:5), "Hungry and thirsty, [their souls are enwrapped in them]." Why does a person hunger and thirst? Because this person's soul is enwrapped— that is, desires—the food and drink.

Rabbi Yisrael Ba'al Shem Tov, *Keter Shem Tov* 194

Text 3b

שֶׁכָּל דָּבָר שֶׁאָדָם לוֹבֵשׁ, אוֹ אוֹכֵל, אוֹ מִשְׁתַּמֵּשׁ בִּכְלִי . . . וְיֵשׁ שָׁם נִיצוֹצוֹת קְדוֹשׁוֹת הַשַּׁיָּכִים לְשֹׁרֶשׁ
נִשְׁמָתוֹ. (וְשָׁמַעְתִּי כִּי זֶהוּ הַטַּעַם שֶׁיֵּשׁ אָדָם שֶׁאוֹהֵב דָּבָר זֶה, וְיֵשׁ אָדָם שֶׁשּׂוֹנֵא דָּבָר זֶה וְאוֹהֵב דָּבָר
אַחֵר.) וּכְשֶׁהוּא מִשְׁתַּמֵּשׁ בְּאוֹתוֹ הַכְּלִי, אוֹ אוֹכֵל מַאֲכָל אֲפִלּוּ לְצוֹרֶךְ גּוּפוֹ, הוּא מְתַקֵּן הַנִּיצוֹצִין.
כִּי אַחַר כָּךְ עוֹבֵד בְּכֹחַ הַזֶּה שֶׁבָּא לְגוּפוֹ מֵאוֹתוֹ מַלְבּוּשׁ אוֹ מַאֲכָל אוֹ שְׁאָר דְּבָרִים, וּבְזֶה הַכֹּחַ עוֹבֵד
לְהַשֵּׁם יִתְבָּרֵךְ, נִמְצְאוּ מְתֻקָּנִים.

אור תורה, ע' תי"ג

There are sparks of holiness within everything that a person wears, eats, or otherwise uses . . . which belong to the person's soul. (I have also heard that this is why some people enjoy a particular thing, while others dislike it and prefer something else.) When a person makes use of that particular item, or eats that particular food—even merely to satisfy bodily needs—this person rectifies the sparks therein. This is so because through the energy that the body received from the food or object, the person is able to serve God.

Rabbi Dovber of Mezritch, *Or Torah*, p. 413

Text 4

וְעוֹד זֹאת בְּמַאֲכָלוֹת אֲסוּרוֹת, שֶׁלְּכָךְ נִקְרָאִים בְּשֵׁם אָסוּר, מִפְּנֵי שֶׁאַף מִי שֶׁאָכַל מַאֲכַל אָסוּר בְּלֹא הוֹדַע לְשֵׁם שָׁמַיִם לַעֲבֹד ה' בְּכֹחַ אֲכִילָה הַהִיא, וְגַם פָּעַל וְעָשָׂה כֵן וְקָרָא וְהִתְפַּלֵּל בְּכֹחַ אֲכִילָה הַהִיא, אֵין הַחַיּוּת שֶׁבָּהּ עוֹלָה וּמִתְלַבֶּשֶׁת בְּתֵבוֹת הַתּוֹרָה וְהַתְּפִלָּה, כְּמוֹ הַהֶתֵּר, מִפְּנֵי אִיסוּרָהּ בִּידֵי הַסִּטְרָא אַחְרָא מִשָּׁלֹשׁ קְלִפּוֹת הַטְּמֵאוֹת.

תניא, פרק ח

Moreover, the following explains why forbidden foods are called ossur [chained]:

Even if one ate a forbidden food unwittingly with the intention to eat it for the sake of Heaven, that is, in order to serve God with the energy derived from it . . . still, the vitality contained in the food will not ascend on High with the words of Torah and prayer. This is true even if one actually does study Torah and pray with the energy derived from that food.

This is because, unlike permitted foods, the vitality within forbidden foods is irretrievably bound by its husk.

Rabbi Shne'ur Zalman of Liadi, *Tanya*, ch. 8

Text 5

הַדָּשׁ, וְהַזּוֹרֶה, הַבּוֹרֵר, הַטּוֹחֵן, וְהַמְרַקֵּד, וְהַלָּשׁ, וְהָאוֹפֶה.

משנה, שבת ז,ב

Threshing, winnowing, sorting, grinding, sifting, kneading, and baking.

Mishnah, Tractate Shabbat 7:2

Text 6

עָבִיד קוּדְשָׁא בְּרִיךְ הוּא עַלְמָא תַּתָּאָה כְּגַוְונָא דְעַלְמָא עִילָאָה

זהר א, לח,א

God made the physical world to mirror the spiritual world.

Zohar 1:38a

III. Eating in Context

Text 7

הָאוֹכֵל בְּשַׂר שְׁמֵנָא דְתוֹרָא וְשׁוֹתֶה יַיִן מְבָשָּׂם לְהַרְחִיב דַּעְתּוֹ לַה' וּלְתוֹרָתוֹ כְּדְאָמַר רָבָא, חַמְרָא וְרֵיחָא כו', אוֹ בִּשְׁבִיל כְּדֵי לְקַיֵּם מִצְוַת עֹנֶג שַׁבָּת וְיוֹם טוֹב, אֲזַי נִתְבָּרֵר חַיּוּת הַבָּשָׂר וְהַיַּיִן . . . וְעוֹלֶה לַה' כְּעוֹלָה וּכְקָרְבָּן . . .

אַךְ מִי שֶׁהוּא כְּזוֹלְלֵי בָשָׂר וְסוֹבְאֵי יַיִן לְמַלֹּאת תַּאֲוַת גּוּפוֹ וְנַפְשׁוֹ הַבַּהֲמִית . . . הִנֵּה עַל יְדֵי זֶה יוֹרֵד חַיּוּת הַבָּשָׂר וְהַיַּיִן שֶׁבְּקִרְבּוֹ, וְנִכְלָל לְפִי שָׁעָה בְּרַע גָּמוּר.

תניא, פרק ז

If one eats fat beef and drinks spiced wine to broaden one's mind for God and for His Torah—as Rava said, "Wine and fragrance [make my mind more receptive]"—or to fulfill the commandment to enjoy the Shabbat and festivals, then the vitality of the meat and the wine . . . ascend to God as an offering.

On the other hand, if a person gluttonously eats meat and quaffs wine to satisfy one's bodily appetites and animal soul . . . then the vitality of the meat and wine that is ingested is thereby degraded and absorbed temporarily in utter evil.

Tanya, op. cit., ch. 7

LEARNING INTERACTION 1

Take a moment to think about your experiences. Which specific foods help you to meet a specific and worthwhile objective?

a)_____

b)_____

c)_____

Text 8a

מַאן דְּבָעֵי לְנַחֲמָא עַל פּוּם חַרְבָּא יֵיכוֹל.

זהר ג, קפח,ב

One who desires bread should eat it with the blade of a sword.

Zohar, op. cit., 3:188b

Text 8b

שְׁעַת אֲכִילָה—שְׁעַת מִלְחָמָה.

זהר ג,רעב,א

The time of eating is a time of battle.

Ibid., 3:272a

Text 9

שֶׁהָיָה כֹּחַ זֶה שֶׁל עֵץ הַחַיִּים וְעֵץ הַדַּעַת טוֹב וָרַע בְּכָל עֲצֵי הַגָּן. וְאִם הָיָה טוֹעֵם מֵעֵץ הַחַיִּים, הַיְינוּ שֶׁלֹּא בַּהֲנָאַת הַגּוּף, אָז הָיָה מַרְגִּישׁ בְּכָל אֲכִילָתוֹ מִכָּל הָעֵץ שֶׁהָיָה אֹכֵל קְדֻשַּׁת עֵץ הַחַיִּים, וְהָיְינוּ אֲכִילָה בִּקְדֻשָּׁה . . . אֲבָל כֵּיוָן שֶׁאָכַל מֵעֵץ הַדַּעַת, הַיְינוּ שֶׁהִרְגִּישׁ הֲנָאַת הַגּוּף בַּאֲכִילָה, עַל יְדֵי זֶה נַעֲשָׂה עִרְבּוּב, וְכָל אֲכִילוֹת שֶׁאָכַל הִרְגִּישׁ מֵעֵץ הַדַּעַת טוֹב וָרַע, הֲנָאַת הַגּוּף.

פרי צדיק, פרשת בראשית ח

All the trees in the garden possessed the potential of both the Tree of Life and the Tree of Knowledge of Good and Evil. . . . Had Adam eaten from "the Tree of Life"—that is, had he eaten appropriately, and not merely to indulge his body—he would have experienced the holiness of the Tree of Life in his eating. . . . But because he ate from the Tree of Knowledge, that is, with the awareness of his sensory pleasure, all subsequent eating was tainted with the desire for bodily gratification.

Rabbi Tzadok Hakohen Rabinowitz, *Pri Tzadik, Parshat Bereishit* 8

Question for Discussion

How does this interpretation differ from the ordinary understanding of the biblical story?

Text 10

"וְאַנְשֵׁי קֹדֶשׁ תִּהְיוּן לִי". וְאָמַר הָרַבִּי מִקּוֹצְק: כָּךְ אָמַר ה': "מַלְאָכִים וּשְׂרָפִים וְחַיּוֹת הַקֹּדֶשׁ יֵשׁ לִי דַי מִבַּלְעֲדֵיכֶם, אֵינִי זָקוּק שֶׁתִּהְיוּ לִי מַלְאָכִים. אֶלָּא 'וְאַנְשֵׁי קֹדֶשׁ תִּהְיוּן לִי', שֶׁתִּהְיוּ בְּנֵי אָדָם וְתִחְיוּ כִּבְנֵי אָדָם, וּכְבְנֵי אָדָם תִּהְיוּ לִי קְדוֹשִׁים וְאַנְשֵׁי קֹדֶשׁ".

לתורה ולמועדים, שמות כה,ב

"You shall be holy people unto Me." The Rebbe of Kotsk said: This is what God is saying: "I have enough angels without you; I have no need for you to be angelic. Instead, 'You shall be holy people unto Me.' Be human, live as humans do—but be holy humans, a holy people."

Rabbi Shlomo Yosef Zevin, *LeTorah Ulemo'adim*, Shemot/Exodus 25:2

IV. A Spiritual Diet

Text 11

אָסוּר לוֹ לָאָדָם שֶׁיֵּהָנֶה מִן הָעוֹלָם הַזֶּה בְּלֹא בְּרָכָה . . . כָּל הַנֶּהֱנֶה מִן הָעוֹלָם הַזֶּה בְּלֹא בְּרָכָה, כְּאִלּוּ נֶהֱנָה מִקָּדְשֵׁי שָׁמַיִם, וּכְתִיב (תהלים כד,א), "לַה׳ הָאָרֶץ וּמְלוֹאָהּ".

תלמוד בבלי, ברכות לה,א

It is forbidden to enjoy anything of this world without reciting a blessing. . . . To enjoy anything of this world without a blessing is like making personal use of things consecrated to Heaven, because it says, "The earth and all that is in it belongs to God (Tehilim/Psalms 24:1)."

Talmud, Berachot 35a

Hebrew Word	Transliteration	Translation	Kabbalistic Meaning
בָּרוּךְ	Baruch	Blessed	**Baruch** can also mean to draw down. The act of reciting a blessing draws the Divine into our consciousness and into our world.
אַתָּה	Atah	Are You	"You" refers to the way God transcends everything, even a name. Yet, "You" also connotes a relationship. Even before we say His name, we have an up-close and personal relationship with Him.
י-ה-ו-ה	Ado-nai	Lord	The four-letter name of God marks the flow of Divine energy from the infinite to the finite.
אֱלֹקֵינוּ	Elo-heinu	Our God	This name of God expresses God's presence in nature.
מֶלֶךְ הָעוֹלָם	Melech ha'olam	King of the universe	God is King over **olam**, a cognate of **he'elem**—concealment. Yet, through our actions, including this **berachah**, we draw light into the concealment.
שֶׁהַכֹּל נִהְיָה בִּדְבָרוֹ	Shehakol nihiyah bidvaro	By whose word all things came to be.	His word is the Divine spark that is no longer held hostage in the physical matter, which is now able to express itself.

Key Points

1   According to Kabbalah, all physical matter contains a spiritual core that can be described as sparks of holiness. These sparks are trapped within their material crusts, which conceal their sanctity. Our souls descend into corporal bodies on this material planet in order to free the Divine sparks and allow them the freedom of expression.

2   Eating is one of the primary ways we accomplish this. By eating kosher food with proper intent—to perform *mitzvot* and lead a healthy and spiritual life—we can reveal the holiness buried within this physical world.

3   The laws of *kashrut* revolve around this idea. Some sparks are compromised by their crusts and far too attached to be freed via consumption. Items containing such sparks are not kosher.

4   Many of the activities involving food preparation are forms of refining and sorting between the desirable and the undesirable. This is a reflection of the spiritual concept of eating—to free the spark from its state of concealment within its husk.

5   We elevate these sparks when we give our eating a context that is deeper than the physical act. This is accomplished by eating only what we need, only as we need it, with the intention of achieving positive and spiritual accomplishments.

6   In ordinary dieting, the repercussions of unhealthy eating are often in the distant future. Spiritual eating means realizing that the consequences of healthy/unhealthy eating are immediately present.

7   Reciting a blessing before we eat can help us overcome the challenge of eating properly, by focusing on the awareness that what we are about to do is more than just a physical act.

Bibliography

Text 1a – Rabbi Chaim ben Yosef Vital (1542–1620). Born in Israel, lived in Safed, Jerusalem, and later Damascus. Vital was the principal disciple of Arizal, though he studied under him for less than two years. Before his passing, Arizal authorized Vital to record his teachings. Acting on this mandate, Vital began arranging his master's teachings in written form, and his many works constitute the foundation of the Lurianic school of Jewish mysticism, which was later universally adopted as the kabbalistic standard. Thus, Vital is one of the most important influences in the development of Kabbalah. Among his most famous works are *Ets Chayim*, and *Sha'ar Hakavanot*.

Text 3a – Rabbi Yisrael ben Eliezer (1698–1760). Rabbi and mystic, better known as the "Ba'al Shem Tov" or by the acronym "Besht"; founder of the chassidic movement. Born in Okupy, Ukraine, he was orphaned as a child. The Ba'al Shem Tov served as a teacher's assistant and clay-digger before founding the Chasidic movement. Although he never committed his ideas to writing, the Ba'al Shem Tov's teachings were gathered by his disciples in various volumes.

Text 3b – Rabbi Dovber "the Magid" of Mezeritch (d. 1772). Was the primary disciple and eventual successor of the Ba'al Shem Tov. Amongst his disciples were the founders of various Chasidic dynasties, including Rabbi Nachum of Chernobyl, Rabbi Levi Yitschak of Berditchev, and Rabbi Shne'ur Zalman of Liadi. His teachings, recorded by his students, appear in various volumes including the *Magid Devarav Leya'akov.*

Text 4 - Rabbi Shne'ur Zalman of Liadi (1745–1812). Chasidic rebbe and founder of the Chabad movement, also known as "the Alter Rebbe" and "the Rav." Born in Liozna, Belarus, he was among the principal students of the Magid of Mezeritch. His numerous works include the *Tanya*, an early classic containing the fundamentals of Chasidism; *Torah Or; Likutei Torah*; and *Shulchan Aruch HaRav*, a reworked and expanded code of Jewish law. He is interred in Hadiach, Ukraine, and was succeeded by his son, Rabbi Dovber of Lubavitch. **Text 5 – Mishnah, Shabbat**

Text 6 - Zohar. The most seminal work of Kabbalah, Jewish mysticism. It is a mystical commentary on the Torah, written in Aramaic and Hebrew. According to Arizal, the Zohar consists of the teachings of Rabbi Shimon bar Yocha'i who lived in the Land of Israel during the 2nd century. The Zohar has become one of the indispensable texts of traditional Judaism, alongside and nearly equal in stature to the Mishnah and Talmud.

Additional Readings

Is Kosher Food Safer?

by Deborah Kotz

Not only Jews look for the kosher symbol on food these days. In a surprising turn of events, "kosher" has become the most popular claim on new food products, trouncing "organic" and "no additives or preservatives," according to a recent report. A noteworthy 4,719 new kosher items were launched in the United States last year—nearly double the number of new "all natural" products, which placed second in the report, issued last month by Mintel, a Chicago-based market research firm.

In fact, sales of kosher foods have risen an estimated 15 percent a year for the past decade. Yet Jews, whose religious doctrine mandates the observance of kosher dietary laws, make up only 20 percent of those buying kosher products. What gives? "It's the belief among all consumers that kosher food is safer, a critical thing right now with worries about the integrity of the food supply," says Marcia Mogelonsky, a senior research analyst at Mintel.

Whether kosher foods are actually less likely to be contaminated with, say, *E. coli* bacteria remains up for debate. While research is scant in this area, experts say it makes sense that kosher food could be safer because it's more closely monitored. "Jews aren't allowed to ingest bugs, so produce must go through a thorough washing and checking to ensure that no bugs are found within the leaves or on the surface of the fruit or vegetable," says Moshe Elefant, a rabbi and chief operating officer of the Orthodox Union, a ko-sher certification organization based in New York. But bacteria can remain even after this type of washing, so consumers can't assume they're less likely to get food poisoning with bagged spinach marked kosher than with a conventional bag.

The same caveat applies to poultry and beef. A salting process that removes blood from the meat has antibacterial effects, but salmonella and *E. coli* can still survive, says Joe Regenstein, a professor of food science who teaches a course on Jewish and Muslim food laws at Cornell University. Kosher beef, though, is much less likely to contain the misshapen proteins that cause mad cow disease, rare as that is, probably because the animals are slaughtered young, before the disease sets in.

Another selling point of kosher foods is that they're easily decoded by those looking to avoid dairy or meat. "One of the fundamental rules of kosher certification is that you can't mix meat and milk," says Elefant. So each product is labeled either dairy or meat—or "pareve" (also spelled parve) if it contains neither. Pareve foods can't even be manufactured on equipment previously used for dairy or meat products. "People with severe dairy allergies are looking for that pareve designation," Elefant says. They might also turn to kosher salami and hot dogs, since nonkosher cured meats often contain a preservative made from milk sugar, though [they] may simply buy kosher because they prefer the stricter supervision that goes into certifying kosher foods. "Food companies agree to allow a third-party inspector to come in unannounced, at essentially any time," says Regenstein. These inspectors check, among other things, that products are being manufactured only with those ingredients listed on the label. Companies, he says, must carefully keep records of where ingredients come from—not always the case for small non-kosher food manufacturers—which allows for quick recall if a product gets contaminated with a nonkosher ingredient or food-borne pathogen. "That alone is worth the price of kosher," Regenstein opines. Contrary to what some folks think, however, a rabbi doesn't bless the food. "Kosher dietary laws are actually just a simple set of rules," explains Elefant, "and the kosher certification helps those who make a commitment to live under those rules."

U.S. News and World Report, January 11, 2008

Reprinted with permission of the publisher

Spiritual Molecules

by Dr. Velvl Greene

Most of us "believe" in molecules.

Hardly any one of us has ever seen a molecule, and unless we have studied a lot of chemistry and physics and physical chemistry, we probably don't understand the tests and criteria used by scientists to detect molecules, analyze them, identify them or describe their structure. Still, we believe they exist, have definable structures, weights and shapes and possess predictable properties. We have been taught that all molecules are made up of a hundred or so elemental atoms—just as all words are made up of the same basic letters. The countless and varied molecules that make up our physical world differ from each other only with respect to the type of atoms they contain, the numbers of atoms

present, their pattern of organization and their location in the molecular structure—just as all of the words in our language differ from each other only with respect to the letters they contain and their sequence. And the same words can be used to write a psalm or a political pamphlet—just as the same molecules can be found in an ant or an elephant.

There is nothing mystical about this anymore. It isn't imaginary or hypothetical. The concept of molecules and atoms and their reactions is as accepted as are things we can see and judge with our own senses.

If a chemist tells us that a given molecule has three carbon atoms and another molecule has six, we believe him. If the chemist tells us that the six carbon atoms of one molecule are in a ring, while in another molecule they are forked, we believe him. Sometimes we believe because it makes sense. More often, we believe because we have no reason to disbelieve. Most of the time we believe because we have a basic confidence in the chemist's honesty and competence.

Chemists and their colleagues have more credibility in our eyes than merchants, lawyers and most of the public servants we choose to run our country. And much of the confidence is justified. Molecular theory and manipulation are the very basis of the exciting discoveries being made almost daily in physiology, genetics, microbiology and pharmacology. The chemist has used his molecular models quite effectively to make predictions and products that have changed our lives.

For example, people long ago discovered, by empirical trial and error, that certain foods were nutritious while others were poisonous; certain beverages were intoxicating while others were innocuous; certain diets were fattening while others, which also satisfied hunger, were less so. In the early years of this century nutritionists learned that the absence of certain foodstuffs from normal diets resulted in pathological consequences. About the same time, allergists learned that adding certain ingredients to normal diets also resulted in pathological consequences. It wasn't until the chemists provided us with "metabolic maps" that we started to sort out the mass of confusing empirical data. These metabolic maps described the molecular pathways involved in food digestion and cell synthesis. They showed how the complex minerals, proteins carbohydrates and lipids present in our dietary foodstuffs could be broken down into simpler and simpler molecules; concurrently, these simple molecules could be utilized by our own bodies for putting together the proteins, minerals, carbohydrates and lipids that constitute our tissues. The maps showed how the whole process was regulated by other molecules (vitamins). The molecular models explained how and why certain foods generated toxic responses and other foods generated allergic responses; the bases of some classical deficiency diseases like rickets, pellagra, goiter and beriberi; the rationale of weight-reducing diets; and dozens of other physiological and pharmacological phenomena.

It can be fairly said that molecular chemistry and molecular biology established nutrition, physiology and nutritional pathology as sciences and took them out of the grasp of alchemists and quacks.

Kashrut and Chemistry

Thoughts of this nature kept intruding as I was reviewing the Torah portion *Shemini* (Leviticus 9-10), wherein the Jewish people were commanded, eternally, to avoid certain foods while being permitted to consume others.

The Torah itself gives no reason for these laws. But anyone familiar with the modern molecular theories of nutrition and nutritional pathology can hardly avoid the temptation of creating molecular models and maps to explain everything in this field.

But it is futile speculation . . .

In his classic volume on biblical and talmudic medicine, written 73 years ago. Dr. Julius Preuss introduced his discussion on *kashrut* (dietary laws) with the following statement:

The biblical dietary laws are included in the chapter on "Hygiene" solely because we can conceive of no reason other than sanitary for their ordination. It must be emphasized, however, that the Torah gives us no reason at all for these laws and the later sources do so only rarely. Thus, nearly everything which one alleges to be the reason for the dietary laws is only a hypothesis and is read into the sources . . .

This statement establishes precisely the frustrating paradox confronting anyone who would like to explain the laws of kashrut using modern knowledge of nutrition and public health as a model. We don't know why certain animals, birds and fish are permitted for food while others are banned; we don't know why the permitted quadrupeds and birds must be slaughtered in a given fashion; we don't know why blood, certain fatty tissues and the sciatic nerve are forbidden; we don't know the hazards associated with cooking and/or consuming meat and milk; and we don't know why certain specific anatomical imperfections render an animal or fowl *traifa* (not kosher) and thus prohibited. We are provided with remarkably detailed guides and instructions about the criteria that distinguish between prohibited and acceptable, but nothing about why. Though we very much want to know why, any rational explanation is simply an exercise in human imagination.

The greatest minds ever produced by the human race have struggled for thousands of years to explain these laws. Dozens, if not hundreds of hypotheses have been proposed to elucidate these mysteries. Why is the ox kosher and the camel not? Why cannot a Jew eat pork and benefit from the well-known nutritional quality of swine flesh? Why is carp acceptable while eels are not? The rational mind yearns to understand and unfortunately, because it cannot understand, sometimes decides to ignore the laws altogether!

In the last hundred years or so, it has become fashionable to explain kashrut with analogies from public health. The basic argument is that Moses was really a primitive health commissioner, and the Parshah of *Shemini* was an early model of current Pure Food and Drug laws. It is an intriguing concept, but its adherents today are mainly Jews who do not want to observe the dietary restrictions in the first place. Very little support for this point of view will be found in authentic public health research. Rabbits are as nutritious as chickens; gefilte fish can be made as well from sturgeon as from trout; there isn't that much difference—microbiologically or chemically—between lamb and pork.

It would be easier to understand (and adhere to?) the dietary restrictions if we would find a chemical reason. It would be easier particularly if we could isolate some kind of substance or harmful chemical from a forbidden food that is not present in a permitted food. Or if we could show that the processes described in the *Shulchan Aruch* (Code of Jewish Law) inhibit some

obscure molecular reaction which produces a toxin. That would make sense. We have a lot of empirical experience with food poisoning and allergies. Undoubtedly our ancestors did also. There are certain foodstuffs in nature that are intrinsically poisonous—certain mushrooms, for example, some fish and some mollusks. It would be quite reasonable for a primitive lawmaker to ban them as food for his tribe. We also know that foods, if improperly stored or processed, can become vehicles for transmission of infectious agents or their toxins. Thus a primitive lawgiver, concerned with the physical health of his tribe, would also ordain laws about processing and storing the materials which have been permitted as food.

If non-kosher foods or improper processing resulted in food poisoning or infection or skin eruptions, we could understand.

But they really don't. From a nutritional and toxicological perspective, there is no difference between a kosher and non-kosher diet. The answer certainly is not chemical. It isn't the physical atoms and molecules of pork that render it inedible for Jews. Otherwise, why is it not forbidden to non-Jews? Is it possible that there are chemical receptors or Jewish cells that are sensitive to molecules of *traifa* foods? It is not beyond medical experience. Some humans are allergic to strawberries while others are not. Indeed, the only difference between the allergic and the retractile is a subtle molecular reaction that occurs in the former and not in the latter. A better example might be the genetic (some say racial) inability of some humans to digest bovine milk while others literally thrive on it. Thus there are molecular reactions, in the realm of nutritional pathology and which are hereditary that can serve as a justification for dietary taboos.

Unfortunately, it doesn't wash clean. Jewish racial qualities are more a Nazi myth than a chemical reality today. When the dietary prohibitions were announced, the 12 tribes encamped around Sinai several thousand years ago certainly shared a similar genetic make up. But in the thousands of years since then and particularly in the thousands of years of diaspora, the genetic homogeneity became significantly diluted. Jews today differ greatly in blood types and immunological make up and physiological response to nutrients. Today a chemical explanation of kashrut—which remains extremely binding despite the gradual genetic diversification is—simply an inadequate hypothesis. A convert to Judaism is obligated to observe the kashrut laws as soon as she or he becomes a Jew, even if he or she has thrived physiologically on the now-forbidden foods until that very moment.

Spiritual Molecules

Many of the rabbinic commentators make reference, while humbly denying that they know the true answer, to the "spiritual damage" that derives from non-kosher foods. For example. Rabbi Shimshon Raphael Hirsch comments on the Torah portion *Kedoshim* (Leviticus 19-20) as follows:

You must . . . conscientiously keep . . . the choice of nourishment . . . as the very first preliminary . . . for spiritual, mental and moral clarity, purity and holiness . . . right from the beginning, at the actual forming of the tissues of your body, the physical formation of the fibers of your brain, nerves and muscles . . .

The forbidden foods are thus not materially poisonous, but they are harmful to our soul. The dangerous components of pork cannot be detected by chemists, and the toxicological effects of its consumption cannot be diagnosed by physicians, but the damage does certainly occur. If we want to think in terms of molecules, we must think about "spiritual molecules."

In this respect, I once read that there are spiritual poisons in certain proscribed foods that dull the spiritual senses or, as is put so well in Yiddish, "stuff up the nose and ears of the soul" to the extent that the individual can no longer receive spiritual messages. I also heard that the animals forbidden as food by Torah possess certain spiritual characteristics which the consumer is in danger of acquiring. Whatever the rationale, spiritual molecules make more sense than chemical ones.

But they make sense only to one who already believes in the authority of Torah and that person is already willing to obey the rules without any rationalizations. To the rest of the world, spiritual molecules are too much the subject of mystery and superstition. In the spiritual realm, according to those who consider themselves modern and scientific there are no rules and no logic—just a lot of fairy stories, visions, magic, witchcraft and gurus.

Of course, real molecules are also invisible and intangible to most of us. Real molecules are also the subjects of speculation by the gurus (of science) who wear their priestly garments and who officiate in their esoteric temples (called laboratories) after years of apprenticeship. But spiritual molecules are too much for the twentieth century.

(Parenthetically, I wonder if our rabbis would be more successful in getting their message across if they exchanged their black frocks for white lab coats? I wonder if the observance of kashrut would be enhanced by impressive lab equipment and periodic tables and diagrams of covalent electron bonds or their spiritual equivalent? Probably not. The contemporary Jewish non-observer is too sophisticated for that; he wouldn't fall for such gimmicks. If he doesn't obey the rules when G-d Himself issues them, why would he change because a rabbi put on a white coat?

Then why does he believe in molecules made up of carbon atoms? But that's another story . . .)

I submit that the real barrier to accepting the role of spiritual molecules derives from two handicaps in conceptualization:

1) The lack of immediate empirical proof of spiritual harm when the laws are disregarded;

2) The matter of particularism, i.e., the selective nature of the dietary laws which permit the majority of humans to eat and benefit from a given food while denying the same opportunity to a very small group of people who are indistinguishable in any detectable way from the majority and who also seem to benefit from the food.

PKU—a Medical Model of Kashrut?

We are taught in Chassidism that the spiritual world and the material world are parallels of each other. Thus phenomena experienced in the flesh and blood universe are modeled on spiritual phenomena. Similarly, the spiritual universe is reflected in things and events which are detected by our mortal senses.

This permits us to postulate the existence of spiritual molecules based on our knowledge of chemical structures. Indeed, there are those who would say that the material molecules we study and teach about in chemistry courses are really the reflection of the intangible spiritual molecules the Creator used as a blueprint!

With this in mind I present the natural history of a rare genetic disease that might provide some kind of answer to those who reject kashrut because they lack empirical proof of harm and feel uncomfortable with strict particularism.

Medicine is familiar with a condition called phenylketonuria or PKU. First described fifty years ago, this hereditary metabolic disorder affects about one out of 15,000 children born in the northern hemisphere and leads, among other things, to an irreversible and severe retardation.

The newborn child appears healthy and normal. He cannot really be distinguished during a routine physical examination, from his 14,999 unaffected peers. He has a normal appetite and an apparently unremarkable metabolism. He eats, sleeps, cries and does all of the other things babies are expected to do. But gradually—over the course of several years—he develops a characteristic appearance and brain damage.

Many years after the disease was first described, physiologists determined that the brain damage was a result of the accumulation in the body of a certain amino acid—phenylalanine—which is a common molecule in many proteins. Normal people have the ability to metabolize phenylalanine and to convert it to other, non-harmful (and essential) nutrients. But one child in 15,000 lacks the necessary enzyme and the phenylalanine accumulates and accumulates until it harms the developing brain.

About 35 years ago, a chemist named Guthrie described a blood test which permits the early diagnosis of PKU, within a few days after birth, long before the neurological damage has occurred. This test is now compulsory in most Western countries (including Israel). Every baby born in a hospital is tested for PKU. If the results suggest that the condition is present, the mother is provided with nutritional advice and counseling. If the diet is modified early enough, if the phenylalanine-containing protein is replaced with a synthetic substitute and fed for the first four or five years, the retardation can usually be avoided. The solution isn't simple; it is also inconvenient, unappetizing and expensive. But, it is effective.

Now consider the following scenario: a public health nurse visits a young mother who has just come home from the hospital with her precious newborn baby. The nurse conveys the frightening news that according to the lab tests the baby has PKU. She also provides the mother with a list of prescribed foods and instructions for preparing a suitable preventive diet.

Neither the nurse nor the mother is a chemist. The mother knows nothing about molecules or physiology or metabolism. She knows what she sees—a healthy, normal baby, like any other baby in the world, who enjoys eating and is apparently thriving on the diet being provided. The nurse knows a little more. She has studied a little chemistry and understands the best physiology of metabolism. Or at least, she believes the teachers who taught her. The nurse doesn't really know the basis of the diagnostic tests; nor could she prescribe a diet out of her own experi-

ence. All she is doing is her job of transmitting the information she was taught. She believes she is acting in the best interests of the child and the community. But she is mostly acting out of duty and acceptance of higher authorities—such as doctors, chemist and nutritionists—who have studied more and know more and have better sources of knowledge.

The mother refuses to accept the diagnosis or the diet. She doesn't believe in the mysteries of chemistry or accept the authority of the doctors. Doesn't her baby look normal? Isn't the baby happy? Besides, the recommended diet is too expensive and inconvenient and unappetizing. What is all this nonsense about molecules anyway?

I end with the following question:

If you were the nurse, what would you do when the mother demands, "Show me the danger now! Show me the difference between my baby and all the others!"

B'Or Ha'Torah Journal: Science, Art and Modern Life in the Light of Torah 6 (1987): 159-164

www.borhatorah.org, info@borhatorah.org

Reprinted with permission of the publisher

IV

When More Makes Merrier
A Holistic Approach to Pursuing Happiness

ROSH**CHODESH**
society

Introduction

In his 2007 book, *Happiness and the Human Spirit: The Spirituality of Becoming the Best You Can Be*, Rabbi Dr. Abraham Twerski makes the following keen observation (p. 5):

> For anyone in the early 1900s, the vision that crippling polio would be eliminated; that the contagious diseases of childhood would be a rarity; that the trip from Chicago to Los Angeles would be a trip of four rather than sixty hours; that the Atlantic Ocean could be traversed in seven hours; that, on the hottest days of summer, we could relax in the comfort of air-conditioned homes, watching a football game being played three thousand miles away, or a choice of movies on DVD—that would be paradise on Earth!

> If you could tell such a person that, in the twenty-first century, the workweek would be thirty-seven hours; that most of the work would be done by electronically controlled machines; that preparation of meals would be facilitated by the availability of instant foods, microwaves, and fast-food vendors; that fax machines, cell phones, and e-mail would enable instant communication; that humans would orbit Earth and walk on the moon; that computers would make the most complex calculations in a fraction of a second and predict the weather with great accuracy; that diseased livers and kidneys would be replaced by healthy organs; that the Internet would put all the knowledge in the world at our fingertips—they would see such a future as pure bliss! Surely, with so many of the sources of distress and suffering eliminated, the human race would finally be able to achieve the goal of happiness. The pursuit would be over!

> So here we are, in the twenty-first century, the beneficiaries of heretofore unimaginable miracles of science and technology, yet happiness continues to elude us.

In this lesson, we discuss what happiness *really* is and how we can go about finding it.

I. Understanding Happiness

Text 1

כְּמוֹ שֶׁנִּצָּחוֹן לְנַצֵּחַ דָּבָר גַּשְׁמִי, כְּגוֹן שְׁנֵי אֲנָשִׁים הַמִּתְאַבְּקִים זֶה עִם זֶה לְהַפִּיל זֶה אֶת זֶה, הִנֵּה אִם הָאֶחָד הוּא בְּעַצְלוּת וּכְבֵדוּת יְנוּצַּח בְּקַל וְיִפּוֹל, גַּם אִם הוּא גִּבּוֹר יוֹתֵר מֵחֲבֵירוֹ, כָּכָה מַמָּשׁ בְּנִצָּחוֹן הַיֵּצֶר, אִי אֶפְשָׁר לְנַצְּחוֹ בְּעַצְלוּת וּכְבֵדוּת הַנִּמְשָׁכוֹת מֵעַצְבוּת וְטִמְטוּם הַלֵּב כָּאֶבֶן, כִּי אִם בִּזְרִיזוּת הַנִּמְשֶׁכֶת מִשִּׂמְחָה וּפְתִיחַת הַלֵּב וְטָהֳרָתוֹ מִכָּל נִדְנוּד דְּאָגָה וְעֶצֶב בָּעוֹלָם.

תניא, פרק כו

Overcoming negative tendencies is similar to overcoming a physical opponent.

If two individuals are wrestling with each other, each striving to defeat the other, but one is lazy and lethargic—he will be defeated easily, even if he is stronger than his opponent.

The same applies regarding the conquest of one's negative tendencies: It is impossible to conquer them with laziness and heaviness that stem from sadness and a heart dulled like a stone, but rather with alacrity that stems from happiness, from a heart that is free and cleansed from any trace of worry and sadness in the world.

Rabbi Shne'ur Zalman of Liadi, *Tanya*, ch. 26

Text 2

Thanks to cutting-edge science, we now know that happiness is the precursor to success, not merely the result. And that happiness and optimism actually fuel *performance and achievement....*

We become more successful when *we are happier and more positive. For example, doctors put in a positive mood before making a diagnosis show almost three times more intelligence and creativity than doctors in a neutral state, and they make accurate diagnoses 19 percent faster. Optimistic salespeople outsell their pessimistic counterparts by 56 percent. Students primed to feel happy before taking math achievement tests far outperform their neutral peers.* It turns out that our brains are literally hardwired to perform at their best not when they are negative or even neutral, but when they are positive.

Professor Shawn Achor, *The Happiness Advantage: The Seven Principles of Positive Psychology That Fuel Success and Performance at Work*, pgs. 3-4, 15

LEARNING INTERACTION 1

Can you think of a time in your life when a degree of positivity or optimism affected your success in overcoming a challenge or exerting self-control?

_____

_____

_____

LEARNING INTERACTION 2

a. If you were writing a dictionary, how would you define "happiness"? _____

Take a moment to go around the room, allowing students to share their definitions. It will probably become evident that the definition of happiness is a bit nebulous. Then move on to the next stage of this interaction:

b. Complete the following sentence: "If _____ *then I would be a happier person."*

LEARNING INTERACTION 3

Peruse the following list and put a star or mark next to the three definitions that resonate the most with you.

1.　　Happiness is when what you think, what you say, and what you do are in harmony.
　　　— *Mahatma Gandhi*

2.　　Many persons have a wrong idea of what constitutes true happiness. It is not attained through self-gratification, but through fidelity to a worthy purpose.
　　　— *Helen Keller*

3.　　Success is getting what you want. Happiness is wanting what you get.
　　　— *Dale Carnegie*

> > >

4.   *Happiness lies in the joy of achievement and the thrill of creative effort.*
     — Franklin D. Roosevelt

5.   *The person born with a talent they are meant to use will find their greatest happiness in using it.*
     — Johann Wolfgang von Goethe

6.   *Happiness can exist only in acceptance.*
     — George Orwell

7.   *Happiness: a good bank account, a good cook, and a good digestion.*
     — Jean-Jacques Rousseau

8.   *People say that money is not the key to happiness, but I always figured if you have enough money, you can have a key made.*
     — Joan Rivers

9.   *True happiness is . . . to enjoy the present, without anxious dependence upon the future.*
     — Lucius Annaeus Seneca

10. *By happiness is intended pleasure and the absence of pain.*
     — John Stuart Mill

11. *What can be added to the happiness of a man who is in health, out of debt, and has a clear conscience?*
     — Adam Smith

12. *The happiness of a man in this life does not consist in the absence but in the mastery of his passions.*
     — Alfred Lord Tennyson

13. *Happiness: an agreeable sensation arising from contemplating the misery of another.*
     — Ambrose Bierce

14. *Happiness consists in activity. It is running steam, not a stagnant pool.*
     — Oliver Wendell Holmes Sr.

15. *When what we are is what we want to be, that's happiness.*
     — Malcolm Forbes

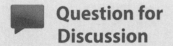

Question for Discussion

What would you consider the happiest day of your life? Why?

Text 3

כָּל שִׂמְחָה הוּא מִפְּנֵי הַשְׁלֵימוּת, כִּי כַּאֲשֶׁר אֶחָד בִּשְׁלֵימוּת אָז בָּא הַשִּׂמְחָה. וְאֵין אָדָם בִּשְׁלֵימוּת כַּאֲשֶׁר אֵין לוֹ אִשָּׁה, וּלְכָךְ שָׁרוּי בְּלֹא שִׂמְחָה.

מהר"ל, חידושי אגדות, שם

Happiness is a result of wholeness. When a person is complete, happiness ensues. A person is not complete without a spouse, which is why an unmarried person lacks happiness.

Rabbi Yehudah Loew (Maharal of Prague), *Chidushei Agadot* on Talmud, Yevamot 62b

Text 4

Every living creature comes into the world in a state of potentiality. Except for human beings, nature has endowed every creature with the instincts that can lead to its actualization. We humans are the exception. In order to become the best we can be, we need to focus our efforts in that direction, to intentionally exercise and implement the traits of the human spirit to the best of our abilities. This process—whether we call it actualization, self-improvement, personal growth, or self-fulfillment—is spirituality. Failure to embrace spirituality leaves us in a state of incompleteness and discontent.

Our happiness depends on being complete people.

Rabbi Dr. Abraham J. Twerski, *Happiness and the Human Spirit: The Spirituality of Becoming the Best You Can Be*, p. 151

Text 5

כַּד אִתְבְּרֵי אָדָם מַה כְּתִיב בֵּהּ "עוֹר וּבָשָׂר תַּלְבִּישֵׁנִי" וְגוֹ' (איוב י,יא). אִי הָכִי הָאָדָם מַהוּ? אִי תֵּימָא דְּאֵינוֹ אֶלָּא עוֹר וּבָשָׂר וְעַצָמוֹת וְגִידִים, לָאו הָכִי, דְּהָא וַדַּאי הָאָדָם לַאו אִיהוּ אֶלָּא נִשְׁמָתָא, וְאִלֵּין דְּקָאמַר עוֹר וּבָשָׂר עַצָמוֹת וְגִידִים כָּלְהוּ לֹא הֲווֹ אֶלָּא מַלְבּוּשָׁא בִּלְחוֹדוֹי, מָאנִין אִינוּן דְּבַר נַשׁ וְלָאו אִינוּן אָדָם.

זוהר ב, עה,ב–עו,א

When Adam was created, what is written concerning him? "Thou hast clothed me with skin and flesh (Iyov/Job 10:11)."

What, then, is a human being? Does a person consist solely of skin, flesh, bones, and sinews?

Nay, the essence of a person is his soul; the skin, flesh, bones, and sinews are but an outward covering, the mere garments, but they are not the person.

Zohar 2:75b–76a

II. If I Were a Rich Man

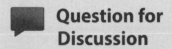

Question for Discussion

"Money doesn't buy happiness" is the old wise saying. Is it true?

Text 6a

In 1978, a trio of psychologists curious about happiness assembled two groups of subjects. In the first were winners of the Illinois state lottery. These men and women had received jackpots of between fifty thousand and a million dollars. In the second group were victims of devastating accidents. Some had been left paralyzed from the waist down. For the others, paralysis started at the neck.

The researchers asked the members of both groups a battery of questions about their lives. On a scale of "the best and worst things that could happen," how did the members of the first group rank becoming rich and the second wheelchair-bound? How happy had they been before these events? How about now? How happy did they expect to be in a couple of years? How much pleasure did they take in daily experiences, such as talking with a friend, hearing a joke, or reading a magazine? . . . For a control, the psychologists assembled a third group, made up of Illinois residents selected at random from the phone book.

When the psychologists tabulated the answers, they found that the lottery group rated winning as a highly positive experience and the accident group ranked victimhood as a negative one. Clearly, the winners realized that they'd been fortunate. But this only made the subsequent results more puzzling. The winners considered themselves no happier at the time of the interviews than the members of the control group did. In the future, the winners expected to become slightly happier, but, once again, no more so than the control-group members. (Even the accident victims expected to be happier than the lottery winners within a few years.) Meanwhile, the winners took significantly less pleasure in daily activities—including clothes-buying—than the members of the other two groups.

Elizabeth Kolbert, "Everybody Have Fun," *The New Yorker*, March 22, 2010

Text 6b

Over the past three and a half decades, real per capita income in the United States has risen from just over seventeen thousand dollars to almost twenty-seven thousand dollars. During that same period, the average new home in the U.S. grew in size by almost fifty percent; the number of cars in the country increased by more than a hundred and twenty million; the proportion of families owning personal computers rose from zero to seventy per cent; and so on. Yet, since the early seventies, the percentage of Americans who describe themselves as either "very happy" or "pretty happy" has remained virtually unchanged. Indeed, the average level of self-reported happiness, or "subjective well-being," appears to have been flat going all the way back to the nineteen-fifties, when real per capita income was less than half what it is today.

Ibid.

Text 6c

Carol Graham, a professor of public policy at the University of Maryland, reports on some of the findings. . . .

Take the case of Nigeria. The country's per capita G.D.P. last year was about fourteen hundred dollars. (In real terms, this is significantly lower than it was when the nation declared its independence, in 1960.) Yet the proportion of Nigerians who rate themselves happy is as high as the proportion of Japanese, whose per-capita G.D.P. is almost twenty-five times as great. The percentage of Bangladeshis who report themselves satisfied is twice as high as the percentage of Russians, though Russians are more than four times as rich, and the proportion of happy Panamanians is twice as high as that of happy Argentines, though the Argentines have double the income. Research that Graham has done in Afghanistan shows that, despite three decades of war and widespread destitution, Afghans are, on average, a pretty cheerful lot. (The most cheerful areas of the country tend to be those in which the Taliban's influence is stronger.) Graham's research in Latin America shows that the very poor are often remarkably upbeat. "Higher per capita income levels do not translate directly into higher average happiness levels," she writes.

Ibid.

Text 7

The notion that money can't buy happiness has been around a long time—even before yoga came into vogue. But it turns out there is a measurable connection between income and happiness; not surprisingly, people with a comfortable living standard are happier than people living in poverty.

The catch is that additional income doesn't buy us any additional happiness on a typical day, once we reach that comfortable standard. The magic number that defines this "comfortable standard" varies across individuals and countries, but in the United States, it seems to fall somewhere around $75,000. Using Gallup data collected from almost half a million Americans, researchers at Princeton found that higher household incomes were associated with better moods on a daily basis — but the beneficial effects of money tapered off entirely after the $75,000 mark.

Elizabeth Dunn and Michael Norton, "Don't Indulge. Be Happy." *The New York Times*, July 7, 2012

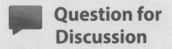 **Question for Discussion**

Why do you think it is that, past a certain point, higher income levels do not translate into higher happiness levels?

Text 8a

וְהָיָה אִם שָׁמוֹעַ תִּשְׁמַע בְּקוֹל ה' אֱלֹקֶיךָ לִשְׁמֹר לַעֲשׂוֹת אֶת כָּל מִצְוֹתָיו אֲשֶׁר אָנֹכִי מְצַוְּךָ הַיּוֹם. . .

וְהוֹתִרְךָ ה' לְטוֹבָה בִּפְרִי בִטְנְךָ וּבִפְרִי בְהֶמְתְּךָ וּבִפְרִי אַדְמָתֶךָ עַל הָאֲדָמָה אֲשֶׁר נִשְׁבַּע ה' לַאֲבֹתֶיךָ לָתֶת לָךְ.

יִפְתַּח ה' לְךָ אֶת אוֹצָרוֹ הַטּוֹב אֶת הַשָּׁמַיִם לָתֵת מְטַר אַרְצְךָ בְּעִתּוֹ וּלְבָרֵךְ אֶת כָּל מַעֲשֵׂה יָדֶךָ וְהִלְוִיתָ גּוֹיִם רַבִּים וְאַתָּה לֹא תִלְוֶה.

דברים כח,א-יב

And it will be if you obey the Lord, your God, to observe and fulfill all His commandments which I command you this day. . . .

And the Lord will grant you good surplus in the fruit of your womb, in the fruit of your livestock, and in the fruit of your soil, on the land that the Lord swore to your forefathers, to give you.

The Lord will open up for you His good treasury, the Heaven, to give your land its rain in its right time, and to bless everything you do. And you will lend to many nations, but you will not [need to] borrow.

Devarim/Deuteronomy 28:1–12

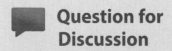 **Question for Discussion**

If the objective of Torah is to introduce people to spirituality, why would the Torah promise physical rewards for its adherents?

Text 8b

כָּל אוֹתָן הַדְּבָרִים אֱמֶת הָיוּ וְיִהְיוּ. וּבִזְמַן שֶׁאָנוּ עוֹשִׂים כָּל מִצְוֺת הַתּוֹרָה, יַגִּיעוּ אֵלֵינוּ טוֹבוֹת הָעוֹלָם הַזֶּה
כּוּלָן . . . וְאַף עַל פִּי כֵן אֵין אוֹתָן הַטּוֹבוֹת הֵם סוֹף מַתַּן שְׂכָרָן שֶׁל מִצְוֺת . . .

אֶלָּא כָּךְ הוּא הֶכְרֵעַ כָּל הַדְּבָרִים: הַקָּדוֹשׁ בָּרוּךְ הוּא נָתַן לָנוּ תּוֹרָה זוֹ עֵץ חַיִּים הִיא, וְכָל הָעוֹשֶׂה כָּל
הַכָּתוּב בָּהּ, וְיוֹדְעוֹ דֵּעָה גְּמוּרָה נְכוֹנָה, זוֹכֶה בָּהּ לְחַיֵּי הָעוֹלָם הַבָּא . . . וְהִבְטִיחָנוּ בַּתּוֹרָה שֶׁאִם נַעֲשֶׂה
אוֹתָהּ בְּשִׂמְחָה וּבְטוֹבַת נֶפֶשׁ, וְנֶהֱגֶה בְּחָכְמָתָהּ תָּמִיד, שֶׁיָּסִיר מִמֶּנּוּ כָּל הַדְּבָרִים הַמּוֹנְעִים אוֹתָנוּ
מִלַּעֲשׂוֹתָהּ, כְּגוֹן חוֹלִי, וּמִלְחָמָה, וְרָעָב, וְכַיּוֹצֵא בָּהֶן, וְיַשְׁפִּיעַ לָנוּ כָּל הַטּוֹבוֹת הַמַּחֲזִיקוֹת אֶת יָדֵינוּ
לַעֲשׂוֹת הַתּוֹרָה, כְּגוֹן שׂוֹבַע, וְשָׁלוֹם, וְרִבּוּי כֶּסֶף וְזָהָב, כְּדֵי שֶׁלֹּא נַעֲסוֹק כָּל יָמֵינוּ בִּדְבָרִים שֶׁהַגּוּף צָרִיךְ
לָהֶן, אֶלָּא נֵשֵׁב פְּנוּיִים לִלְמוֹד בְּחָכְמָה וְלַעֲשׂוֹת הַמִּצְוָה כְּדֵי שֶׁנִּזְכֶּה לְחַיֵּי הָעוֹלָם הַבָּא.

משנה תורה, הלכות תשובה ט,א

All of the Torah's statements regarding physical rewards have indeed been realized in the past and will be realized in the future. When we fulfill all the mitzvot in the Torah, we will acquire all of the benefits of this world. . . .

Nevertheless, those benefits are not the ultimate reward for the mitzvot. . . .

Rather, the resolution of the matter is as follows: God gave us this Torah, which is a tree of life. Whoever fulfills what is written within it and comprehends it with complete and proper knowledge will merit the life of the World to Come. . . .

Yet, we are promised by the Torah that if we fulfill it with joy and good spirit and meditate on its wisdom at all times, then God will remove all the obstacles that prevent us from fulfilling it, such as sickness, war, famine, and the like. He will grant us all the good, such as plenty, peace, and an abundance of silver and gold in order that we need not be involved throughout all our days in mundane matters. This will reinforce our performance of the Torah, as we will be unburdened and thereby have the opportunity to study wisdom and perform mitzvot, so that we will merit a share in the World to Come.

Rabbi Moshe ben Maimon (Maimonides/Rambam), *Mishneh Torah*, Laws of Repentance 9:1

Text 9

אֵיזֶהוּ עָשִׁיר הַשָּׂמֵחַ בְּחֶלְקוֹ.

משנה אבות ד,א

Who is rich? He who is happy with his lot.

Mishnah, Avot 4:1

Text 10

רוּחָנִיּוּת וְגַשְׁמִיּוּת זַיינֶען הַפָּכִים בְּעֶצֶם מְהוּתָם. דָאס וואָס עֶס אִיז אַ מַעֲלָה אִין גַשְׁמִיּוּת, אִיז אַ חִסָּרוֹן אִין רוּחָנִיּוּת.

אִין גַשְׁמִיּוּת אִיז אַ שָׂמֵחַ בְּחֶלְקוֹ דֶער גְרֶעסְטֶער בַּעַל מַעֲלָה. אוּן דוּרְךְ עֲבוֹדָה וועט אַזאַ אֵיינֶער צוּקוּמֶען צוּ דִי הֶעכְסְטֶע מַדְרֵיגוֹת. אִין רוּחָנִיּוּת אָבֶּער אִיז אַ שָׂמֵחַ בְּחֶלְקוֹ דֶער גְרֶעסְטֶער חִסָּרוֹן, אוּן עֶר וועֶרְט, רַחֲמָנָא לִיצְלָן, אַ יוֹרֵד וְנוֹפֵל.

היום יום, ל׳ סיון

Spirituality and physicality are intrinsically opposites. A material virtue is a spiritual disadvantage.

In material matters, one who is "satisfied with his lot" is an individual of the highest quality. A person possessing this trait will, through Divine service, attain the highest levels. In spiritual matters, however, to be satisfied with one's lot is the greatest failing, and causes one to decline and fall [spiritually], God forbid.

Rabbi Yosef Yitzchak Schneersohn, cited in *Hayom Yom*, 30 Sivan

III. Knowing Where to Look

Text 11

בְּעִנְיָנִים הַגַּשְׁמִיִּים צָרִיךְ לְהִסְתַּכֵּל בְּמִי שֶׁהוּא לְמַטָּה מִמֶּנּוּ, וּלְהוֹדוֹת לְהַשֵּׁם יִתְבָּרֵךְ כִּי טוֹב עַל חַסְדּוֹ אִתּוֹ עִמּוֹ.

בְּעִנְיָנִים הָרוּחָנִיִּים צָרִיךְ לְהִסְתַּכֵּל בְּמִי שֶׁהוּא לְמַעְלָה מִמֶּנּוּ, וּלְהִתְחַנֵּן לַה' שֶׁיִּתֵּן לוֹ דֵעָה טוֹבָה לְהִתְלַמֵּד מִמֶּנּוּ וְכֹחַ וְעֹז שֶׁיּוּכַל לַעֲלוֹת בְּעִלּוּי.

היום יום, כד חשון

In material matters, a person should look at someone less fortunate than himself and thank God for His kindness toward him.

In spiritual matters, one should look at someone who is on a higher level than himself, and plead with God to give him the proper understanding to learn from that person, and the strength and fortitude to rise higher, level after level.

Ibid., 24 Cheshvan

Text 12

רַבִּי עֲקִיבָא אִיתְקַדְּשַׁת לֵיהּ בְּרַתֵּיהּ דְּכַלְבָּא שָׁבוּעַ. שָׁמַע כַּלְבָּא שָׁבוּעַ, אַדְּרָהּ הֲנָאָה מִכָּל נִכְסֵיהּ. אָזְלָא וְאִיתְנְסִיבָה לֵיהּ בְּסִיתְוָא.

הֲוָה גָּנוּ בֵּי תִּיבְנָא, הֲוָה קָא מְנַקֵּיט לֵיהּ תִּיבְנָא מִן מַזְיֵיהּ.

אָמַר לָהּ: "אִי הֲוַאי לִי, רָמֵינָא לִיךְ יְרוּשְׁלַיִם דְּדַהֲבָא".

אָתָא אֵלִיָּהוּ אִידְּמֵי לְהוֹן כְּאֱנָשָׁא וְקָא קָרֵי אַבָּבָא, אָמַר לְהוּ: "הַבוּ לִי פּוּרְתָּא דְּתִיבְנָא, דִּילְדַת אִתְּתִי וְלֵית לִי מִידַעַם לְאַגּוּנָהּ".

אָמַר לָהּ רַבִּי עֲקִיבָא לְאִנְתְּתֵיהּ: "חֲזִי גַּבְרָא דְּאֲפִילּוּ תִּיבְנָא לָא אִית לֵיהּ".

תלמוד בבלי, נדרים נ,א

> > >

The daughter of Kalba Savua was betrothed to Rabbi Akiva. When Kalba Savua heard this, he pronounced a vow prohibiting her from benefiting from any of his possessions. In spite of this, she went and married Rabbi Akiva in the winter.

[As a result of their poverty,] they would sleep in the straw shed and Rabbi Akiva would pluck the straw from her hair.

He said to her, "If I had the means, I would place upon you a Jerusalem of gold."

Eliyahu/Elijah [the Prophet] came appearing to them in the guise of a person, and he called out at the door. [Eliyahu] said to them, "[Please] give me a little straw, for my wife has given birth and I have nothing upon which to lay her down."

Rabbi Akiva said to his wife, "See, here is a person who lacks even straw!"

Talmud, Nedarim 50a

Text 13

Every week, the study's participants kept a short journal. They either briefly described, in a single sentence, five things that they were grateful for that had occurred in the past week (the gratitude condition), or they did the opposite, describing five daily hassles from the previous week (the hassles condition) that they were displeased about. The neutral group was simply asked to list five events of circumstances that affected them in the last week, and they were not told to accentuate the positive or negative aspects of those circumstances (the events condition)....

At the end of ten weeks, we examined differences between the three groups.... Participants in the gratitude condition...were a full 25 percent happier than the other participants.

Robert Emmons, *Thanks! How Practicing Gratitude Can Make You Happier*, pp. 27–30

Text 14

בָּרוּךְ אַתָּה ה׳ אֱלֹהֵינוּ מֶלֶךְ הָעוֹלָם. פּוֹקֵחַ עִוְרִים.

בָּרוּךְ אַתָּה ה׳ אֱלֹהֵינוּ מֶלֶךְ הָעוֹלָם. מַתִּיר אֲסוּרִים.

בָּרוּךְ אַתָּה ה׳ אֱלֹהֵינוּ מֶלֶךְ הָעוֹלָם. זוֹקֵף כְּפוּפִים.

בָּרוּךְ אַתָּה ה׳ אֱלֹהֵינוּ מֶלֶךְ הָעוֹלָם. מַלְבִּישׁ עֲרֻמִּים.

בָּרוּךְ אַתָּה ה׳ אֱלֹהֵינוּ מֶלֶךְ הָעוֹלָם. הַנּוֹתֵן לַיָּעֵף כֹּחַ.

ברכות השחר, סידור תהלת ה׳

Blessed are You, Lord our God, King of the universe, Who grants us vision [literally: "opens the eyes of the blind"].

Blessed are You, Lord our God, King of the universe, Who grants us mobility [literally: "releases the bound"].

Blessed are You, Lord our God, King of the universe, Who grants us the ability to stand [literally: "straightens the bowed"].

Blessed are You, Lord our God, King of the universe, Who grants us clothing [literally: "clothes the naked"].

Blessed are You, Lord our God, King of the universe, Who gives strength to the weary.

Siddur Tehilat Hashem, Morning Blessings,

LEARNING INTERACTION 4

Make a list of three things that you are grateful for today.

_____

_____

_____

Key Points

1   Happiness leads to success. When we are happy, we are able to overcome challenges and exert more self-control. Even sadness resulting from a previous wrongdoing is detrimental to one's motivation to improve.

2   To be happy means to be complete. God did not create us in a complete state. We must journey to it on our own. We must work to be whole.

3   People achieve completion, and hence happiness, when they integrate their spiritual essence, the soul, into their daily living.

4   The pursuit of material possessions is counterproductive when sought as an end for itself. As a means to an end, however, it is fully consistent with one's spiritual core and therefore can lead to happiness.

5   Giving to others lies at the heart of one's mission in life according to the Torah. In such behavior, there is harmony between body and soul, which leads to happiness.

6   When a person transcends his or her limitations and strives to attain more spirituality, this person becomes more complete, and therefore finds more happiness.

7   In material matters, one who is "satisfied with his lot" is an individual of the highest quality. In spiritual matters, however, to be satisfied with one's lot is the worst deficiency.

8   We are advised to look at a person greater than us in spiritual achievement, in order to engender a desire to do more. In material matters, one should look at someone whose situation is worse than one's own.

9   Consistently counting blessings has been proven to increase happiness.

Bibliography

Text 1 - Rabbi Shne'ur Zalman of Liadi (1745–1812). Chasidic rebbe and founder of the Chabad movement, also known as "the Alter Rebbe" and "the Rav." Born in Liozna, Belarus, he was among the principal students of the Magid of Mezeritch. His numerous works include the *Tanya*, an early classic containing the fundamentals of Chasidism; *Torah Or; Likutei Torah*; and *Shulchan Aruch HaRav*, a reworked and expanded code of Jewish law. He is interred in Hadiach, Ukraine, and was succeeded by his son, Rabbi Dovber of Lubavitch.

Text 4 – Rabbi Abraham Twerski, MD (1930–). Born in Milwaukee; scion to the Chernobyl Chasidic dynasty. A well-known expert in the field of substance abuse, Rabbi Twerski has authored over 50 books on self-help and Judaism, and has served a pioneering role in heightening awareness on the issues of addiction, spousal abuse, and low self-esteem. He served as medical director of the Gateway Rehabilitation Center in Pittsburgh, and associate professor of psychiatry at the University of Pittsburgh School of Medicine.

Text 5 – Zohar. The most seminal work of Kabbalah, Jewish mysticism. It is a mystical commentary on the Torah, written in Aramaic and Hebrew. According to Arizal, the Zohar consists of the teachings of Rabbi Shimon bar Yocha'i who lived in the Land of Israel during the 2nd century. The Zohar has become one of the indispensable texts of traditional Judaism, alongside and nearly equal in stature to the Mishnah and Talmud.

Text 8b – Rabbi Moshe ben Maimon (1135–1204). Better known as Maimonides or by the acronym Rambam; born in Cordoba, Spain. After the conquest of Cordoba by the Almohads, he fled Spain and eventually settled in Cairo, Egypt. There, he became the leader of the Jewish community and served as court physician to the vizier of Egypt. His rulings on Jewish law are considered integral to the formation of halachic consensus. He is most noted for authoring the *Mishneh Torah,* an encyclopedic arrangement of Jewish law, and for his philosophical work, *Guide for the Perplexed.*

Text 10 – Rabbi Yosef Yitschak Schneersohn (1880–1950). Chasidic rebbe and 6th leader of the Chabad movement. Rabbi Schneersohn's activities in defense of Russian Jewry led to his arrest by both Czarist and Communist authorities. After he was liberated from Soviet prison and exile, he moved to Riga, Latvia, and later to Warsaw, Poland, from where he fled the Nazi occupation and arrived in New York in 1940. Settling in Brooklyn, Rabbi Schneersohn worked to revitalize American Jewish life. His son-in-law, Rabbi Menachem Mendel Schneerson, succeeded him as the leader of the Chabad movement.

Text 12 – Babylonian Talmud. A literary work of monumental proportions that draws upon the legal, spiritual, intellectual, ethical, and historical traditions of Judaism, the thirty-eight tractate Babylonian Talmud contains the teachings of the Jewish sages from the period after the destruction of the Second Temple through the fifth century CE. It has served as the primary vehicle for the transmission of the Oral Law and the education of Jews over the centuries; it is the entry point for all subsequent legal, ethical, and theological Jewish scholarship.

Additional Readings

A Blessed Day

By Shirley Coles

It is said that the reward of a mitzvah is the mitzvah itself. There are so many ways of expressing this. It is only in recent years, as I've grown older and begun to try to make sense of my world, that the concept of "mitzvah" has intrigued and guided me. It reminds me of finding my way out of a forest when I am lost, only to realize that I have come full circle to the place where I began. It reminds me of the path of a boomerang, thrown into the wind only to return to me. I began to learn about mitzvot. There is the story, for example, of the man who set out to find a treasure, spending his life seeking its secret hiding place. When, at the end of his time, he finds it in his own home... it had been in his possession the whole time. It is in my possession now; it always has been. And I have a powerful need to know what that treasure is, how to keep it in my life, and how to pass it on to my children, for we are the descendants of those who, through the ages, have kept alive the word of Gd. That word has kept us united as a people through holy ritual and ethical choices.

To perform a mitzvah is to experience the sheer joy of doing something for someone else, or for Gd, but more than that, it is the experience of living a Jewish life. How does one come to do a mitzvah? Is it a commandment from the Almighty? Is it a choice we come to make? I have learned that there are different sources of inspiration and guidance. We do mitzvot when we follow rituals. They bind us together as a people so that wherever we travel throughout the world, we are never lost or alone.

I have a dear and valued friend, Lila, who is sharing with me her midlife quest for understanding of what it means to be a Jewish woman. One day, during a typical marathon phone call, she told me that she had decided not to go to work that day; she was tired, somewhat unable to focus her thoughts, and depressed without knowing why. She is the friend who once said that she likes to do things for other people... because it makes her happy. I sat quietly while she took in what she had just said. Getting joy from doing for another. It was the very essence of mitzvah...when you do something for someone else or for Gd, it brings you joy as well. Mitzvah begets mitzvah...whether it is a ritual deed or an ethical one.

On this particular day of her feeling downcast and spent, I suggested to her that she do a mitzvah for herself. It was a beautiful autumn day. The air was sweet, invigorating and inviting, and just about perfect for someone who enjoyed driving out into the countryside. She asked if I would consider joining her. I knew she seldom had the opportunity to be by herself, to hear her own thoughts. It took a good deal of persuasion to convince her that she deserved the luxury of setting forth on this adventure, alone. "What shall I do all day?" she wondered. "Just be," I answered. "Just let yourself be."

I learned later that my friend had experienced a blessed day. Not long into her drive along the shore, she happened upon a large seagull that lay on the side of the road in obvious distress, his weak bleating testament to his suffering. She was tempted to drive by, not knowing what she would find, or what to do about it, and was actually frightened that the bird would mistake her ministrations for aggression and hurt her with its sharp beak. She found herself pulling over to the shoulder of the road, leaving her truck, and slowly approaching the gull. She talked to him quietly and was able to get close enough to kneel beside and see that he was completely tangled in some kind of net. His struggles had made it worse and his strength was spent. Would he let her help him? There seem to be times when one stops reasoning intellectually and simply does what needs doing. Talking to him all the while, she managed to work him free, stroked his feathers gently and set him on his feet. For a few moments, they both looked at each other, nothing more. And then, with a great flapping of his wings, the gull took to the sky. If she expected gratitude, there was none forthcoming, but it almost seemed as if her heart took flight with him, and she was glad.

Later that day, on her way home, my friend noticed a young man with two young children walking along the dunes. He was waving to her, and holding up a water container. She pulled up and stopped her truck, uneasy about the circumstances, but reassured by the presence of the children who seemed to cling to his hands and join him in waving her to stop. In a few minutes, it became clear that the fellow was father of the children. They were city folk unused to the wise preparation for a day out in the country. They had been out hiking in the area, gotten lost, and needed a ride into town and needed to replenish their water supply. My friend, still high on her previous encounter with the gull, invited the three to get into the back of the truck, and shared her water with them. When they finally

pulled into a mall area where the young man had left his car, he thanked my friend profusely, explaining that he had spent such wonderful time with his children that day, and had not been able to afford more than what they had done.

My friend sat in her truck, watching the little family settle into their car and the thoughts of her own family were strong. She had not been spending much time with them lately. Her work took up most of her waking time. Trying to succeed in her firm and also trying to be a good mother and wife, she had expended her strength until there was little left not only for her children, but even for her parents. They were quite elderly now; it had been a month since she had called them and since the children had seen their grandparents. Picking up her cell phone, she dialed their number.

Lila was rather surprised that, not only was she resolute about calling her parents, but that she had more than enough energy to do so. Her mother answered the call, as usual taking several rings to do so, since her advanced years had markedly slowed her down. They exchanged news of family and friends. Lila found herself eager to tell about the gull and the family. There was an exhilaration in the telling. This from a woman whose life had been overtaken with by work, stress, and a distancing from her husband who missed the vibrant, loving woman he married. In her usual conversations with her mother, Lila would seek reassurance and nurturing, and, if her aging parents needed her in some ways, she had little to give.

Her mother was silent for a few moments and then said, "Lila, you sound so happy... do you know? You have had a blessed day... you have done some wonderful things today... mitzvot... and you are having the blessings of these things because all mitzvot come back as gifts from Gd." Listening to these words, my friend felt a sudden lifting of a heavy burden and she knew the truth in her mother's words. She returned to my house and we sat talking for a long time. Actually, I listened and she talked.

I listened and I thought, *there had been a tsunami of mitzvot today, actually starting with me!* I had recognized that my friend was in need and, in essence, had given her permission to spend a day nurturing herself. Lila had recognized a living creature in trouble and pain; she had set it free without giving thought to her own safety. She had recognized a family, lost and thirsty, and she had taken the time and trouble, not only to supply them with water, but to drive out of her way to show them the beauty of the area and have fun doing so. In the process, Lila had found a source of happiness within herself, and she went on to share some of that happiness with her parents. By the time she returned to me, Lila was glowing. But, having started a domino effect of goodness and kindness, I think I felt the best of all.

Joy on Demand? How Can I Become a Happier Person?

By Rabbi Simon Jacobson

Dear Rabbi Simon Jacobson,

Purim always intimidates me. Serious days I can handle—days of study or introspection. Fast days and days of mourning are also accessible—I can always find something to feel sad about. But Purim and Simchat Torah, these are the holidays that I find daunting. I'm supposed to be joyous, happy and exuberant! How do I access joy? Do I have joy inside of me that I can turn on like a tap for 24 hours—joy on demand? Happiness

on demand! Bottled Joy! People may suggest using alcohol but I'm concerned that either I'll fall asleep or be a melancholic drunk.

Sometimes I walk down the street and I say to myself, "Be joyous, get in touch with your joy," and I immediately think of at least ten reasons not to be joyous: eg. "I'm not married, I'm not married, I'm not married . . . " (ten times).

As I understand it, on Purim, I should be joyful because 2500 years ago, a nice Jewish girl (Esther) married a non-Jewish king (Ahashverosh) whose viceroy (Haman) decided it would be a good idea to kill all the Jews. 2500 years ago, the Jews were saved and so I am here today. I guess that's a fair reason to celebrate—that I exist. But really 2500 years is a long way to travel back in time in order to find a reason to be happy. Isn't there an incident a little more current in Jewish history about which I can feel unadulterated Joy?

Seriously though, how do I access Purim?

Eda Rozensweig

Dear Eda,

Great question. This would make for an excellent topic for discussion at the Purim table.

Here are some of my thoughts: For one, Purim allows us the opportunity to ask the questions you pose: how can we have joy in our lives, especially when we are not in the mood of it and have many reasons not to be joyful?

There is a short-term solution and a long-term one. First, the long-term. The question is why are some people naturally happy and others not? Is joy genetic? Natural and inherent, or acquired? Nature or nurture?

The answer of the Torah—which I believe is the blueprint for life—is that joy is natural and inherent to every person. Just witness the natural happiness and cheerfulness of a young child. The bright joyous face of a child is something that any adult vies for. A child begins to lose his natural cheer due to external causes. His inherent joy starts to erode when he begins to experience the disappointments and tragedies of life events, the despondent attitudes of parents, educators and other adults affecting the child.

Purim is the time of year when the window of opportunity of accessing our inner joy opens up. The celebration of Purim is not merely due to the historical events that occurred 2500 ago, but a celebration of an event that is happening in our lives today, on the day of Purim. (Time is a cyclical energy. Each day recreates the energy flow of that respective day in years past). The Baal Shem Tov puts it this way: If one reads the Purim Megillah as if it is an event that happened in the past and not in the present, the mitzvah has not been performed.

How do we access the inner joy innate in each of us? By accessing the cheer and enthusiasm of our inner child—the part of us connected to G-d that precedes the sadness that life circumstances imposed and continues to impose upon us. That is what Purim is all about: the celebration of our inner child. The enchantment and magic of our souls.

Purim is a day of joyous abandon that transcends conventional boundaries. We are told to celebrate "ad de lo yado"—which means to be joyous until you reach a place beyond the doors of perception, where we transcend dark and light, even the pains and disappointments of our lives. The story of Purim teaches us that despite how dark it gets, even when all hope seems to be lost, the joy of the inner child surfaces in an eruption of joy. It is a delight that transcends any pain you may be dealing with in life, whether it is the lack of a marriage or a challenging marriage.

Long term—one needs to cultivate the inner soul child. Purim is a day when a window opens up that allows us deep inside of ourselves. Meditating and internalizing the feeling that G-d put you on Earth for a unique purpose, that you have an indispensable contribution to make, realizing that all else in life pales in comparison to the essential power of your soul -- is a sure cause for being joyous. Short term—on Purim day listen to the Megillah, participate in a Purim festivity meal, send food gifts to friends, and give charity to the needy. These are all methods and tools to excavate the inner resources of our soul child that are available to us on Purim.

Joy is contagious. Often when we can't access it on our own, a way of igniting it is by celebrating in dance and song with others. Behavioral change, acting joyous (even when you don't feel like it), coupled with the fact that deep inside (or not so deep) lies a reservoir of pure joy, is a way to actually become joyous.

May G-d give you the strength to see your child, to access the inner joy, and to celebrate.

Happy Purim,

Simon Jacobson

Posted on April 3, 2005

Reprinted from www.algemeiner.com

The Key to Happiness

By Rabbi Simon Jacobson

Man can never be happy if he does not nourish his soul as he does his body.

— The Rebbe

What is your life like?

If you are like most people, it is made up of countless bits and pieces of fragmented activity: exercise, work, eating, conversations, entertainment, sleep. Add up the pieces day after day, year after year, and you end up with an entire life split into millions of fragments, with no connecting thread. Fragmentation rattles our peace of mind, creating untold tension and anxiety. Over time, the fragments pile up and begin to suffocate your soul, the inner you that craves focus, purpose and direction. Is it any wonder that after forty or fifty years of slogging through such disjointed days we wake up and suddenly wonder, "Is this what life is about? Am I really happy?"

A happy life is synonymous with a meaningful life, and we all want to live meaningful lives. We constantly strive to make our mark on humanity, to contribute something worthwhile to our world.

By acknowledging that within your body is a G-dly soul, a soul that can give your life purpose and lift it above the mundane pursuits of everyday life, you begin to put the pieces of your fragmented life in order. You see your life from a larger perspective, sanctifying every moment of your life—not only while you are studying or praying or doing charitable deeds, but while you are eating and sleeping, at home or at work, while traveling or on vacation. Instead of carrying out your daily activities by rote, you discover the G-dliness within each of them.

The Key to Happiness: Uniting Body and Soul

To be a happy, wholesome and healthy person, your body and soul must work in perfect harmony. This means uniting the body and soul to fulfill the mission for which we were all put on earth: to lead a meaningful, productive, and virtuous life by making this physical world a home for G-d.

The body and soul, however, are in constant conflict: the body basically looking to satisfy its needs with the soul looking for transcendence and unity. The first step in dealing with this conflict is to acknowledge that the struggle exists, and be aware of the two distinct forces. Thinking that we are a single entity leads to confusion and despair: One day we are virtuous and the next we are selfish; one day we are motivated, the next we procrastinate.

The only way to unite body and soul is to accept that G-d is far higher than our limited selves. The soul, because of its transcendent nature, can rise above selfishness more easily than the body, and can discipline the body, through study and prayer, to recognize its true mission. Only then can the body rise to its true prominence—when it serves as a vehicle for the soul instead of acting under its own power, with its selfish wants and needs. Once the body recognizes the soul's dominance and makes peace with its twin sister, the tension can be properly harnessed.

Happiness Requires Action

It is not enough to acknowledge your soul, you must actualize it by partnering it with the body to help a neighbor in need, to listen to a friend in distress, to help provide food or clothing to someone who cannot afford it. These become more than simple good deeds; they become vital nourishment for your soul and a means of putting your physical body to good spiritual use.

True happiness is the fusion of body and soul dedicated to a higher cause, a cause that benefits humankind and gives meaning and inner peace to the individual in the process.

Action

When you awake in the morning, while you are still lying in bed, think for a moment: What does it mean to be awake and alive? Begin each day with a prayer; thank G-d for the new day. Acknowledge your soul. Think about what you would like to accomplish that would make today a meaningful day. If you train yourself to do this every morning, you will immediately begin to see your life in a new, sharper focus.

You should end your day just as you begin it. As you prepare for sleep, review the day and how you used it opportunities. Recognize that G-d has put you here for a purpose, and that all your activities should express that purpose. Go to sleep with the resolve that no matter how good—or bad— today was, tomorrow will be better. By doing so, your sleep will be more peaceful, and your waking more meaningful.

"Every person has both a body and a soul," said the Rebbe. "It is like a bird and its wings. Imagine if a bird were unaware that its wings enabled it to fly, they would only add an extra burden of weight. But once it flaps its wings, it lifts itself skyward. We all have wings—our soul—that can lift us as high as we need go. All we have to do is learn to use them."

(excerpt from *Toward a Meaningful Life—The Wisdom of the Rebbe* by Rabbi Simon Jacobson)

© 2006 The Meaningful Life Center. All rights reserved. http:www.meaningfullife.com

The Gift of Humor

By Shirley Coles

When I think of things funny, thigh-slapping, fall-down funny, my thoughts inevitably turn to two women, my grandmothers Bella and Rachel. As the years have passed, they seem to have blended and resemble one another more and more, becoming my generic imprint for that wonderful word… grandmother. The woman I see is about five feet three inches tall. She has steel gray hair caught in a neat bun, soft and round body, low-heeled black shoes, belted flowered dress and always a cardigan sweater. Her delicious aroma is that of baking bread and lavender. The laugh lines are deeply etched and her accented English peppered with Yiddish idiom was the music of my childhood.

When I think of things funny, I also think of being Jewish and, although I am profoundly aware of the history of my people, I never cease to marvel how, along with the terror and the misery, we have produced a multitude of comics who set the groundwork for courage through humor. The list is endless of the funny Jewish men who filled the theaters and resorts with laughter. I remember when, as a teenager, I would race to the home of my uncle on Sunday evenings where I could watch famous comedians on the only TV set in the family. No one dared interrupt while Uncle Izzy, in his big easy chair would laugh so hard his face would turn bright red. It became a rite of passage to say you had seen the show.

I was never quite sure of how much my grandmothers understood of the dialogue, but they understood the action and the gestures, and they understood laughter. History has immortalized incredibly clever comedians who were performing not only in this country during WWII, but also overseas for the troops. In the early 1900's, they appeared in resorts and theaters and the Yiddish theater, with its plays and burlesque, was a huge draw for newly arrived immigrants from Europe. Radio and television brought them into our homes. I used to marvel at the sight of tears rolling down faces which may have been tears of sadness only hours before when they learned of relatives denied entry into this country or families torn apart during the efforts to eradicate our people. Down through the centuries, history repeated itself… and down through the centuries, music and laughter were thriving and becoming part of our identity.

Of course, other ethnic groups can rightly claim to have their comic heroes as well, but somehow there is a flavor and persistence to Jewish humor which weaves its way into our everyday lives, our language, and our interaction with each other. It makes harsh events softer and bad things bearable. How can one remain angry or hopeless when, with a giant shrug of the shoulders, and a frown turned upside down, there is no place to go except ahead to prevail against adversity.

I still laugh when I remember how, one very hot day at the beach, my two cousins and I decided to play a trick on Grandma Rachel. She was wearing what seemed more like a heavy black short dress than a bathing suit, and she had her cardigan sweater on over her shoulders. We generously offered to walk with her to the water's edge and each placed a steadying arm around her back. We had noticed earlier that the very-worn sweater had a loop of wool hanging down and the plan was to give gentle tugs to it as we walked. We kept up a light conversation to distract her as the back of the sweater became shorter and shorter. The sharp cold of the water

on her toes brought the joke down on us. The silence as we stood there staring at one another was loud. Grandma Rachel pulled the tattered sweater down, took a long hard look at it and began to laugh. She scooped up handfuls of water, doused us thoroughly, and somehow we all wound up sitting in the wet sand.

Visits to the other funny and deeply loving woman in my life meant walks to the corner deli, being allowed to drink coffee-flavored milk, curing my poison ivy with pickle juice, and sitting up late into the night drawing pictures and learning how to read the headlines in the Jewish newspaper. On one of these nights, something I tried to read struck her funny. Her laughter shook her from stem to stern and the bed itself. Just as Grandpa came down the hall to see what was happening, the mattress caved in, leaving us caught in the middle. If it had been a summer night, with the windows open to carry our helpless screeches, I'm sure it might have caused the neighbors to come running.

I have never forgotten how to laugh because of these two women. And, yet, it was to them that I also came with my most serious of problems and sadness.

When they embraced me with sage advice and encouragement, there was always a kiss and a pinch on the cheek, as well as the ever present hope and humor in her tone. As a woman, I found that I emulated them with my own children, and they with theirs. To this day, it causes raised eyebrows, but it's too late to change the heart of this woman. I am funny.

Reprinted with permission from the author and Chabad.org

It's About Time

V

Empathically Speaking
A Jewish Approach to Effective Communication

ROSHCHODESH
society

Introduction

There is much to be said about words. They make the world go 'round; sometimes clockwise, other times otherwise. History has proven that words are one of humankind's most powerful tools. A word can launch a revolution. A word can bring reconciliation. Words are pearls of poetry waiting for an artist.

We have all witnessed the power of the spoken word in our personal lives. Perhaps a teacher, parent, or friend saw in us a potential that we never dreamed possible, and unleashed it with a thoughtful word. Perhaps they exclaimed, "You are a great writer!" and you suddenly believed you could be and paid more attention to your writing. Perhaps they insisted, "You have a beautiful voice!" and your heart found a home in your vocal cords. "You are so kindhearted and considerate," they gushed, and you made a point of being so from then on.

We have also witnessed the opposite effect of words on our lives. Perhaps it was a moment of vulnerability, made infinitely worse by someone blaming us carelessly, telling us we would never make it, or that we had no talent or use in this world—and the words cut deep enough to make us loosen our grip on our goal. Most of us have experienced an incident in which we were cut into a million pieces by the devastating blows of an overly sharp tongue.

A marriage is born or buried on the weight of a word breathed in passion or fury. A student is encouraged or destroyed by a teacher's considered or careless remark. A parent's choice of response determines whether their child will receive a lifetime of self-worth or whether their confidence will be nipped in the bud of life. Words can heal and bless. Words can cause distress.

In this lesson, we will take a look at the guidelines of the Torah and Jewish philosophers regarding the words we choose to use.

I. The Articulate Being

FIGURE 5.1

Uniqueness of Human Biology

Posture	Humans are unique among the primates in that walking fully upright is our chief mode of locomotion. This frees our hands for using tools.
Fingers	We can bring our thumbs all the way across the hand to our ring and little fingers. We can also flex the ring and little fingers toward the base of our thumb. This gives humans a powerful grip and exceptional dexterity to hold and manipulate tools.
Speech	The larynx, or voice box, sits lower in the throat in humans than in chimps, one of several features that enable human speech. We also possess a descended hyoid bone—this horseshoe-shaped bone below the tongue—unique in that it is not attached to any other bones in the body. It enables us to articulate words.
Brains	Humans do not have the largest brains in the world; those belong to sperm whales. We do not even have the largest brains relative to body size. Many birds have brains that make up more than 8 percent of their body weight, compared to only 2.5 percent for humans. Yet the human brain, weighing only approximately three pounds when fully grown, gives us the ability to reason and think, and provided the works of Mozart, Einstein, and many other geniuses.
Blushing	Humans are the only species known to blush. Blushing helps keep people honest, benefiting our social interaction.
Childhood	Humans must remain in the care of their parents for much longer than other living primates.
Life	Most animals reproduce until they die, but human females can survive long after ceasing reproduction.

source: www.livescience.com

Text 1a

וַיִּיצֶר ה' אֱלֹקִים אֶת הָאָדָם עָפָר מִן הָאֲדָמָה,
וַיִּפַּח בְּאַפָּיו נִשְׁמַת חַיִּים, וַיְהִי הָאָדָם לְנֶפֶשׁ
חַיָּה.

בראשית ב,ז

*God formed man of dust from the
ground, and He breathed into his nostrils
the soul of life, and man became a living
spirit.*

Bereishit/Genesis 2:7

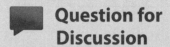

Question for Discussion

Which of these characteristics is most significant to the identity of the human being?

Text 1b

וּבְרָא ה' אֱלֹקִים יָת אָדָם עַפְרָא מִן אַדְמְתָא, וּנְפַח בְּאַנְפּוֹהִי נִשְׁמָתָא דְחַיֵּי, וַהֲוַת בְּאָדָם לְרוּחַ מְמַלְלָא.

תרגום אונקלוס, שם

*God created man of dust from the ground, and He breathed into his nostrils the soul of life,
and man became an articulating spirit.*

Targum Onkelos, ad loc.

Text 1b

וּבְרָא ה' אֱלֹקִים יָת אָדָם עַפְרָא מִן אַדְמְתָא, וּנְפַח בְּאַנְפּוֹהִי נִשְׁמָתָא דְחַיֵּי, וַהֲוַת בְּאָדָם לְרוּחַ מְמַלְלָא.

תרגום אונקלוס, שם

*God created man of dust from the ground, and He breathed into his nostrils the soul of life, and
man became an articulating spirit.*

Targum Onkelos, ad loc.

FIGURE 5.2

The Four Kingdoms

Silent (Inanimate)	דּוֹמֵם
Vegetation	צוֹמֵחַ
Life (Animal)	חַי
Articulator (Human)	מְדַבֵּר

Text 2

*Speech is unique because it is the only human faculty not constrained by self—one speaks with **another**.*

Speech is not self-serving. On the contrary, speech is rooted in the depths of the human soul, a level unrestricted by any sort of restraints, including the restraints of self-absorption.

Speech is what reveals the limitless quality of the human soul. This is why humans are called "articulators."

Rabbi Menachem Mendel Schneerson, *Likutei Sichot* 6:116

Text 3

The great apes—chimpanzees, bonobos, gorillas and orangutans—communicate almost exclusively for the purpose of getting others to do what they want. Human infants, in addition, gesture and talk in order to share information with others—they want to be helpful. They also share their emotions and attitudes freely—as when an infant points to a passing bird for its mother and squeals with glee.

Michael Tomasello, Ph.D., "How Are Humans Unique?" *The New York Times*, May 25, 2008

II. A Verbal Wrong

Text 4

וְכִי תִמְכְּרוּ מִמְכָּר לַעֲמִיתֶךָ אוֹ קָנֹה מִיַּד עֲמִיתֶךָ אַל תּוֹנוּ אִישׁ אֶת אָחִיו . . .

וְלֹא תוֹנוּ אִישׁ אֶת עֲמִיתוֹ וְיָרֵאתָ מֵאֱלֹקֶיךָ.

ויקרא כה,יד–יז

When you make a sale to your fellow or make a purchase from the hand of your fellow, you shall not wrong one another. . . .

A person shall not wrong a fellow; and you shall fear your God.

Vayikra/Leviticus 25:14–17

Text 5

הָא כֵּיצַד? אִם הָיָה בַּעַל תְּשׁוּבָה, אַל יֹאמַר לוֹ "זְכוֹר מַעֲשֶׂיךָ הָרִאשׁוֹנִים".

אִם הָיָה בֶּן גֵּרִים, אַל יֹאמַר לוֹ "זְכוֹר מַעֲשֵׂה אֲבוֹתֶיךָ".

אִם הָיָה גֵּר וּבָא לִלְמוֹד תּוֹרָה, אַל יֹאמַר לוֹ "פֶּה שֶׁאָכַל נְבֵלוֹת וּטְרֵיפוֹת שְׁקָצִים וּרְמָשִׂים בָּא לִלְמוֹד תּוֹרָה שֶׁנֶּאֶמְרָה מִפִּי הַגְּבוּרָה".

אִם הָיוּ יִסּוּרִין בָּאִין עָלָיו, אִם הָיוּ חֳלָאִים בָּאִין עָלָיו, אוֹ שֶׁהָיָה מְקַבֵּר אֶת בָּנָיו, אַל יֹאמַר לוֹ כְּדֶרֶךְ שֶׁאָמְרוּ לוֹ חֲבֵירָיו לְאִיּוֹב . . .

אִם הָיוּ חַמָּרִים מְבַקְשִׁין תְּבוּאָה מִמֶּנּוּ, לֹא יֹאמַר לָהֶם "לְכוּ אֵצֶל פְּלוֹנִי שֶׁהוּא מוֹכֵר תְּבוּאָה", וְיוֹדֵעַ בּוֹ שֶׁלֹּא מָכַר מֵעוֹלָם.

תלמוד בבלי, בבא מציעא נח,ב

> > >

What are examples [of oppressing someone with words]?

Do not say to a penitent, "Remember your former deeds!"

Do not say to a descendant of converts, "Remember your ancestors' deeds!"

Do not say to a convert who wishes to study Torah, "A mouth that ate non-kosher meats, reptiles, and insects now wishes to utter God's holy words?"

Do not speak [unsympathetically] to one who is hurting, struck by disease, or bereaved of children, as Iyov's/Job's friends spoke to Iyov. . . .

Do not say to donkey drivers who ask you for grain, "Go to So-and-So," although you know that he has never sold grain.

Talmud, Bava Metzia 58b

Text 6

גָּדוֹל אוֹנָאַת דְּבָרִים מֵאוֹנָאַת מָמוֹן . . . זֶה
בְּגוּפוֹ וְזֶה בְּמָמוֹנוֹ . . . זֶה נִיתַּן לְהִישָׁבוֹן,
וְזֶה לֹא נִיתַּן לְהִישָׁבוֹן.

תלמוד בבלי, שם

Oppressing someone with words is worse than oppressing someone monetarily. . . .

The former is an affront to his person; the latter, only to his finances. . . .

The former cannot be restituted; the latter can be restituted.

Ibid.

Text 7

"וְלֹא תוֹנוּ אִישׁ אֶת עֲמִיתוֹ": כַּאן הִזְהִיר עַל
אוֹנָאַת דְּבָרִים . . .

וְאִם תֹּאמַר, מִי יוֹדֵעַ אִם נִתְכַּוַּנְתִּי לְרָעָה?
לְכַךְ נֶאֱמַר "וְיָרֵאתָ מֵאֱלֹקֶיךָ", הַיּוֹדֵעַ
מַחֲשָׁבוֹת הוּא יוֹדֵעַ.

רש"י, ויקרא כה,יז

"A person shall not wrong a fellow." Here, Scripture is warning against wronging another verbally. . . .

Should you say, "Who can tell whether I had evil intentions [when I offended or verbally oppressed my fellow]?" Therefore, it says, "and you shall fear your God": The One who knows all thoughts knows [the truth].

Rashi, on Vayikra 25:17

III. Words That Wound

Text 8

A word is dead when it is said, some say. I say it just begins to live that day.

Emily Dickinson, Complete Poems, Part One: Life

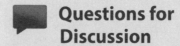

Questions for Discussion

1. In what way is a word "dead when it is said"?

2. How does it begin "to live that day"?

Text 9

Gossip occurs everywhere in our social world. One need only glance at the covers of magazines in supermarkets or log onto the most popular Internet websites to realize that the gossip market thrives on publishing intimate details about the lives of celebrities. Aside from public forums, gossip is also hard to avoid in our face-to-face social interactions. Emler's (1994) empirical work suggests that up to two-thirds of all conversations include some reference to third-party doings. Dunbar (2004) reports similar findings from a series of studies on the content of everyday conversation, noting that gossip accounts for approximately 65% of speaking time, with only limited variations across age and gender.

Travis Grosser, Virginie Lopez-Kidwell, Giuseppe (Joe) Labianca, "A Social Network Analysis of Positive and Negative Gossip in Organizational Life," *Group & Organization Management*, Volume 35 (2): 177

Text 10a

לֹא תֵלֵךְ רָכִיל בְּעַמֶּיךָ.

ויקרא יט,טז

You shall not go around as a rachil *amongst your people.*

Vayikra 19:16

Text 10b

אֵי זֶהוּ רָכִיל? זֶה שֶׁטּוֹעֵן דְּבָרִים וְהוֹלֵךְ מִזֶּה לָזֶה וְאוֹמֵר "כָּךְ אָמַר פְּלוֹנִי", "כָּךְ וְכָךְ שָׁמַעְתִּי עַל פְּלוֹנִי". אַף עַל פִּי שֶׁהוּא אֱמֶת, הֲרֵי זֶה מַחֲרִיב אֶת הָעוֹלָם.

רמב"ם, הלכות דעות ז,ב

Who is considered a rachil? *He who peddles tidbits from one person to another, saying, "Mr. A said such and such; I heard such and such about Mrs. B." Even if it is true, the gossip destroys the world.*

Rabbi Moshe ben Maimon (Maimonides/Rambam), *Mishneh Torah*, Laws of Temperaments 7:2

Text 10c

יֵשׁ עָוֹן גָּדוֹל מִזֶּה עַד מְאֹד, וְהוּא בִּכְלַל לָאו זֶה, וְהוּא לְשׁוֹן הָרַע, וְהוּא הַמְסַפֵּר בִּגְנוּת חֲבֵירוֹ אַף עַל פִּי שֶׁאוֹמֵר אֱמֶת. אֲבָל הָאוֹמֵר שֶׁקֶר נִקְרָא מוֹצִיא שֵׁם רַע עַל חֲבֵירוֹ.

רמב"ם, שם

There is a more serious wrongdoing included in this prohibition: lashon hara—*speaking disparagingly about others, even if speaking the truth.*

However, one who speaks lies concerning his fellow is called motzi shem ra—*a defamer of character.*

Ibid.

FIGURE 5.3

Three Forms of Prohibited Speech

Hebrew term	Definition	Is the information false?	Is the information negative?
Rechilut	Gossip	No	No
Lashon hara	Negative gossip	No	Yes
Motzi shem ra	Slander	Yes	Yes

Text 11

וְאִם הוֹצִיא עָלָיו שֵׁם רַע, אֵינוֹ צָרִיךְ לִמְחוֹל לוֹ בְּכָל עִנְיָן, אֲפִילוּ אִם יְבַקֵּשׁ מִמֶּנּוּ כַּמָּה פְּעָמִים. מִשּׁוּם דְּאֶפְשָׁר שֶׁיֵּשׁ בְּנֵי אָדָם שֶׁשָּׁמְעוּ הוֹצָאַת הַלַּעַז עָלָיו, וְלֹא שָׁמְעוּ הַפִּיּוּס, וְיִדְמֶה לָהֶם שֶׁאֶפְשָׁר שֶׁהַלַּעַז הוּא אֱמֶת, וְלֹא יָצָא עֲדַיִן אָדָם זֶה נָקִי מֵחֲשָׁד.

וּמִכָּל מָקוֹם מִדַּת עֲנָוָה לִמְחוֹל אֲפִילוּ בְּהוֹצָאַת שֵׁם רַע.

שולחן ערוך הרב, אורח חיים תרו,ד

One need not forgive a person who slandered him, even if the slanderer repeatedly asks for forgiveness. The reason: It is possible that people heard the slander but were not aware of the placation. These people might believe the slander to be true, and the reputation of the slandered person will continue to be harmed.

Yet, it is a trait of humility to forgive, even in the case of slander.

Rabbi Shne'ur Zalman of Liadi, *Shulchan Aruch HaRav, Orach Chayim* 606:4

Text 12

מוֹרִי זלה"ה הָיָה נוֹהֵג כְּשֶׁנָּפְלָה לוֹ אֵיזֶה הַשָּׂגָה בְּמוֹחוֹ, הָיָה אוֹמְרָהּ בְּפֶה, אַף שֶׁלֹּא יָבִינוּ הַשּׁוֹמְעִים כָּל כָּךְ, שֶׁהָיָה מְדַבְּרָהּ רַק כְּמוֹ בִּפְנֵי עַצְמוֹ כו'. וְהַטַּעַם לָזֶה הוּא בִּכְדֵי לְהַמְשִׁיךְ אֶת הַהַשָּׂגָה שֶׁנָּפְלָה לוֹ בְּזֶה הָעוֹלָם בִּבְחִינַת יְצִיאַת הַדִּבּוּר כְּשֶׁמְּדַבְּרָהּ בְּפִיו, עַל יְדֵי זֶה שֶׁמְּדַבְּרָהּ בְּצִירוּפֵי אוֹתִיוֹת הַדִּבּוּר מַמְשִׁיכָהּ לָעוֹלָם הַזֶּה. וְאֲזַי כְּשֶׁיַּמְשִׁיכֶנָּה לָעוֹלָם הַזֶּה, יוּכַל אַחֵר, אַף שֶׁהוּא בְּסוֹף הָעוֹלָם, לְהַשִּׂיגָהּ עַל יְדֵי יְגִיעָתוֹ בְּתוֹרָה וַעֲבוֹדָה . . . אֲבָל אִם לֹא הָיָה מַמְשִׁיכָהּ לָעוֹלָם הַזֶּה עַל יְדֵי הַדִּבּוּר כו', אַף שֶׁיִּיגַע אַחֵר הַרְבֵּה לֹא יַשִּׂיגֶנָּה בְּמוֹחוֹ, שֶׁאֵינָהּ נִמְצֵאת בְּזֶה הָעוֹלָם, שֶׁהִיא בַּשָּׁמַיִם.

מאמרי אדמו"ר הזקן הקצרים, ע' 474

Whenever my master [Rabbi Dov Ber of Mezritch] conceived an original [Torah] thought, he would voice it aloud, although those present could not understand him. He would speak as if to himself. By articulating the idea, he would draw it into this world.

Once the idea was present in this world, it could occur to another person—even one at the other end of the world—who was laboring in the study of Torah and the service of God... . Had it not been drawn into this world, even if the other were to toil mightily, he would not arrive at this idea—for it would still be in Heaven.

Rabbi Shne'ur Zalman of Liadi, *Ma'amarei Admur Hazaken Haketzarim*, p. 474

Text 13

The nature of speech is that of revealing something that was previously concealed in thought. Thus, when another's evil is revealed through speech, it has the capacity to do spiritual harm to the person about whom the evil is spoken; were this evil not to have been revealed through speech, it may well have remained dormant and not elicited the unfortunate ensuing results of its revelation.

It is axiomatic that "positive actions have a greater degree of efficacy than negative actions." If speaking of another's evil qualities and traits harms that individual, surely speaking of the other's good qualities and traits has a positive influence upon the person so praised.

Rabbi Sholom B. Wineberg, *The Chassidic Dimension* (Brooklyn N.Y.: Kehot Publication Society, 2003), 5:145

Text 14

לִישָׁנָא תְּלִיתָאי קָטִיל תְּלִיתָאי: הוֹרֵג לְאוֹמְרוֹ, וּלְמְקַבְּלוֹ, וּלְאוֹמְרִין עָלָיו.

תלמוד בבלי, ערכין טו,ב

Evil gossip slays three: the speaker, the listener, and the subject of the gossip.

Talmud, Arachin 15b

Text 15

וְנֶזֶק הָרְכִילוּת חָדַל לִסְפּוֹר כִּי אֵין מִסְפָּר. כִּי הוּא מַרְבֶּה שִׂנְאָה בָּעוֹלָם, וּמַכְשִׁיל אֶת בְּנֵי אָדָם
לַעֲבוֹר עַל מַה שֶׁכָּתוּב בַּתּוֹרָה "לֹא תִשְׂנָא אֶת אָחִיךָ בִּלְבָבֶךָ" (ויקרא יט,יז). וְהִנֵּה הָעוֹלָם
קַיָּם עַל הַשָּׁלוֹם. וּמִפְּנֵי הַשִּׂנְאָה נְמוֹגִים אֶרֶץ וְכָל יוֹשְׁבֶיהָ . . . וּפְעָמִים רַבּוֹת יִתֵּן הָרָכִיל חֶרֶב
בְּיַד חֲבֵרוֹ לַהֲרוֹג אֶת רֵעֵהוּ.

שערי תשובה ג,רכב

The damage caused by rechilut *is incalculable. It multiplies hate in the world and causes
people to violate the commandment, "You shall not hate your brother in your heart." The
world rests on [a foundation of] peace. As a result of hate, the earth and all its inhabitants
tremble. . . . Many times, the gossiper puts a sword in the hand of a person to kill his peer.*

Rabbi Yonah ben Avraham of Gerona, *Sha'arei Teshuvah* 3:222

Text 16a

הוֹלֵךְ רָכִיל מְגַלֶּה סּוֹד, וְנֶאֱמַן רוּחַ מְכַסֶּה דָבָר.

משלי יא,יג

A gossipmonger reveals secrets, but one who is trustworthy of spirit conceals a matter.

Mishlei/Proverbs 11:13

Text 16b

שֶׁהָרָכִיל מִמְדּוֹתָיו וּמִפְּעֻלוֹתָיו לְגַלּוֹת סוֹד, רְצוֹנוֹ לוֹמַר אַף מַה שֶׁהוּזְהַר עָלָיו לְהַסְתִּירוֹ וּלְכַסּוֹתוֹ. אֲבָל נֶאֱמָן רוּחַ לֹא דַיּוֹ לְכַסּוֹת סוֹד, רְצוֹנוֹ לוֹמַר מַה שֶׁהוּזְהַר מִמֶּנּוּ, אֲבָל אֲפִילוּ הַדְּבָרִים שֶׁשָּׁמַע בְּמִקְרֶה מִבְּלִי שֶׁיּוּזְהַר עַל הֶסְתֵּרָם, אַחַר שֶׁיֵּדַע וְיַכִּיר שֶׁיֵּשׁ צוֹרֶךְ בְּהֶסְתֵּרָם, יְכַסֶּה אוֹתָם וְיַסְתִּירֵם.

חיבור התשובה א,ד

A rachil is one who reveals secrets—even those that they were commanded to keep secret and conceal. A trustworthy person not only conceals a secret they were ordered to conceal, but even something heard by chance that they were not ordered to conceal. They do so because they intuitively understand the need to keep overheard information confidential.

Rabbi Menachem Meiri, *Chibur Hateshuvah* 1:2

IV. Effective Communication

Text 17

אַל תְּרַצֶּה אֶת חֲבֵרֶךָ בְּשַׁעַת כַּעֲסוֹ, וְאַל תְּנַחֲמֵהוּ בְּשָׁעָה שֶׁמֵּתוֹ מוּטָל לְפָנָיו.

משנה, אבות ד,יח

Do not placate your fellow in the moment of his anger; do not comfort him while his dead lies before him.

Mishnah, Avot 4:18

Text 18

מֵשִׁיב דָּבָר בְּטֶרֶם יִשְׁמָע, אִוֶּלֶת הִיא לוֹ וּכְלִמָּה.

משלי יח,יג

He who answers a word before he understands—that is his folly and shame.

Mishlei, op. cit. 18:13

Text 19

שִׁבְעָה דְבָרִים בְּגוֹלֶם וְשִׁבְעָה בְּחָכָם . . . וְאֵינוֹ נִכְנָס לְתוֹךְ דִּבְרֵי חֲבֵירוֹ.

משנה, אבות ה,ז

There are seven hallmarks that distinguish the mature human being. . . . The mature person does not interrupt while another is speaking.

Mishnah, Avot 5:7

FIGURE 5.4

- "Silence is the best medicine."—Talmud, Megilah 18a.

- "Silence is the fence [that guards] wisdom."—Mishnah, Avot 3:13.

- "All my days I grew up among the sages and did not find anything better for one's person than silence." —Mishnah, Avot 1:17.

- "Whoever engages in excessive talk invites sin."—Mishnah, Avot 1:17.

- "Always teach students in a concise manner."—Talmud, Pesachim 3b

- "Silence is fitting for the wise, and all the more so for fools."—Talmud, Pesachim 99a

- "Be wise and remain silent." —Talmud, Yoma 7a.

V. Modeh Ani

Text 20

מוֹדֶה אֲנִי לְפָנֶיךָ מֶלֶךְ חַי וְקַיָּם. שֶׁהֶחֱזַרְתָּ בִּי נִשְׁמָתִי בְּחֶמְלָה. רַבָּה אֱמוּנָתֶךָ.

מודה אני, סידור תהלת ה'

I offer thanks before You, living and eternal King, for You have mercifully restored my soul within me. Your faithfulness is great.

Siddur Tehilat Hashem, Laws Relating to One's Conduct upon Rising in the Morning

Key Points

1 In Jewish thought, the uniqueness of human beings is expressed in their ability to speak. While animals communicate, humans are uniquely able to use their communication to extend beyond themselves, to form relationships with others.

2 Judaism has laws that encourage the use of communication to enhance relationships, not to undermine them.

3 *Ona'at devarim* is the prohibition again telling a person something that they will find hurtful or insensitive.

4 *Motzi shem ra* is the prohibition against speaking slanderously.

5 *Lashon hara* is the prohibition against negative gossiping, even when the information is factually true. Aside from the practical harm, Jewish mysticism teaches that such speech has the ability to reveal and actualize negative potential within the subject of the gossip.

6 *Rechilut* is the prohibition of innocuous gossip that discloses information without permission, even when the information is not negative in content. This is prohibited because it could lead to unintentionally harming the subject of the gossip.

7 Avoiding harmful talk is only the first step. The second step is using our speech to forge positive relationships.

8 Helpful tips for communication: Be aware that listening is occasionally preferable to speaking. Understand the issue before joining a conversation. Avoid cutting someone off in mid-speech. Avoid saying more than is necessary.

Bibliography

Text 1b – Onkelos (ca. 35–120 CE). Famous convert to Judaism in mishnaic times. According to traditional sources, he was a prominent Roman nobleman and a nephew of the Roman emperor Titus. Author of *Targum Onkelos*, an Aramaic translation of the Bible. His *Targum* is an exposition of the interpretation of the Torah, as received by Rabbi Eliezer and Rabbi Yehoshua.

Text 2 – Rabbi Menachem Mendel Schneerson (1902–1994). Known as "the Lubavitcher Rebbe," or simply as "the Rebbe." Born in southern Ukraine. Rabbi Schneerson escaped from the Nazis, arriving in the U.S. in June 1941. The towering Jewish leader of the 20th century, the Rebbe inspired and guided the revival of traditional Judaism after the European devastation, and often emphasized that the performance of just one additional good deed could usher in the era of Mashiach.

Text 5 – Babylonian Talmud. A literary work of monumental proportions that draws upon the legal, spiritual, intellectual, ethical, and historical traditions of Judaism, the thirty-eight tractate Babylonian Talmud contains the teachings of the Jewish sages from the period after the destruction of the Second Temple through the fifth century CE. It has served as the primary vehicle for the transmission of the Oral Law and the education of Jews over the centuries; it is the entry point for all subsequent legal, ethical, and theological Jewish scholarship.

Text 7 – Rabbi Shlomoh Yitschaki (1040–1105). Better known by the acronym Rashi. Rabbi and famed author of comprehensive commentaries on the Talmud and Bible. Born in Troyes, France, Rashi studied in the famed *yeshivot* of Mainz and Worms. His commentaries, which focus on the simple understanding of the text, are considered the most fundamental of all the commentaries that preceded and followed. Since their initial printings, the commentaries have appeared in virtually every edition of the Talmud and Bible. Many of the famed authors of the *Tosafot* are among Rashi's descendants.

Text 10b – Rabbi Moshe ben Maimon (1135–1204). Better known as Maimonides or by the acronym Rambam; born in Cordoba, Spain. After the conquest of Cordoba by the Almohads, he fled Spain and eventually settled in Cairo, Egypt. There, he became the leader of the Jewish community and served as court physician to the vizier of Egypt. His rulings on Jewish law are considered integral to the formation of halachic consensus. He is most noted for authoring the *Mishneh Torah,* an encyclopedic arrangement of Jewish law, and for his philosophical work, *Guide for the Perplexed.*

Text 11 - Rabbi Shne'ur Zalman of Liadi (1745–1812). Chasidic rebbe and founder of the Chabad movement, also known as "the Alter Rebbe" and "the Rav." Born in Liozna, Belarus, he was among the principal students of the Magid of Mezeritch. His numerous works include the *Tanya*, an early classic containing the fundamentals of Chasidism; *Torah Or; Likutei Torah*; and *Shulchan Aruch HaRav*, a reworked and expanded code of Jewish law. He is interred in Hadiach, Ukraine, and was succeeded by his son, Rabbi Dovber of Lubavitch.

Text 15 – Rabbi Yonah ben Avraham of Gerona (d. 1263). Born in the late 12th century in Gerona, Spain. A talmudist and teacher of ethics, he also served as dean of the yeshivah in Barcelona. He was a cousin and friend of Nachmanides, and a teacher of the Rashba and Re'ah. Authored works on Tanach, Mishnah, and Talmud, but is most famous for his *Sha'arei Teshuvah*, a work on ethics and repentance.

Text 16b – Rabbi Menachem Me'iri (1249–1310). Born in Provence, France. His monumental work, *Beit Habechirah,* summarizes in a lucid style the discussions of the Talmud along with the commentaries of the major subsequent rabbis. Despite its stature, the work was largely unknown for many generations, and thus has had less influence on subsequent halachic development than would have been expected given its stature.

Additional Readings

How to Reach People

By Simon Jacobson

December 2002

A young but dynamic speaker once called me frantically. He was about to deliver a lecture on a certain topic and he had an attack of 'stage fright'. "How can I get up there and speak with authority to an educated audience about subjects that they may know more about than I do"? he asked. "I feel like a fraud", he continued, "totally inadequate talking about science and history to scientists and historians".

Before I share our conversation with you, let us learn from the greatest communicator of all how to speak to others.

In this week's Torah portion (Shmot) Moses is chosen by G-d to redeem the Jewish people from their oppression under Pharaoh and the Egyptians. In his classical dialogue with G-d – a fascinating dialogue that teaches us volumes about establishing a relationship with G-d – Moses resists becoming G-d's messenger. Among his arguments he says to G-d: "I am not a man of words…my speech is difficult and my tongue is difficult" (Exodus 4:10). I find it difficult to speak and find the right language. To which G-d replies with a resounding statement: "Who gave man a mouth … Is it not I, G-d? Now go, and I will be your mouth" (4:11-12).

What happens? Moses approaches Pharaoh and gets G-d's message across; he succeeds in freeing the Jews from Egypt. Moses then becomes the supreme teacher and communicator. Moshe

Rabeinu. Moses receives the Torah at Sinai and proceeds to teach it to the people. This man of 'no words' becomes the source of Divine words for all of time. An entire book of the Torah is even named "Devorim" – "these are the words that Moses spoke". It is the words of Moses, the 'man of no words', that are remembered forever. Is there anyone else in history whose every word is known and analyzed as those of Moses in the Bible? How many books and commentaries have been written to understand every utterance that came out Moses' mouth?

Why? Because true communication is not about brilliant ideas, eloquent oratory skills, compelling presentations; it is about '*bittul*', about recognizing that you are a channel – a transparent conduit – to convey a truth that is greater than yourself. And the more transparent you are, the better your communication will be. Conversely, the more your ego is in the way, the less resonance your message will have. When your personality stands between your message and the listeners then your personality dilutes (distorts?) the message.

Moses was the greatest communicator because he had the deepest self suspension (*bittul*). G-d chose Moses precisely because he didn't want the 'job'. G-d didn't want someone who was enamored with themselves and their speaking abilities. He didn't want a leader who was interested in emanating great light and energy (*ohr*); He wanted someone who would excel at absorbing Higher wisdom, Divine knowledge, and someone who would therefore appreciate the containers (*keilim*) more than the lights. Because as great as your own light can be, it still (and always) remains *your* light, and is defined and limited as such. However, when you become an absorber, you can then retain and convey knowledge and light much greater than yourself.

And this is what I told my dear friend: True speaking is listening. It is not about *you* (the speaker and teacher); it is about the truth, the knowledge, and about the people you are speaking to. Before you get up to speak, as yourself this question: "Are the words I am about to say important for the audience to hear"? "Is the next hour (or whatever time your talk will take) the single most important thing that the audience (and you, the lecturer) can be doing?

If your answer is no, then you shouldn't be giving this talk. It means that you don't respect your audience and also yourself. Why should they be spending their precious time and energy listening to you now and not do more important things? The only right you have to speak to others – including those more educated, refined and experienced than yourself – is because you are not sharing your own thoughts and ideas; you are sharing wisdom and truth that you have heard and absorbed, coming from a higher place.

Preface your lecture by saying just that. Your only right to speak is because you have listened – listened to teachers and masters, who in turn listened to their masters, all links in an unbroken chain of listeners (not 'chachomim', but 'talmidei chachomim', *pupils* of wise ones), going back to the first listener – and thus, speaker – Moses.

Communication is about trust. About opening up channels between you and your listeners, so that they are *receptive* to hear your words. The only way to help an audience get beyond stereotypes and others psychological blocks, is to get out of the way and allow the higher and inner truth resonate. The more you are into yourself, the less you are invested in the message and the audience. And your listeners *will* know – they will feel it. They will be able to sense the truth of the message – and get beyond their own resistance – only if you allow them to by getting your own personality out of the way. Words from the heart enter the heart, our sages teach us. Words that come only from the mouth or even the mind, enter one ear and out the other.

True, there are speakers we listen to for their brilliance, for their advice on medical, financial, or other issues. Though they may be arrogant speakers, we still listen to what they have to say, because we want their information. In exchange for their 'goods' we may be willing to tolerate their egos and even obnoxiousness (not for long, and sometimes not even for a moment). But even then, no true communication has taken place; only (at best) a transactional imparting of information.

This may be true regarding cold facts and hard information. But when it comes to communicating *truth*, emotional and spiritual tools to help people live better lives, then ego, arrogance and the likes, all block the way for healthy communication.

This was the gist of the conversation between myself and my friend about the nature of communication – a discussion, mind you, that is part of my own ongoing struggle as a writer and a teacher.

And may I add that my friend has since become a world famous lecturer, mesmerizing audiences everywhere. Not due to our conversation alone, but to his own evolution and maturation process, which will surely continue to grow.

If you are a teacher or public speaker, here is a guaranteed test to determine your rate of success with your students or audiences. Ask yourself the following questions:

~ Is my talk or class the most important thing that the listeners can be doing during this time?

~ Do I respect my audience? Am I sincerely interested in their welfare?

~ Am I conveying a truth greater than my own?

~ Do my listeners trust me? And if not, how will I establish trust?

~ Are my words coming from the heart?

The same is true about communication between friends, spouses and any close relationships. Communication is not about being right, getting your point across, persuasion and convincing others in the validity of your message. All those aspects may be important and the end result of good communication. But the root of excellent communication we learn from Moses:

Be first a person of 'no words', then your words will be worth listening to.

Reprinted with permission from meaningfullife.com

Soul Inscription

The most famous statement ever uttered in all of history – The Ten Commandments – begins with an unusual four-letter word: *Anochi*. The word means "I", referring to G-d – I the Lord Your G-d took you out of Egypt…" But "*ani*" is the common Hebrew pronoun for "I".

Explains the Talmud (Shabbat 105a), that *Anochi* is an acronym for *Ana Nafshi Ketovit Yehovit. Simply translated:* I Myself wrote [these words and] gave [them to you]. But on closer inspection the actual translation is far more intriguing: I wrote down My very Soul and gave it to you. Or more poetically: My Soul is inscribed in these words that I gave you.

As the opening word of the Ten Commandments, *Anochi* clearly must carry profound significance, which sets the tone and captures the essence of all the commandments and of the entire Torah. Indeed, the Rebbe Yosef Yitzchak emphasizes that the entire Torah is encompassed in the Ten Commandments; the Ten Commandments are all contained in the first two commandments, which in turn are contained in the first commandment; and the first commandment is reflected in microcosm in the first word, *Anochi*. And since all of existence originates from and is included in the Torah, which is the blueprint with which the Cosmic Architect constructed the universe, we can conclude that *Anochi* illuminates for us a fundamental aspect of our entire reality.

Anochi captures the essence and purpose of all existence: To inscribe and reveal the soul in our every word and in our every experience.

No small feat. We live in a highly fragmented and compartmentalized universe. The greatest dichotomy is between body and soul, matter and spirit. Yet, beneath the fissured surface an underlying unity connects all the pieces. Initially we seem all separate from one another – each of us with our own range of experiences, different exposures and life trajectories. But when we begin to communicate with each other, we discover common threads, shared reactions, mutual interests, which transcend our differences. As diverse as we may be, we learn that we celebrate similar milestones, smile at similar experiences, shed the same tears, suffer over the same pains.

Human compartmentalization is acutely and powerfully expressed in the words of Bertrand Russell. When asked how he, as a professor of ethics, could behave unethically, Russell said, "I am also a teacher of mathematics and I am not a triangle". Academics often take pride in their detachment: "I can be completely knowledgeable of a given topic and it does not affect my behavior". Contrast this attitude with Maimonides' words, that a true scholar is recognized in his actions: how he talks, walks, sleeps and does business. A seamless flow between knowledge and behavior.

Russell was following nothing less that the natural laws of all beings – "the way of all flesh" – driven by and justifying fundamental compartmentalizing between ideals and actions. What you teach is not necessarily what you do, and vice versa. Your writing does not necessarily reflect your soul. Maimonides, on the other hand, was following the lead of *Anochi* – seamless integration between soul and words.

The opening of the Ten Commandments, *Anochi*, defines the essence of life's purpose, of all our interactions and of all our words – to manifest the unifying soul in our fragmented universe.

Had G-d not inscribed His soul into the words, our relationship with the Divine would remain detached. The same is true on a human level. If all our interactions were commercial and mundane, we would never connect, truly connect, with one another.

By inscribing His Spirit in His words, every word, now imbued with profound spirituality, evoked a unifying tranquility in all of existence. As the Midrash beautifully describes the state of the universe when *G-d spoke all these words* (Exodus 20:1): No bird twittered, no fowl flew, no ox lowed, none of the angels stirred a wing, the seraphim did not say "Holy, Holy", the sea did not roar, the creatures spoke not, the whole world was hushed into breathless silence and the voice went forth: "I am G-d your G-d".

[As an aside, Ten Commandments is not an accurate translation of the original Hebrew "Aseres ha'Dibrot", which actually means Ten Words, or Ten Statements. Words seem so much more comforting than commandments…].

We too can and ought to learn this from of communication: To inscribe our souls into our words, so that our every utterance becomes a transparent channel for our souls expression.

True communication is not merely the process of conveying messages, ideas and feelings. It is about a relationship – a connection and bond between the parties communicating with each other.

A writer, a speaker, a composer inscribes – engraves – his soul in his work. This allows him to reach into the soul of the reader or listener. Words from the heart enter the heart. A work that is lacking sincerity and soulfullness will not resonate.

Think of it this way: During an average day how many of our conversations are about superficial subjects, spoken with hollow words? How many of our interactions and transactions are transitory experiences? How many of our desires and craving are fleeting and short-lived?

Our mission – taking the cue from G-d etching His soul into the Divine words He imparted to us – is to reach deeper into ourselves, to reveal the soul in every one of our experiences, even casual or trivial ones.

Imagine how people would react to you if they heard your spirit singing instead of your body whining; your beckoning soul instead of your hawking mouthpiece; your gentle words instead of aggressive demands.

Speak from your heart and soul and you too can bring soothing stillness to a chaotic and turbulent world.

Reprinted with permission from meaningfullife.com

The Stutterer

Sensitivity, Leadership and the Secret of Communication

Russian Translation

He spoke slowly and deliberately. Every word seemed carefully measured, as if he was being charged by the syllable. Nothing more than necessary was said and nothing less. Rarely did I hear a speaker so focused and precise.

Even more impressive was his refinement and humility. He spoke about the challenges each of us face – some of us are coming off personal loss, others hurting from psychological scars and yet others challenged by physical handicaps. The familiarity and empathy with which he expressed the inner loneliness associated with these wounds showed that he had suffered much in his life.

"Be patient with yourself", he said, "don't rush things and don't get caught up with the whizzing forces around you. Let yourself be – and always know that you have a beautiful soul inside of you, despite the outer scars you may carry. When your skin gets burned it hurts, but it doesn't make you feel inadequate or unworthy. The same is with our emotional pains and

insecurities. They are what they are, and do not reflect are your inherent value".

As he concluded his moving talk, suddenly and quite deliberately, he quickened the pace of his words. "Now let me share with you my… li-li-li-li-li-little s-s-s-secret", he stammered, barely able to finish the sentence. "From the time I was a li-li-li-ttle child, I s-s-s-stuttered. But", and he slowed down again, "with hard work and patience I have learned to control my inclination. You can too".

He slowly walked away from the podium. The entire audience sat stunned.

I felt so sad. I remembered a classmate who stuttered. It would always break my heart to witness his stammering voice, the facial contortions, struggling to express himself. But then I remembered that this man just spoke for 40 minutes expressing from the depths of his heart a most powerful and needed message. "What a display of courage"? I thought to myself. "What strength of character to be so vulnerable in front of a crowd!"

* * *

Who was the first documented stutterer in history?

This week's Torah portion tells us. Moses is chosen by G-d to redeem the Jewish people from their oppression under Pharaoh and the Egyptians. In his classical dialogue with G-d, one that teaches us volumes, Moses resists becoming G-d's messenger.

Three times and with three different expressions Moses declares that he cannot speak: "I am **not a man of words** – not yesterday, not the day before, not from the very first time You spoke to me. **My speech is difficult** and **my tongue** is difficult" (Exodus 4:10). "The children of Israel did not listen to me. How then will Pharaoh listen to me, seeing that I am of **closed lips**"? (6:12;30).

Moses was the communicator par-excellence; the one chosen to transmit the Torah to his generations and generations to come. Why, of all people, did G-d make it so that the ultimate communicator was "not a man of words", a man whose speech and tongue were "difficult"?!

Explains the Zohar (II 25b), that in the Egyptian exile Moses' "speech was in exile". Moses, who in his selflessness was a seamless channel for the Divine, a totally integrated spirit and body, could not be duplicitous: In a world of pain – a depraved Egyptian exile, imposing slavery and genocide on an innocent people – Moses transparently reflected the reality around him, and could therefore physically not speak clearly; his "speech was in exile" together with the people who were in Egyptian exile. With suffering all around him Moses' mouth was literally locked.

A more callous person, whose life does not necessarily reflect the pain of others – can continue speaking and pontificating even when he should be silent. As we unfortunately see all the time how we can easily go about smiling and celebrating while the city around us is burning. People are usually out to protect themselves and couldn't care less about the suffering of others.

But Moses, the faithful shepherd, could not rest when he witnessed others in pain. His physical body ached and his mouth quivered from all the suffering the Jewish people endured in Egypt.

On a spiritual level, the mystics explain that in the root Moses originated from a dimension that is beyond expression. Moses' soul was from the hidden world of "thought", which cannot be ex-

pressed in the revealed world of "speech". Moses therefore argued that he is not the person to redeem the people from the conscious world (speech).

G-d, however, disagreed. "Who gave man a mouth ... Is it not I, G-d? Now go, and I will be your mouth and direct what you say" (4:11-12). Precisely because Moses was the epitome of selflessness, because he felt the pain of others and was a soul that transcended expression (in words), therefore he was the one that G-d chose to redeem the people from their exile.

And the power to do so came from the Divine "I will be your mouth", which imbued Moses with the power to transcend his "stutter" and communicate effectively with Pharaoh and finally free the Jewish nation from the Egyptian exile.

Ultimately, once they were redeemed from their misery in Egypt and they began integrating the Divine into their material lives, Moses too was healed and was able to express in words the deepest dimensions of the Divine.

In other words, a man of selfless bittul always reflects the reality around him. In a world of suffering, in exile, a schism develops between his thoughts and words, and he falls silent. In a world of redemption he is becomes channel between the supra-conscious world of thought and the conscious world of words.

As we see that Moses becomes the greatest communicator in all of history. Following the exodus from Egypt, Moses receives the Torah at Sinai and proceeds to teach it to the people. This man of "no words" becomes the source of Divine words for all of time. An entire book of the Torah is even named "Devorim" – "these are the words that Moses spoke". The words of Moses, the man of "no words", are remembered forever. Is there anyone else in history whose every word is known and analyzed as those of Moses in the Bible? How many books and commentaries have been written to understand every utterance that came out Moses' mouth?

How is it possible that the most powerful communicator is a man of "no words"? Because true communication is not about brilliant ideas, eloquent oratory skills, compelling presentations; it is about "*bittul*" (selflessness), about recognizing that you are a transparent conduit to convey a truth that is greater than yourself. Moses epitomized this *bittul*; he was more of an absorber of truth than a "speaker". His transparency was therefore the key to his communicative skills. See "The Art of Communictation".

Everything about Moses manifested "bittul" and sensitivity – as the chapter documents:

"Moses was a shepherd" (3:1): The Midrash explains that G-d tests his leaders with sheep (as He later does with David). One sheep once wandered away from the entire flock. Moses sensed the missing sheep, and went searching, only to find the young animal sipping water from a nearby brook. Moses carried the sheep back to the flock. "Ahh", G-d' said. "If Moses is that sensitive to a single sheep amongst thousands, even when no one is watching, how much more so he will be sensitive to my people. He is worthy of being my chosen leader.

Earlier Moses witnesses an "Egyptian kill one of his fellow Hebrews. He looked all around and saw no one, then he killed the Egyptian" (2:11-12). "He looked all around and saw no one" can be interpreted to mean that he saw no one cared – no one was concerned about the travesty being perpetrated against their fellow men. Moses however *did* care. So he proceeds to do what is

necessary to protect innocent people from brutal genocide.

The next day Moses sees "two Hebrew men fighting". "Why are you beating your brother"? he asked them (2:13). Moses here too showed concern about the divisiveness among the Hebrews – though he received the classical response: "who made you our prince and judge", another way of saying mind your own business.

Ironically, in our information age, we have much to learn from Moses. With all our amazing advancements in communications technology, we have also an unprecedented level of miscommunication – between spouses, parents and children, neighbors, communities and nations. E-mail, forums, IM, blogs, VoIP has turned everyone into pundits – speaking and discussing about everything and nothing.

But are we really speaking? Are we really communicating? Who is it that said "today people read more and more about less and less"?

Moses may have been a man of "no words" but he teaches us that speaking – true speaking – is about communicating. And communicating is about listening as much as (if not more than) it is about speaking. The more transparent you are, the better your communication will be. Conversely, the more your ego is in the way, the less resonance your message will have. When your personality stands between your message and the listeners then your personality dilutes (and distorts) the message.

Most of us have been blessed with the power of lucid speech. A great gift indeed. But do we use this gift to communicate truth? Are our words kind and loving and ones that elicit love? Are we able to convey in words our innermost feelings and deepest spiritual desires? Or are our words deceptive? How often do we lie? How often do we use offensive language – words that hurt, divide and conceal, rather than words that heal, unite and reveal? Does our body's speech speak the words of our soul? Or is it the other way around: Our soul's energy is forced to speak the narcissistic words of materialistic pursuits? Physically we may speak clearly, but spiritually are we all not stuttering in one way or another?

As long as there is no seamlessness between our spirits and our words we stutter along, once in a while hopefully sharing a true word or two?

Stuttering is a reflection of a misalignment. In our distorted world, where spirit and matter have yet to fuse, where our material investments do not necessarily mirror our soul's needs, we all stutter.

We stutter in our search for love and intimacy, we stutter through our fears and insecurities, and we stutter when we are called upon to speak truth to our children and students. We stutter when we need to show kindness to friends and when we need to welcome and respect strangers.

The only difference is that some of us have mastered the art of concealing our stutters beneath an elegant "façade" of words. Whether it is the "gift of gab" or excellent "sales skills", "spin", "buzz", "hype" or "hooks" – we know how to convincingly "sell" something even if it has no true benefit (or we know how to convince ourselves that it has benefit even if it doesn't). Not to suggest that every "sale" is worthless, but it's a far cry from transparent selflessness.

We live in a world of politicians, actors, models and performers – who pride themselves in their ability to project all sorts of images and standards with not the slightest stutter or blink.

Stuttering reflects the dichotomy of existence, the split between the inner and the outer.

But stuttering has another side to it. Every stutter is also a challenging opportunity to discover selflessness (bittul), and a brilliance that transcends mere words (as it was with Moses), as the stutterer in our opening story demonstrated with his profound empathy.

This may also explain why stuttering affects four times as many males as females. Brain scans show that in women the connective tissue that allows communication between the two hemispheres of the brain tends to be thicker, perhaps facilitating interchange. In a study made by Simon Baron-Cohen, the director of the autism research center at Cambridge University and the author of "The Essential Difference: The Truth About the Male and Female Brain", he tries to explain that the brain structure in women may be the reason why one study from Yale found that when performing language tasks, women are likely to activate both hemispheres, whereas males (on average) activate only the left hemisphere.

He goes on to argue that psychological tests also reveal patterns of male/female differences. On average, males tend to score higher on mechanics tests than females do. Females, on the other hand, average higher scores than males on tests of emotion recognition, social sensitivity and language ability.

Many of these differences are seen in adults, which might lead to the conclusion that all they reflect are differences in socialization and experience. But some differences are also seen extremely early in development, which may suggest that biology also plays a role. For example, on the first day of life, male and female newborns pay attention to different things. On average, at 24 hours old, more male infants will look at a mechanical mobile suspended above them, whereas more female infants will look at a human face. Girls tend to talk earlier than boys, and in the second year of life their vocabularies grow at a faster rate. One-year-old girls also make more eye contact than boys of their age.

Cohen summarizes these differences by saying that "males on average have a stronger drive to systemize, and females to empathize".

Perhaps with their extra measure of empathy, women can counter some of the stuttering effects of a systemized universe out of touch with its soul.

Moses on the other hand, because of his absolute empathy, actually absorbs and reflects the dichotomy of the universe, in order to help repair it.

By introducing the soul into our lives and its profound empathy we can redeem the forces that lock our speech in "exile". We can reveal the brilliance that often lies concealed within the "stutters" of our lives.

There is something compelling about silence. Take silent films: With no sound to rely upon, actors have to communicate with facial expressions and body language. This is the first language that we all – as young children – are exposed to. Only later do we learn the language of words. Another way of putting it: Just as white space is more important than the actual letters of the printed word, the spaces and silence between words are more critical than the spoken sounds.

"Just as it was in the days when they left Egypt [so too in the future] I will show you wonders". Let us learn sensitivity from Moses how to heal a fractured world.

The lessons are simple but profound:

Never be complacent. Care about those around you. Take a stand against injustice. Protect the innocent. Fight those that are ready to hurt others. Show concern and act forcefully in face of terrorism. Stand up against any form of divisiveness.

Above all: be humble and sensitive.

Allow Moses into our lives and just as then, so today, we will experience wonders.

Reprinted with permission from meaningfullife.com

VI Knowing the Unknowable
Bridging the Gap Between Faith and Reason

ROSH**CHODESH**
society

Introduction

Every worthwhile endeavor can be enhanced and exponentially deepened through being in touch with one's innermost self. While a person can accomplish much in life, being in touch with one's essential humanness allows them to break out of all sorts of limitations, to maintain ultimate self-control, to live a life fully in consonance with their inner convictions, and to experience boundless joy.

The same holds true with regard to the individual relationship we each have with God. As we will demonstrate in this lesson, perhaps one need not be a very soulful person to be convinced of God's existence and have a rudimentary relationship with God. But the ultimate and most genuine relationship with God is an experience that can only emanate from the deepest reaches of one's essence. This lesson will explore how to realize this sort of relationship.

I.   Letting Him In

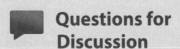
Questions for Discussion

1. Are both approaches—intellectual and faith-based—viable ways to approach God?

2. If they are both viable approaches, is one of them preferable over the other? Why?

II.   A Rationalist Approach

Text 1

מַעֲשֶׂה שֶׁבָּא מִין וְאָמַר לְרַבִּי עֲקִיבָא: הָעוֹלָם הַזֶּה מִי בְּרָאוֹ? אָמַר לוֹ: הַקָּדוֹשׁ בָּרוּךְ הוּא. אָמַר לוֹ: הַרְאֵינִי דָּבָר בָּרוּר. אָמַר לוֹ: לְמָחָר תָּבֹא אֵלִי. לְמָחָר בָּא אֶצְלוֹ. אָמַר לוֹ: מָה אַתָּה לוֹבֵשׁ? אָמַר לוֹ: בֶּגֶד. אָמַר לוֹ: מִי עֲשָׂאוֹ? אָמַר לוֹ: הָאוֹרֵג. אָמַר לוֹ: אֵינִי מַאֲמִינְךָ, הַרְאֵינִי דָּבָר בָּרוּר. אָמַר לוֹ: וּמָה אַרְאֶה לְךָ? וְאֵין אַתָּה יוֹדֵעַ שֶׁהָאוֹרֵג עֲשָׂאוֹ? אָמַר לוֹ: וְאַתָּה אֵינְךָ יוֹדֵעַ שֶׁהַקָּדוֹשׁ בָּרוּךְ הוּא בָּרָא אֶת עוֹלָמוֹ? נִפְטַר אוֹתוֹ הַמִּין. אָמְרוּ לוֹ תַּלְמִידָיו: מָה הַדָּבָר בָּרוּר? אָמַר לוֹ: בָּנַי כְּשֵׁם שֶׁהַבַּיִת מוֹדִיעַ עַל הַבַּנַּאי, וְהַבֶּגֶד מוֹדִיעַ עַל הָאוֹרֵג, וְהַדֶּלֶת עַל הַנַּגָּר, כַּךְ הָעוֹלָם מוֹדִיעַ עַל הַקָּדוֹשׁ בָּרוּךְ הוּא שֶׁהוּא בְּרָאוֹ.

מדרש תמורה, אוצר המדרשים (אייזנשטיין) ע׳ 580

Once, a heretic came to Rabbi Akiva and asked, "Who created the world?"

"God," replied Rabbi Akiva.

"Prove it," said the man.

Rabbi Akiva replied, "Return to me tomorrow."

On the morrow, the man returned. "What are you wearing?" asked Rabbi Akiva.

> > >

"A piece of clothing," the man replied.

"And who made it?" asked Rabbi Akiva.

"The weaver," the man replied.

"I don't believe you; show me proof!" Rabbi Akiva demanded.

"What should I show you?" exclaimed the man. "Don't you know that the weaver made it?"

"And don't you know that God created His world?" Rabbi Akiva responded.

The heretic departed.

Rabbi Akiva's students then asked their teacher, "What is your proof?"

Rabbi Akiva replied, "My sons, just as a home is evidence of its builder, and a piece of clothing evidence of its weaver, and a door evidence of its carpenter, so too, the world is evidence of God Who created it.

Medrash Temurah, Otzar Hamedrashim (Eisenstein) pg 580

Text 2

This most beautiful system of the sun, planets, and comets could only proceed from the counsel and dominion of an intelligent and powerful Being.

Sir Isaac Newton, *Principia* [Philadelphia: Running Press, 2002], p. 426

Text 3

וּכְבָר דִּמּוּ אֲנָשִׁים כִּי הָעוֹלָם נִהְיָה בִּתְחִלַּת הַוָּיָתוֹ בְּמִקְרֶה מֵאֵלָיו, בְּלִי בּוֹרֵא שֶׁבְּרָאוֹ אוֹ יוֹצֵר שֶׁיְּצָרוֹ. וּמִן הַתָּמַהּ בְּעֵינַי שֶׁיַּעֲלֶה עַל לֵב בַּעַל הַגִּיּוֹן בִּזְמַן שְׂפִיּוּתוֹ כָּרַעְיוֹן הַזֶּה . . . וּמִן הַיָּדוּעַ אֶצְלֵנוּ, כִּי הַדְּבָרִים שֶׁהֵם נֶעְדָּרִים כַּוָּנַת מְכַוֵּן בִּפְרָט אֶחָד מֵהֶם, אֵין אֶפְשָׁרוּת שֶׁיִּמָּצְאוּ בָהֶם עִקְּבוֹת הַחָכְמָה וְהַיְכֹלֶת.

הֲלֹא תִרְאֶה, אִלּוּ יָצַק הָאָדָם דְּיוֹ עַל נְיָר בְּבַת אַחַת, לֹא יִתָּכֵן שֶׁיִּצְטַיֵּר מִמֶּנּוּ עָלָיו כְּתָב סָדוּר וְשׁוּרוֹת נִקְרָאוֹת כְּאוֹתוֹ הַנַּעֲשֶׂה בָּעֵט. וְאִלּוּ הִגִּישׁ לְפָנֵינוּ אָדָם כְּתָב מְסֻדָּר, מִמַּה שֶׁאֵין אֶפְשָׁרוּת שֶׁיִּהְיֶה שֶׁלֹּא עַל יְדֵי עֵט, וְדִימָּה שֶׁהוּא יָצַק אֶת הַדְּיוֹ עַל הַנְּיָר וְנִצְטַיֵּר הַכְּתָב עָלָיו מֵאֵלָיו, הָיִינוּ מְמַהֲרִים לְהַכְחִישׁוֹ וְשֶׁלֹּא יִתָּכֵן שֶׁנַּעֲשָׂה שֶׁלֹּא בְּכַוָּנַת מְכַוֵּן.

וְכֵיוָן שֶׁמָּצְחָשׁ בְּעֵינֵינוּ שֶׁיִּרְטֹט תָּבְנִיּוֹת שֶׁנִּקְבְּעוּ בְּהַסְכָּמָתֵנוּ, הָאַךְ יִתָּכֵן לוֹמַר בְּמַה שֶׁהוּא בְּעֵינֵינוּ יוֹתֵר דַּק בַּעֲשִׂיָּתוֹ וְעָמֹק בְּשִׁכְלוּלוֹ לְלֹא גְבוּל, שֶׁהוּא נִתְהַוָּה בְּלִי כַּוָּנַת מְכַוֵּן, וְחָכְמַת חָכָם, וִיכֹלֶת יָכֹל?

חובות הלבבות (מהדורת קאפח), שער היחוד ו

There are people who presume that the universe came into being by chance and of itself, without a creator creating it or an artisan designing it. I find it astounding that an intellectual person at a moment of lucidity should entertain such a thought.... Common sense dictates that anything that is not the product of thoughtful design—down to the last detail—cannot possibly contain the impression of wisdom and faculty.

Consider: Were a person to haphazardly pour ink on paper, it is inconceivable for this to result in orderly lines of script, as is produced by a pen. Were a person to present before us a paper containing orderly lines of script, which can only possibly be produced with a pen, claiming that he simply poured ink on the paper and the result was this script, we would quickly reject this assertion and [explain that] this script must be the product of thoughtful design.

If it is beyond belief that a simple script [can be a product of chance], how is it conceivable that something which is infinitely more subtle and complex should have come into existence without thoughtful design and the wisdom and capacity of a wise and capable being?[2]

Rabbeinu Bachya ibn Pakuda, *Duties of the Heart, Sha'ar Hayichud 6*

III. A Faith-Based Approach

Text 4

הַנְּשָׁמָה הוּא מִן הָעֶלְיוֹנִים, חֵלֶק אֱלוֹקָהּ
מִמַּעַל.

עץ הדעת טוב, פרשת ואתחנן

*The soul is from the supernal realm; it is
a part of God from above.*

Rabbi Chaim Vital, *Etz Hada'at Tov, Parshat Va'etchanan*

Text 5

זֶה שֶׁיִּשְׂרָאֵל מַאֲמִינִים בֶּאֱלָקוּת בֶּאֱמוּנָה
פְּשׁוּטָה וְאֵין צְרִיכִים רְאָיוֹת עַל זֶה הוּא
מִצַּד . . . דְּשׁוֹרֶשׁ הָאֱמוּנָה הוּא מֵעֶצֶם
הַנְּשָׁמָה . . . דְּזֶה שֶׁעֶצֶם הַנְּשָׁמָה מְקֻשֶּׁרֶת
בֶּאֱלָקוּת הִיא הִתְקַשְּׁרוּת עַצְמִית.

ספר המאמרים מלוקט ו,קלב

*The Jew's[5] simple faith in God, which
requires no supporting evidence . . .
finds its origin in the essence of the soul,
which is inherently connected to God.*

Rabbi Menachem Mendel Schneerson,
Sefer Hama'amarim Melukat 6:132

Text 6a

*Its genesis: inside the kingdom of night, I witnessed a strange trial. Three rabbis—all erudite
and pious men—decided one winter evening to indict God for allowing His children to be
massacred. I remember: I was there, and I felt like crying. But there nobody cried.*

Elie Wiesel, *The Trial of God* [New York: Schocken Books, 1986], p. XXV

Text 6b

By the time he was fifteen, Elie Wiesel was in Auschwitz, a Nazi death camp. A teacher of Talmud befriended him by insisting that whenever they were together they would study Talmud—Talmud without pens and pencils, Talmud without paper, Talmud without books. It would be their act of religious defiance.

One night the teacher took Wiesel back to his own barracks, and there, with the young boy as the only witness, three great Jewish scholars—masters of Talmud, Halakhah, and Jewish jurisprudence—put God on trial, creating, in that eerie place, "a rabbinic court of law to indict the Almighty." The trial lasted several nights. Witnesses were heard, evidence was gathered, conclusions were drawn, all of which issued finally in a unanimous verdict: The Lord God Almighty, Creator of Heaven and Earth, was found guilty of crimes against creation and humankind. And then, after what Wiesel describes as an "infinity of silence," the Talmudic scholar looked at the sky and said, "It's time for evening prayers," and the members of the tribunal recited Maariv, *the evening service.*

Ibid., Introduction by Robert McAfee Brown

IV. Know Thy Creator

Text 7

מַה שֶּׁאֲנַחְנוּ חוֹקְרִים וּמְעַיְּנִים בְּעִנְיְנֵי
אֱמוּנָתֵנוּ הוּא . . . כְּדֵי שֶׁתִּתְאַמֵּת לָנוּ בְּפֹעַל
מַה שֶּׁיָּדַעְנוּ מִפִּי נְבִיאֵי ה' בִּידִיעָה.

אמונות ודעות (מהדורת קאפח), הקדמה, אות ו

We engage in philosophy and intellectually probe the principles of our faith . . . to confirm intellectually that which we already know from God's prophets.

Rabbi Sa'adyah ben Yosef Ga'on (Sa'adyah Ga'on), *Emunot Vede'ot*, Introduction 6

Text 8

יְסוֹד הַיְסוֹדוֹת וְעַמּוּד הַחַכְמוֹת, לֵידַע
שֶׁיֵּשׁ שָׁם מָצוּי רִאשׁוֹן, וְהוּא מַמְצִיא כָּל
הַנִּמְצָא. וְכָל הַנִּמְצָאִים מִן שָׁמַיִם וְאֶרֶץ
וּמַה שֶּׁבֵּינֵיהֶם, לֹא נִמְצְאוּ אֶלָּא מֵאֲמִתַּת
הִמָּצְאוֹ . . .

וִידִיעַת דָּבָר זֶה מִצְוַת עֲשֵׂה, שֶׁנֶּאֱמַר
"אָנֹכִי ה' אֱלוֹקֶיךָ" (שמות כב,ב).

משנה תורה, הלכות יסודי התורה א,א-ו

The foundation of all foundations and the pillar of wisdom is to know that there is a Primary Being Who brings all existence into being. All the creatures

of the Heavens, earth, and what's between them came into existence only from His being. . . .

The knowledge of this concept is a positive commandment, as implied by the verse [Shemot/Exodus 20:2], "I am God, your Lord."

Rabbi Moshe ben Maimon (Maimonides/Rambam), *Mishneh Torah*, Laws of the Foundation of Torah 1:1–6

Text 9

כִּי זֶה כָּל הָאָדָם וְתַכְלִיתוֹ, לְמַעַן דַּעַת אֶת כְּבוֹד ה' וִיקַר תִּפְאֶרֶת גְּדֻלָתוֹ, אִישׁ אִישׁ כְּפִי אֲשֶׁר יוּכַל שְׂאֵת, כְּמוֹ שֶׁכָּתוּב בְּרַעְיָא מְהֵימְנָא פָּרָשַׁת בֹּא: "בְּגִין דְּיִשְׁתְּמוֹדְעוּן לֵיהּ".

תניא, פרק מד

Man's raison d'être *is to know the glory of God and the majestic splendor of His greatness, each according to his or her capacity, as is written in the Zohar (2:42b): "[The purpose of creation] is for the creations to know Him."*

Rabbi Shne'ur Zalman of Liadi, *Tanya*, ch. 42

LEARNING INTERACTION 1

Write down the respective advantages of a faith-based approach to God, and an intellect-based approach.

Advantages of Faith in God	Advantages of Understanding God

V. The Daily Journey

Text 10

מוֹדֶה אֲנִי לְפָנֶיךָ מֶלֶךְ חַי וְקַיָּם, שֶׁהֶחֱזַרְתָּ בִּי נִשְׁמָתִי בְּחֶמְלָה. רַבָּה אֱמוּנָתֶךָ.

סידור תהילת ה', סדר השכמת הבוקר

I am modeh *to You, living and eternal King. You have mercifully restored my soul within me; Your faithfulness is great.*

Siddur Tehilat Hashem, Order Upon Arising in the Morning

Key Points

1   Intellectual arguments for the existence of God have been proposed by philosophers and theologians—including Jewish ones.

2   Intellectual arguments contain an intrinsic failing: "Facts" are based on data and premises that can be mistaken. Hence, even when logic does bring someone to acknowledge God, it cannot be with a potent sense of conviction and surety. Moreover, our goal is having a *relationship* with God, and an intellectual understanding of God's existence will not necessarily create one.

3   Faith in God already exists within every one of us—though sometimes it is covered by layers of dust. It is the deepest definition of who we are and we need only access it.

4   Soul-faith is potent and unwavering inasmuch as it stems from the core of one's being.

5   Soul-faith is accompanied by a desire to cleave to God and to maintain a full relationship with Him through intellect, emotion, and action.

6   The person of faith must endeavor to *understand* God. Only when our soul and mind work in tandem can we have a complete relationship with God, a relationship that encompasses the totality of our being.

Bibliography

Text 1 – Rabbi Moshe ben Maimon (1135–1204). Better known as Maimonides or by the acronym Rambam; born in Cordoba, Spain. After the conquest of Cordoba by the Almohads, he fled Spain and eventually settled in Cairo, Egypt. There, he became the leader of the Jewish community and served as court physician to the vizier of Egypt. His rulings on Jewish law are considered integral to the formation of halachic consensus. He is most noted for authoring the *Mishneh Torah,* an encyclopedic arrangement of Jewish law, and for his philosophical work, *Guide for the Perplexed.*

Text 4 – Rabbi Chaim ben Yosef Vital (1542–1620). Born in Israel, lived in Safed, Jerusalem, and later Damascus. Vital was the principal disciple of Arizal, though he studied under him for less than two years. Before his passing, Arizal authorized Vital to record his teachings. Acting on this mandate, Vital began arranging his master's teachings in written form, and his many works constitute the foundation of the Lurianic school of Jewish mysticism, which was later universally adopted as the kabbalistic standard. Thus, Vital is one of the most important influences in the development of Kabbalah. Among his most famous works are *Ets Chayim,* and *Sha'ar Hakavanot.*

Text 5 – Rabbi Menachem Mendel Schneerson (1902–1994). Known as "the Lubavitcher Rebbe," or simply as "the Rebbe." Born in southern Ukraine. Rabbi Schneerson escaped from the Nazis, arriving in the U.S. in June 1941. The towering Jewish leader of the 20th century, the Rebbe inspired and guided the revival of traditional Judaism after the European devastation, and often emphasized that the performance of just one additional good deed could usher in the era of Mashiach.

Text 6a – Elie Wiesel (1928–). Professor of the humanities at Boston University. Born in Sighet, Transylvania, at the age of fifteen he was deported by the Nazis to Auschwitz. Wiesel is the author of more than 40 books of fiction and non-fiction, including the acclaimed memoir *Night,* which has been published in more than 30 languages. In 1986, Wiesel won the Nobel Prize for Peace. Soon after, Wiesel and his wife established the Elie Wiesel Foundation for Humanity. For his literary and human rights activities he has received numerous awards including the Presidential Medal of Freedom and the U.S. Congressional Gold Medal.

Text 7 – Rabbi Sa'adyah ben Yosef Ga'on (ca. 882–942). Born in Egypt; prominent rabbi, Jewish philosopher, and exegete of the geonic period, he was known for his works on the Torah, Hebrew linguistics, Halachah, and philosophy. Rabbi Sa'adyah came to the forefront of the rabbinic scene through his active opposition to Karaism, a divergent sect that denies the divinity of the Oral Law, as well as his recalibration of the Hebrew Lunar calendar. In 928, the exilarch David ben Zakai invited him to head the illustrious yeshivah in Sura, Babylonia, thereby bestowing upon him the honorific title, Ga'on. His later conflict with the exilarch, however, would eventually create a rift within Babylonian Jewry.

Text 9 - Rabbi Shne'ur Zalman of Liadi (1745–1812). Chasidic rebbe and founder of the Chabad movement, also known as "the Alter Rebbe" and "the Rav." Born in Liozna, Belarus, he was among the principal students of the Magid of Mezeritch. His numerous works include the *Tanya*, an early classic containing the fundamentals of Chasidism; *Torah Or; Likutei Torah*; and *Shulchan Aruch HaRav*, a reworked and expanded code of Jewish law. He is interred in Hadiach, Ukraine, and was succeeded by his son, Rabbi Dovber of Lubavitch.

Additional Readings

Proof

by Rabbi Menachem M. Schneerson

B"H. 25 Iyar, 5719[1]

Mr. Yitzchak Damiel,

Peace and blessing!

I have received your letter, with the enclosed question from the young men and women. Please apologize to them on my behalf for the delayed response. I was especially preoccupied throughout the days and weeks before and after Pesach.

As the question itself cannot be fully dealt with in a letter, I have to limit my response to a number of fundamental points, but I hope that you will be able to add your own explanation to these points in my letter, based on the teachings of our Torah and especially the teachings of Chassidut.

Needless to say, if there are any aspects of my letter which are not sufficiently clear, I am always ready to respond to further inquiries—and even challenges or refutations—which I will endeavor to answer to the best of my ability.

In response to the question:

"Is there a convincing proof for the existence of the Creator that could satisfy us as skeptics beyond the faintest shadow of a doubt"?

[2]At first glance the question seems simple enough, especially since the concepts are straightforward and the terms familiar. But this apparent simplicity is deceptive, and to address the question properly requires clarity of language and careful definition of terms. In particular, what do we mean by "existence" and "proof" of existence? We must start here because these words mean very different things to different people. For example, that which constitutes complete proof for a young child may be totally inadequate for a meticulous scientist, and vice versa.

For instance, some say that for children, existence and proof of existence apply only to tangible objects—"seeing is believing".

Included in this kind of proof is the general idea of a report. This too is a proof based on perception, except that it is someone else's perception. Consider, for example, a person born blind and who has never seen the shade of pink called magenta. Does he have convincing proof for the existence of that color? Surely he will rely on the perceptions of others who tell him that there is such a thing as light, that it comes in various colors, and that these colors come in different shades, one of which is magenta. Although magenta is totally beyond anything in his experience, he has absolutely no trouble believing in this entity because he trusts other people's reported perceptions.

---

1   June 2, 1959

2   At this point, we depart from phrase-by-phrase translation, and revert to the translator's loose rendition of this letter as published in *Fusion: Absolute Standards in a World of Relativity*, Ch. 1. Feldheim Pub., 1990.

At a more abstract level, another perfectly acceptable kind of proof is reasoning from effect to cause. Everyone acknowledges with complete certainty that everything that happens has a reason and cause for happening. Thus when one sees actions, these themselves are proof of an activating force, even though this is not direct proof and superficially there appears to be room for doubt. A classic example is the existence of electric power. Man is a sentient being; his sense of sight verifies the existence of colors, his sense of hearing verifies the existence of sound, etc. These are considered complete, direct proofs; yet, while we can sense current, man has no faculty to perceive electric potential, or voltage. We only see its effects, such as a filament glowing or a voltmeter's needle moving, etc. Still, we are certain of our conclusion that there exists some imperceptible force, which we term electricity, which is the reason behind what we do see. This is considered conclusive proof in the same way one proves the existence of magnetism and other forces. Electricity is a prime example because its existence is totally accepted beyond any shadow of a doubt.

The scientist's faith in cause and effect is so intense that he will accept as undisputed fact the existence of an activating force, even if it plainly contradicts rationality. A case in point is the force of gravity. We are so familiar with the idea of gravity from every science book throughout our school years, that no one would dream of questioning it, even though rationally it is far more difficult to accept than electricity. Electricity is only imperceptible when it is still, but when it flows it can be felt and measured. Not so with gravity; no one has ever seen, felt or measured a wave or particle of gravity. Our only proof that the force of gravity exists is that physical bodies move. But how can a force act from afar with no intermediary whatsoever between the masses? With a remote controlled garage door or toy, there is a flow of measurable infrared or radio waves, but with gravity there is nothing but the simple faith that every action has a cause.

At first scientists tried to explain the force of gravity by assuming the existence of a fine mediating substance called ether. But the idea had to be abandoned because the proposed medium would have necessarily had so many contradictory properties that it became even more implausible than the alternative absurdity of remote action without any connection.

Anyone in the exact sciences who wonders whether the existence of the Creator can be reliably proven should consider another "standard" concept, derived from the realm of physics. This idea is so intellectually challenging that after many decades of study, even the experts admit it is beyond their comprehension. Nonetheless it is accepted by all exact scientists as a reality, and it is a proven fact in the eyes of the public. The idea referred to is that matter is nothing but a particular form of energy, and that it is possible to transform matter into energy and energy to matter. Superficially it may be hard to see what is so difficult about this notion of relativity. However if one takes a moment to consider the degree of similarity between the light now emanating from his bulb, and the shoe on his foot, and then tries to imagine converting one into the other and back again, the problem becomes crystal clear. Everything in our experience leads us to think that matter and energy are as fundamentally different as two things can be. Therefore, to say that they are equivalent does not even sound, say, reasonable-but-difficult; it simply sounds ridiculous.

As with gravity, the only compelling proof for relativity is that we see events that have no apparent explanation and if we accept the theory—they are explained. This is considered a scientific proof and, on this basis alone, relativity is accepted virtually everywhere as conclusively demonstrated beyond the faintest doubt, even though from a strictly rational standpoint, the equivalence of matter and energy is not at all compelling.

People act in accordance with their beliefs, and skeptics are no different. Hence it is reasonable to expect that a skeptic will feel free to use as a basis for action any ideas that are shown to meet his criteria of legitimacy. On this basis, there is not only one, but several proofs for the existence of G-d and, as mentioned, there is no problem if one is forced to say that this existence is not grasped by the senses or the mind, or even if it contradicts rationality. As long as this existence accounts for observed reality and does so better than any other proposition, we have what is usually considered to be conclusive, scientific proof.

In this sense, proving the existence of the Creator is the same as proving anything else, whether in the realm of science or in the context of our daily lives.

Anyone who examines his daily conduct will admit that he doesn't perform a penetrating, thorough analysis assessing the reliability of the information on which he bases his daily activities. If the weather forecast calls for rain, he wears his boots even though he has never met the weatherman or studied meteorology, and furthermore he knows that the weatherman is often wrong. For another example, if Vitamin E is reported to cure baldness, he will take it without knowing for sure how it works or if it works. He'll take it without even knowing what it is. Rather he accepts the words of others who did look into the matter.

Only where there is some doubt that maybe the "information" was faked or that the observer was affected by internal or external factors, or that he wasn't sure himself and took someone else's view, etc … Then one would seek additional evidence. And with every increase in the number of observers, and with every type of variation in position, situation and context relative to the observers, the likelihood of deception becomes more remote and the evidence is strengthened in the form of a scientific and convincing proof. On this basis, the individual and society engage in all kinds of activities and projects, with complete trust that their conclusions are true and established.

So too in our case. The giving of the Torah on Mount Sinai was verified, generation after generation, as a fact proven by the presence of 600,000 adult males. If one includes women, children, Levites, men over sixty, etc., there were present millions of individuals, including Egyptian emigrants, who saw the events with their own eyes and experienced Divine communication personally and simultaneously.

This is not a testimony restricted to a single prophet, a dreamer or an elite group. This testimony was transmitted from parent to child, generation after generation, and everyone acknowledges that there was no interruption in the transmission from then until now. Moreover, there have never been less than 600,000 reporters in any generation, people whose characters were dissimilar and who were by no means afraid to disagree on basic issues, as is well documented from Sinai on. Yet, despite all their differences and arguments, and despite their being dispersed throughout the world for millennia, all the versions of the above historical event are similar in every detail. Is there more reliable and precise testimony than this?

There is a second manner of proof which is also based on the premise above—that everything that happens has a cause, that seeing any event or situation is proof positive that some guiding force exists, even if the event was apparently senseless or destructive. This proof is as follows:

Consider any object. Virtually anything that one can imagine is composed of various parts that are arranged and coordinated with remarkable precision. None of the parts has any inherent control over the others and yet we know that the harmonious and unified functioning of the entire system is itself a phenomenon and must be due to some cause. We conclude from this with complete confidence that there is an external power that binds and unifies all the parts. Moreover, the very fact that it binds and unifies the parts proves that it is stronger than they are since it controls them.

For example, if we were to enter a factory where everything was run automatically and we did not see anyone there, we would not doubt the existence and involvement of a great mechanic whose knowledge encompassed all the machinery and component parts and who controlled them – one who was in charge of their functioning among themselves and who maintained the connection between the parts and the control center. On the contrary—the more concealed the hand of man in such a factory, and the more the operations are automated, the more impressed and convinced we are of the mechanic's remarkable skill.

And if this is the case with a factory, where we are speaking of hundreds, thousands, or even tens of thousands of parts, how much more true is this for natural objects, e.g., a piece of wood or stone, a plant or an animal, and—needless to say—the structure of the human body, as Job states, "From my flesh I will envision …"[3] This is especially so from the scientific perspective that every object is comprised of billions of atoms, with each atom containing even more minute parts. One would think, at first glance, that chaos would reign and yield incomparable disorder. But instead, we see an amazing orderliness and a marvelous fitting of the smaller parts to the larger, up to the very largest as well as the integration of microcosmic and macrocosmic patterns and processes, etc., etc. It is therefore clear beyond any shadow of a doubt that there exists a "Mechanic" responsible for all this.

One might say that all this is governed according to the "laws of nature"—but I think it is important to emphasize that such expressions have no explanatory content, but rather give a convenient summary or description of the existing situation. That is, it is true that natural phenomena are conducted according to definite patterns. But to say that a "Law of Nature" is a being in and of itself without dependence, and that this being rules throughout the cosmos, and that there are thousands of beings like it, according to the number of natural laws, is so absurd that there is not one scientist in the field who would say so. Rather it is the case that such laws are merely convenient, summary expressions for describing a situation, so that one should not be forced to duplicate at every turn a lengthy description of the "simple" facts. But however elegant and sophisticated a law of nature may be, it is clear and obvious that such an expression provides no explanation whatsoever.

---

3 *Iyov* 19:26

Now to the heart of the matter. To put it plainly, everyone has criteria for what can be reliably considered true. If an idea meets those standards, it is fit to be believed and acted upon. If it does not, then it is not suitable for belief or as a basis for action. But one may not adopt certain truth criteria when it is convenient, and then drop them when it is not. Therefore, it is assumed that anyone who is seeking a proof is not merely doing so for the sake of intellectual exercise, but would indeed live by his conclusions.

In this regard it should be noted that the aforementioned proof is much stronger than all those proofs and evidence by which people conduct their daily lives. What simpler illustration is there than the fact that, when retiring at night, one arranges everything for the morning even though there is no logical proof that tomorrow morning the sun will rise yet again and that all natural systems will continue to function as they did yesterday and the day before. It is only that since the world has been working this way for so many days and years, one trusts that these "laws" will also rule tomorrow and the next day.

And on this basis alone, a person strives and troubles himself to prepare his affairs for the following morning, even though he has no logically compelling reason to do so. On the contrary, if chance or random probabilities were running the show, it would be more reasonable to assume that tomorrow will be utterly unpredictable. The conviction that nature will continue to function as it did today is only logically compelling when it is based on the knowledge that there really is a Master of the world.

Although more could be said on everything that was discussed above and certain points could be explained further, this should suffice and provide enough material for consideration and

conclusion. For it is incorrect to maintain that the Creator's existence requires proof, while His Creation itself exists beyond doubt, because in fact the opposite is true! Recent results of scientific research, regarding the existence of the universe and ways to "describe" it, contradict each other in numerous areas and indeed leave room for major doubts. But the most serious, significant and fundamental scientific doubt is as follows:

Who can establish whether the perceived impression of the eyes, of the ears, or of the brain generally, has any reality outside human sensation or thought? This argument poses an insurmountable challenge to the truth of the world's existence but in no way applies to the Creator, nor to the functional reality of event causation and universal order. For this, practically speaking, it doesn't matter whether there exists an independent reality or just the impression of such a reality. The primary consideration of the average person, and according to which he lives his whole life, is that for everything in his world there is a cause which acts, from within or without.

A further note of importance is that often human nature is such that when one is given a simple proof, it is difficult to accept because of its very simplicity. Such irrational rejection is unfortunate because it precludes any effect on personal behavior, while one of the foundations of our faith in the universe's Creator and Director, as well as the stand at Sinai and the receiving of the Torah and its commandments, is that the quality of a person's deeds is what matters most.

I will be pleased to hear responses to all the above, and as mentioned in the enclosed letter, I hope they will feel completely free to present their opinions, even if they disagree with what is written above.

With Blessing

/signature[4]

Mind Over Matter: The Lubavitcher Rebbe on Science, Technology, and Medicine, Translated and edited by Arnie Gotfryd, [Jerusalem: Shamir, 2003], 1-10

Reprinted with the permission of the editor

A Space for Him to Fill

By Jay Litvin

A woman suffering from ovarian cancer wrote me after reading an earlier article I wrote for this publication. In her letter she says, ". . . *sometimes I think I'm acting more positive than I feel because of all the social pressure I experience to 'think positive'. Sometimes people sound like they're saying, 'If you just clap real hard and believe, Tinker Bell will live. And you will be cured of cancer'. Meaning that if I'm not disease free, I'm 'clinging on to negativity.'"*

When discussing my own health condition with people, I have had similar experiences. Should I express anything but my most positive self—should I expose the darker side of my thoughts and fears—I often feel as if I have disclosed an unseemly lack of *bitachon* (trust in G-d) that the listener is quickly trying to rectify with statements such as "think good", "stay strong", or "I'm sure we'll be hearing good news from you soon".

But the larger question is whether there really is a contradiction between expressing the full gamut

of positive and negative emotions, and the belief that only good thoughts produce good results (expressed by the Chassidic adage, "Think good and it will be good").

Do any of us possess such simplicity and sincerity, such innocence and wholeheartedness, such impeccability in our *bitachon* as to eliminate any vestige of doubt or fear? And if we do not, how do we apply the adage "Think good and it will be good" to our flawed lives and selves? How does it apply to us who, in spite of our imperfection, seek such faith to combat illness and other hardship?

To one whose faith and trust is truly without blemish, there would, I imagine, be no negativity in thought or emotion. He or she would think good and it would simply be good. The life of this person would, it seems to me, be filled with such wholehearted acceptance and love that there would be no possibility for a bad outcome. Or, perhaps he or she would perceive every outcome as good. Or, perhaps people like this are not even concerned with outcomes, so filled are they with the awareness of G-d's perfection in each moment.

But for the rest of us, such cracks in faith and trust allow seepage of the darkest kind, especially in times of serious illness, loss, and danger. Most commonly we experience fear or grief, expressed through sadness, anger, blame, or resentment.

For folks like me battling a life-threatening disease, there will be times when we are mad, sad, scared, and downright blue. Are we incapable then or void of *bitachon*?

I propose that rather than seeing our lives linearly, in which these "blue times" are rifts in the otherwise seamless continuity of our trust, we see our lives more spherically, made up of a full spectrum of simultaneously existing, fluctuating emotions

4 *Emunah U'Mada*, pp. 3–8

and thoughts that take their place in the wholeness of who we are. In such a view, dwelling on or giving primacy to our fears would certainly throw our system out of whack; yet acknowledging them appropriately would strengthen the trust and *bitachon* that holds them in balance. In this model, fear becomes the catalyst to courage, weakness the other side of endurance, anxiety the shadow of faith and patience.

I believe that, ironically, such a view strengthens the adage, "Think good and it will be good". For now, when we see fear or anxiety in our friend (or ourselves), we no longer see negativity; rather we recognize the catalyst to strengthen his (and our) faith and trust. When we acknowledge fear in our friend, we affirm, as well, its opposite—the Rock that eternally supports us when life seems so fragile and unstable. When we free, rather than inhibit, our friend to express this side of his/her emotional reality, we create an opportunity to support our friend as he travels through tunnels of darkness, eventually perceiving the glimmer of light that leads ultimately to the faith and trust he or she seeks. Conversely, when we *deny* our friend (or our ourselves) this freedom, we inhibit this discovery; we retard the development or expression of the very *bitachon* our friend so desperately needs.

My friends like it when they see me feeling strong and energetic in spite of the chemotherapy I endure. Little do they know that such strength and energy come precisely from those days when I stop fighting against the extreme weakness I sometimes feel and allow myself to collapse—without resistance—to wallow in my bed, covers pulled over my head, feeling my aloneness, my emptiness and fear. When I do this, I always, *always* emerge renewed and refreshed. My renewed, reinforced faith and trust comes not from denying these feelings, but precisely by allowing them.

In my aloneness I invite G-d's companionship, my emptiness becomes a space for Him to fill. When my fear and trembling cease, they are replaced by a renewed sense of trust and security. By exploring, enduring, and surviving these emotional netherworlds I know once again that their power and reality are illusory, temporary, and insubstantial. They exist only to bring me closer to G-d.

If these fears are illusory, why do they continually return? Because they are so deeply ingrained in our humanity as part of our "nature" that if . . . *if* . . . they are ever to be overcome, it will be the result of a lifetime of work—a lifetime of experience with no escape from the hardships and grief, the fear and anxiety that ultimately spur us closer to the truth. The deeper our fears, the deeper the level of true *bitachon* to which they can lead us.

Thus, in either case—whether we already possess *bitachon* or are flawed seekers of G-d's protection in time of danger—we are forced once again to return to the concepts of wholeheartedness, purity, sincerity, and impeccability. If we are not *tzaddikim* who possess the faith and trust in G-d that precludes all worry and fear, than let us at least possess enough faith and trust in G-d to allow these feelings. Let us acknowledge them in ourselves and our friends not as demonic obstacles but as pathways to *bitachon*, to trust and faith in G-d.

And before we cast platitudes of faith in the face of those who suffer, and risk plunging daggers in their already wounded hearts, let us reflect on the mundane fears and anxieties that daily invade our own lives. Our response to a flat tire on the way to that long-awaited business meeting may be the best measure of how deep our trust in G-d really is. If you trust that G-d will lead you to health and long life but become angry at your wife or husband because he or she doesn't exhibit the perfection you expect, do you really have full trust that G-d determines the life and fate of all His creations, including the fate of someone who is gravely ill and in danger?

Two things may result from this honest self-assessment. First, we may become loving catalysts rather than self-righteous obstacles to the growth of our friends. Second, we may learn how to transform not only our fears into faith, but our platitudes into the truths that were once their mothers.

Reprinted with permission from www.chabad.org

Religious faith reminds us that a happy life is one of altruism, forgiveness, and love.

by Rabbi Jonathan Sacks

One of my favourite contemporary phrases is *mission drift*. First used by the military, it's what happens when in pursuit of an objective people forget what objective they were pursuing. You get sidetracked. The territory turns out to be not like the map. On paper, it looks easy to get from A to B. But once you're down there, there are all sorts of diversions. The going is harder than you thought it would be. You lose your way. The car breaks down. On the brink of your departure, it looked so simple. But then, as someone (no one's quite sure who) once said, "In theory there's no difference between theory and practice. But in practice there is".

That's what the Jewish high holy days, the New Year and the Day of Atonement, are about. They're about life and how we live it; time and how we use it; values and ideals and how, over time, we tend to forget them. It's about mission drift.

In theory it sounded so simple—life, that is. Obey the rules. Do the right and the good. Be a blessing. But in practice we find ourselves cutting corners, compromising principles, searching for quick fixes, too pressured and hassled to look up and see if we're still on the right road.

It helps, once a year, to stop and look at the map again. Soon it becomes clear that we've taken a number of wrong turns. So, we admit our mistakes, apologise, seek atonement, and set out again, hopefully this time to reach our destination. The key word of these days is *teshuvah*. Normally translated as "penitence", it really means "return", getting back on track, a little more determined to get it right this time without getting diverted or delayed.

Is it possible for a whole society, even an entire civilisation, to suffer mission drift? Not only is it possible. It's almost inevitable. Right now we are going through one of the great mission drifts in the history of the West.

The objective long ago was happiness, for which, according to Aristotle, all people aim. Given that, as angry atheists argue, religion makes people miserable, there must be another way. There were four candidates: the state, the market, science, and technology. They all failed.

The state gives us services, not meanings. The principle of liberal democracy is that the state does not tell us how to live. It leaves that choice to us. But since happiness depends on how we live, it cannot be provided by the state.

The market gives us choices, but it does not tell us which choices to make. It sets before us everything money can buy. But as the Beatles sang almost a half century ago, money can't buy me love—or anything else that has value but not a price. Even people who win a fortune experience temporary exhilaration, which lasts, on average, a year, and then they're back to the happiness level they were at before they won.

Science, as Richard Dawkins never lets us forget, tells us where we came from. What it doesn't, and cannot tell us, is where we are going to. Yet happiness is a destination, not a point of departure. It's part of culture, not nature. Therefore, it lies outside the bounds of science.

Technology has indeed removed many causes of unhappiness. Standards of living have risen. So has life expectancy. Technology has abolished distance and made knowledge more accessible than ever before. But at the same time, it has substituted virtual encounters for real ones, Second Life for real life, Facebook for true face-to-face relationships. Watching a screen and living a life are not the same.

All four institutions are invaluable. They rank among the greatest ever inventions of the human mind. But they don't lead, in and of themselves, to happiness. Thinking otherwise is to mistake the means for the end.

The new "science of happiness", a burgeoning discipline, has confirmed some very ancient truths indeed. Happiness involves a sense of meaning and purpose, a network of close and supportive relationships, and an attitude of gratitude. Optimists are healthier than others. So are altruists, those who give time and money to others.

Mission drift happens when people in search of happiness choose routes that go elsewhere. A happy life is a life of altruism, forgiveness and love—which is what religious faith reminds us of on its holy days.

www.timesonline.co.uk

Reprinted with permission

How Do We Know that G-d Exists?

By Tzvi Freeman

Question

I'd like to ask you a question that has really bothered me now for a while. You see, I have become aware through much deep thought that we certainly cannot prove many basic things about the world. For example, I cannot know with certainty that anyone other than myself really exists! Yes, I see people and talk to them, but that could all just be a product of whatever is making my mind run —it could be my own simulated universe, so to speak. My senses might be utterly lying to me, when the truth out there is really an entirely different reality, or perhaps no reality at all . . .

I could go on and on, but I'm sure you get my drift. What I am basically getting at is that anything is possible —there is utterly no way whatsoever to know anything with certainty about this universe!

If that is the case, how can we know that G-d exists? Yes, we can provide mountains of evidence that some being created the world and revealed the Torah at Sinai —but all that evidence is from a "reality" that we have no way of knowing exists at all!

How then is it possible for us to have a meaningful relationship with a being of whose existence we cannot be certain, in a world of whose nature we cannot be certain, etc., etc . . . . It just doesn't seem possible! All this is a great source of frustration to me.

Adam G.

Answer

Dear Adam

You pose some very good questions. Allow me, then, to counter with some questions of my own.

Did you eat breakfast this morning? Did you drive to work? Did you keep the dentist appointment you had for 4:00 pm?

I'm going to assume that the answer to all three questions is "yes". I'm also going to assume that the reason that you ate your breakfast was that you knew that the toast, eggs and juice would satisfy the hunger you felt in your stomach and provide you with the nutrients and the energy to keep you going for the next few hours. And I'll also assume that you knew that your car hasn't been rigged with explosives that your dentist is not a serial killer.

You see, Adam, we use the word "know" in two different ways. We use it one way in philosophical discussions like the one in your question. And we use it in a different way in day-to-day life. In philosophical discussions we play with words, take their definitions to their extremes, and come up with mind-boggling conclusions. In day-to-day life we use a combination of intelligence, experience, common sense and intuition to know certain things. Whether we know these things "absolutely" or "certainly" in the philosophical sense is irrelevant: we know them enough to live by them and make our choices —including life-and-death choices —with this knowledge. With all due respect to philosophy, that's as "absolute" and as "certain" that knowledge can get.

So why this double standard? Why deny you inner life that which you freely and naturally extend to your external life? At the very least, give your knowledge of G-d and of your purpose in life

the same credence that you extend to your breakfast (which you eat based on your knowledge that there's food and not silicone on your plate), your car (which you drive based on your knowledge that it won't explode), and your dentist (in whose chair you allow yourself to be put to sleep based on the knowledge that he's not Ted Bundy).

If it's truly knowledge that you desire, then I can think of no truer definition and criteria for "knowledge" than that which works for you in your everyday existence.

Intellect, by definition, is never sure of anything. Plenty of things that make perfect sense are completely wrong. Plenty of absurdities are true. That is why Torah law goes by experience over logic. But even experience can be misleading. That's where intuitive faith, emunah, comes in. Emunah is a power higher than intellect. Intellect tries to figure out the truth. Emunah is the truth that you already know, the truth inside you.

Ultimately, none of the three, on its own, can serve as a truly functional guide to life—we need all three. We need experience to recognize the patterns along which our lives run, whether or not they can be logically "explained". We need intellect to challenge our knowledge, expose its contradictions, and help us figure out how to apply it. And we need faith to recognize the truth, to open ourselves to that which we intrinsically know simply because that is what is.

Tzvi Freeman

Question

Can you give me an example of a "truth that you already know, the truth inside you"? I've never experienced that. So are we not back to square one?

How may we prove to ourselves we have this inner faith?

Answer

If you had a gun pointed to your head, you would know very clearly, 100% clearly, that you want to live. That's not an intellectual conclusion. That's just raw truth.

There are other things, beside that will to live, of which we have that clear, 100% knowledge. We call that emunah, "faith".

Throughout our history, countless thousands of our fathers and mothers were told, "Deny the oneness of G-d or die!" Including many who may have not been very "religious", or even very "Jewish" in their daily lives up to that moment of truth. Still, their faith was 100%—even more than their belief in life. That's inside of us as well, whether we are aware of it or not.

Reprinted with permission from the Judaism Website--www.Chabad.org

Where Change Begins

by Gordon B. Zacks

In 1969, I was the Chairman of the Young Leadership Cabinet of the national United Jewish Appeal. As such, I was invited to deliver the keynote address to the Council of Jewish Federations and Welfare Funds Annual Conference, being held that year in November in Boston. The theme was "Youth Looks at the Future of the American Jewish Community". I spent six months preparing for this talk. Usually, I speak extemporaneously with at most a one-page outline. This time—because of its importance—I elected to read the entire speech.

In it, I thanked my parents' generation for supporting the creation of the state of Israel and rescuing survivors from the Holocaust. In its aftermath, two million Jews had been delivered through their efforts from lands of oppression and resettled to lands of freedom. Nonetheless, I pointed out that we faced a disaster in the field of Jewish education. We ran the risk of losing more Jews through assimilation than we had saved through affirmation. We needed to address the failure of our Jewish educational system to inspire many young Jews to continue to be Jewish. I recommended that we create a national Jewish research and development venture capital fund to invest risk capital in innovative approaches to make Jewish education relevant to young people and to create an Institute for Jewish Life that would manage the process.

To fund this Institute, I proposed that the Jewish community endow the Institute with $100 million of State of Israel bonds for a period of ten years. The purchasers would receive a tax deduction. At the end of ten years, they would get their principal back. The Institute would get the use of the interest. Annually it would provide about $6 million in revenue. We would have ten years in which to evaluate the results. If the concept didn't produce worthwhile results, that would be the end of the Institute. Ultimately the idea was adopted in an abbreviated form with funding of $3.5 million. In this truncated version, it failed in its mission and was eventually closed. Still, it stimulated a lot of discussion about Jewish education, and placed it right behind rescue as a priority for the American Jewish community.

In December 1969, I received a call from a man named Leibel Alevsky. He was a rabbi with the Lubavitch movement in the Crown Heights section of Brooklyn. He said the Rebbe wanted to meet me. Given the tone of the phone call, I thought I was being invited for a royal audience. I immediately said yes to a date in January, but I didn't even know who the Rebbe was! My rabbi gave me some background and urged me to go ahead with the meeting. On the appointed day in January, Alevsky and I were finishing dinner in his home at 11:15 at night. We got a call that the Rebbe would see me now. I walked with Alevsky to a modest building to find 300 people—from around the world—each waiting at the Rebbe's headquarters, the *Chabad* Center, in the middle of the night for an audience with the Rebbe!

Later I learned that the Rebbe held these audiences three times each week, lasting from sundown often until the middle of the night.

I went in alone to see the Rebbe. In his office, illuminated by a single ceiling light, books were stacked from the floor to the ceiling. He was a slight man with translucent skin and absolutely clear whites of his eyes—the sclera encircling his sparkling blue irises, his beard outlining an impish grin. The Rebbe was sixty-seven at the time. He looked at me in such a penetrating way that I felt like I was being x-rayed.

"Mr. Zacks, I have read your speech", he began, "and it's clear you have taken good care of your mind. I can look at you, and it's clear you have taken good care of your body. *What* have you done to take care of your soul"?

No small talk about how I was or if I had a pleasant trip. I was stunned.

"The Jewish house is on fire", he continued. "We have an emergency, and this is not the time to experiment with new ways to put out the fire. Instead, you call the proven and tested fire department. We *are* that fire department. We—the Lubavitch—don't have drugs or intermarriage problems with our children or kids opting out of Judaism. Our tradition works, and our children are being educated. We have a worldwide outreach program that contacts and impacts non-observant Jews and saves souls. Give us the $100 million, and we will spend it to correct the problems that you are concerned about".

"Rebbe", I asked after pausing for a moment, "what if the house is on fire, but people have forgotten your telephone number"? "G-d will provide", he answered me.

"There are millions of Jews whose houses are on fire", I said to him. "Most of them are Jews who will not call you, either because they have lost your number or *they* won't accept the lifestyle compromises you expect. They're still worthy of saving in their own way, and they are entitled to a quality Jewish education that makes Judaism relevant to their lives. That's why we need this Institute".

"Do you believe in revelation, Mr. Zacks"? he asked me next.

"I believe in G-d and I believe he inspires... but I don't believe he writes", I answered.

"You mean, Mr. Zacks, that there is this vast structure G-d has created of plants, animals, food chains, stars, and planets. And, that the only creature in all of creation that doesn't understand how to fit in and live their life purposefully is the human"?

I told him *yes.*

"What about the complexity of the human body? What about the jewel of the human cell?

How does the body ingest food and renew itself with absolute consistency"?

I had no answer.

"Why, Mr. Zacks, is the nose always where the nose belongs? Why are the eyes always on the face for generation after generation"?

I could only shrug my shoulders, but my respect for him deepened by the moment.

"And, how can you account for the brain and the mind? How do they steer this remarkable system in a purposeful and precise way? And, what about how we fit into the earth's ecosystem, where we inhale the oxygen that plants so wonderfully manufacture for us? Could this all be accidental"?

How could I answer him?

"And, beyond what happens on earth. What about all the heavenly bodies in the sky that seem to follow such a perfect order and don't collide with each other? Is man the only creature on the planet earth without guidelines for living its life? Should man ignore the Torah given to us by G-d as a roadmap to guide us? This is the missing link which connects us to the complexity of Nature!"

So it went. Comment after comment. More times than not, I could not begin to answer his points.

He quoted Kazantzakis' book *Zorba the Greek* to me during our conversation. "Do you remember the young man talking with Zorba on the beach, when Zorba asks what the purpose of life is? The young fellow admits he doesn't know. And Zorba comments, 'Well, all those damned books you read—what good are they? Why do you read them?' Zorba's friend says he doesn't know. Zorba can see his friend doesn't have an answer to the most fundamental question. That's the trouble with you. 'A man's head is like a grocer', Zorba says, 'it keeps accounts.... The head's a careful little shopkeeper; it never risks all it has, always keeps something in reserve. It never breaks the string'. Wise men and grocers *weigh* everything. They can never cut the cord and be free. Your problem, Mr. Zacks, is that you are trying to find G-d's map through your head. You are unlikely to find it that way. You have to *experience* before you can truly feel and then be free to learn. Let me send a teacher to live with you for a year and teach you how to *be* Jewish. You will unleash a whole new dimension to your life. If you really want to change the world, change yourself! It's like dropping a stone into a pool of water and watching the concentric circles radiate to the shore. You will influence all the people around you, and they will influence others in turn. That's how you bring about improvement in the world".

"Rebbe, I'm not ready to do that", I told him. I remained firm despite the incredibly woven tapestry of the universe he presented to me.

"What do you have to lose"? he asked, "One year of your life? What if I'm right? It could gain you an eternity if I'm right, but only cost you one year if I'm wrong".

"I'll think about it", I said as we wrapped up our hour-and-a-half conversation. The normal audience with the Rebbe was thirty seconds to a minute. Three hundred people were still waiting to come in at one in the morning.

The Rebbe took people the way they were. His ultimate goal was to bring you to the ways of Jewish life, but his means were not confrontational and demanding. You could literally feel his warmth and love in addition to the power of his vast intellect. Once he established the *Chabad* Center at 770 Eastern Parkway in Crown Heights, I don't think he ever left it. Yet he was totally wired into the events of the world. I sensed this in my first meeting with the Rebbe. He radiated compassion, love, and respect for others—a servant leader totally committed to serving G-d through helping others.

The Rebbe wrote me letters encouraging me to devote myself to Jewish education. Over a series of years, I received five letters from him saying that he wanted to send his representative to me to spend a year teaching me how to be Jewish. I responded to each of them and declined.

Beginning in 1986, the Rebbe had a receiving line on Sunday in which he passed out a dollar bill to be given by the recipient as *tzedakah* to charity. His reasoning: "When two people meet, something good should result for a third". People waited in line for as long as four hours to be greeted by him and receive his blessing and the dollar bill. The Rebbe was eighty-four when he started doing this. An older woman in the line asked him how he could manage to perform this demanding task. "Every soul is a diamond", he answered. "Can one grow tired of counting diamonds"?

In 1987, my youngest daughter, Kim, had just returned from Israel and she wanted to participate in the custom of Sunday Dollars. I said fine I would take her. I neither called nor told anyone who I was when we arrived. I stood in line with her. It had been seventeen years since I had seen the Rebbe and ten years since he wrote me his last letter. When it was our turn to speak with the Rebbe, he looked at me and asked "What are you doing for Jewish education"? His eyes had the same penetrating look that had scanned me seventeen years earlier and asked, *"What are you*

doing to take care of your soul, Mr. Zacks"? It was as though I had just walked back into his office. In truth, hundreds of thousands of people had filed past him over those years.

"You are amazing!" I exclaimed to him.

"What has that to do with saving Jewish lives? What are you **doing** for Jewish education"? he retorted. He may not have gotten exactly what he wanted from me, but the Rebbe surely taught me the power of changing yourself to influence others. He wanted to enlist me as *his* fundraiser for Jewish education. While I certainly considered his invitation, I declined it. Still he may have been the most charismatic man I ever met. He had an incredible aura to him, partly because he was such a combination of charisma *and* pragmatism. This man came out of the scientific community to return to the religious life. Every Israeli prime minister and Israeli chief of staff found his way to the Rebbe's doorstep when they came to the United States. The most amazing thing? The Rebbe saw himself as perfecting G-d's will. He had no power in the sense that a police commissioner, a general, or a tax collector does. He had no one enforcing his decisions. What he *did* have was the authority of his holiness, which caused others to connect to him. It wasn't his title that gave the Rebbe authority. It was his presence and his profound grasp of bringing the principles of the Torah to life in himself and in others. The Rebbe didn't declare himself a leader. His overpowering presence inspired those around him to declare him their leader and to revere him. Through earning respect and trust, people endowed him with leadership.

About ten years after I first met the Rebbe, I attended a dinner in Cleveland at the home of Leibel Alevsky. At the table with us was the man the Rebbe sent to the Soviet Union to save Jews. When the Rebbe sent him on this mission, he didn't give him a plan or give him money! This was during the Stalin era. The anti-Jewish, anti-Zionist mentality of the Soviets may have been at its very worst. The Rebbe's designate went to the Soviet Union, lived and worked by his wits, and figured out how he could smuggle Jews out to Poland by train. He succeeded. At the same time, he was smuggling in prayer books, religious articles, and calendars for those still in the Soviet Union. And, he set up secret schools to teach Hebrew. The Lubavitchers are incredibly resourceful people, whose outreach is one-on-one.

The Lubavitchers are the essence of true believers. As I traveled abroad, I first noted their presence in Morocco. They ran schools for kids in the ghetto. That may sound noble, but not earth-shattering until you understand the kind of "social security system" that prevailed in Morocco at the time. Children *were* the system. At birth, many infants—Arabs and Jews both—were maimed and deformed by their parents so the kids could beg more effectively! The Lubavitchers *bought* the children from their parents for one more *dirham* than the market value of the child begging on the street for a year, and then they gave the children an education.

You could see the evidence of the Rebbe's positive work all over the world in places like the Soviet Union, Morocco, and Iran. How did these devout Lubavitchers get there? The Rebbe would simply say, "Go to Morocco and save souls". They didn't get a dime or an ounce of organizational help. They saved thousands and thousands of Jews physically, and they spiritually changed many more. The conviction they are doing G-d's work carries them forward. Their passion brings them to college campuses all over the United States. They will send out a repre-

sentative wearing *payos* and a black frock coat and open up a *Chabad* house on campuses like University of California at Berkeley. They get kids off narcotics and give them a spiritual jolt instead of a buzz on drugs. "Get high on G-d!" they preach. Their individual missions are great illustrations of the power of one. The Rebbe's passion for saving Jewish souls lives through them.

Unlike every other Jewish figure in this book, the Rebbe was not a Zionist. Though very supportive of the state of Israel and its defense forces, he felt that redemption would only be ushered in by the Messiah. He also drove home the point that a commitment to the state of Israel does not exempt us from fulfilling age-old Judaic commandments. In fact, it should actually elicit more loyalty to the Torah. The Rebbe was completely devoted to fulfilling G-d's will.

The essence of the Rebbe's teaching is celebration of G-d. The *Chabad* radiate a wonderful joy of life that is a reverberation of the Rebbe's spirit. I wish I could believe the way they do, with their absolute confidence in their answer. Their sheer love in celebrating the Jewish traditions with singing and dancing is unmatched. Nothing equals the celebration of a Shabbat with a Chabadnik. The food is homemade, delicious—though not necessarily healthy for your arteries—but it's only the beginning of the positive energy that flows in each Shabbat from celebrating the birthday of the world!

Gordon B. Zacks. Chairman of R. G. Barry Corporation, a leading footwear company, was general chairman designate of the National United Jewish Appeal (UJA) and a founding member and chairman of the Young Leadership Cabinet of the UJA. An expert on the Middle East, Zacks advised U.S. presidents and foreign heads of state on international relations and global trade policy. He was involved in the rescue and resettlement of millions of Jews in distress from more than one hundred countries to Israel and other free countries.

Defining Moments: Stories of Character, Courage, and Leadership, [New York: Beaufort Books, 2006], 137–148

Reprinted with the permission.

VII
Going the Extra Mile
Tools for Implementing Lasting Change

ROSH**CHODESH**
society

Introduction

A tree bears witness to changing seasons, but do the seasons actually change? Winter has never taught itself to outgrow its chill, nor spring its penchant for pretty plants. A tree constantly expands its waistline, but it continues to do only what trees do best—nothing more. The same is true of animal life: A giraffe can grin or grimace, but it cannot escape its own markings.

What about humans? Are we also imprisoned by nature? Are we as the summer and fall, which follow a cycle but cannot step beyond?

Certainly, we grow and mature from childhood to adulthood and on into seniority. We experience, and we learn. That, however, does not mean that our essential character has changed in the slightest. A small, young human with a particular temperament can develop into a large and more sophisticated human with the identi-cal temperament—a larger version of the same model.

Change means more than that. It whispers to a miser: *You can be generous.* It dares the obnoxious: *You can be pleasant.* It challenges us to defy ourselves and redefine ourselves.

Deep down, there is no doubt that mankind strives for change, even total transformation. Bookstores are lined with books on self-help and transformative meditations. It seems that humans will never make peace with their own inconsistencies and failings. We all want to be perfect, at least more perfect than at present.

In this lesson, we will take a look at the approach of the Torah and Jewish philosophers regarding our ability to work on ourselves, and the options we face in doing so.

I. Is Change Possible?

Text 1

דֵעוֹת הַרְבֵּה יֵשׁ לְכָל אֶחָד וְאֶחָד מִבְּנֵי אָדָם, וְזוֹ מְשׁוּנָה מִזּוֹ וּרְחוֹקָה מִמֶּנּוּ בְּיוֹתֵר. יֵשׁ אָדָם שֶׁהוּא בַּעַל חֵמָה כּוֹעֵס תָּמִיד, וְיֵשׁ אָדָם שֶׁדַּעְתּוֹ מְיוּשֶּׁבֶת עָלָיו וְאֵינוֹ כּוֹעֵס כְּלָל, וְאִם יִכְעַס יִכְעַס כַּעַס מְעַט בְּכַמָּה שָׁנִים. וְיֵשׁ אָדָם שֶׁהוּא גְּבַהּ לֵב בְּיוֹתֵר, וְיֵשׁ שֶׁהוּא שְׁפַל רוּחַ בְּיוֹתֵר. וְיֵשׁ שֶׁהוּא בַּעַל תַּאֲוָה לֹא תִשְׂבַּע נַפְשׁוֹ מֵהֲלוֹךְ בְּתַאֲוָה, וְיֵשׁ שֶׁהוּא בַּעַל לֵב טָהוֹר מְאֹד וְלֹא יִתְאַוֶּה אֲפִילוּ לִדְבָרִים מְעַטִּים שֶׁהַגּוּף צָרִיךְ לָהֶן. וְיֵשׁ בַּעַל נֶפֶשׁ רְחָבָה שֶׁלֹּא תִשְׂבַּע נַפְשׁוֹ מִכָּל מָמוֹן הָעוֹלָם, כְּעִנְיָן שֶׁנֶּאֱמַר "אוֹהֵב כֶּסֶף לֹא יִשְׂבַּע כֶּסֶף" (קהלת ה,ט), וְיֵשׁ מְקַצֵּר נַפְשׁוֹ שֶׁדַּיּוֹ אֲפִילוּ דָּבָר מְעַט שֶׁלֹּא יַסְפִּיק לוֹ וְלֹא יִרְדּוֹף לְהַשִּׂיג כָּל צָרְכּוֹ. וְיֵשׁ שֶׁהוּא מְסַגֵּף עַצְמוֹ בָּרָעָב וְקוֹבֵץ עַל יָדוֹ וְאֵינוֹ אוֹכֵל פְּרוּטָה מִשֶּׁלּוֹ אֶלָּא בְּצַעַר גָּדוֹל, וְיֵשׁ שֶׁהוּא מְאַבֵּד כָּל מָמוֹנוֹ בְּיָדוֹ לְדַעְתּוֹ. וְעַל דְּרָכִים אֵלּוּ שְׁאָר כָּל הַדֵּעוֹת כְּגוֹן מְהוֹלָל, וְאוֹנֵן, וְכִילַי, וְשׁוֹעַ, וְאַכְזָרִי, וְרַחֲמָן, וְרַךְ לֵבָב, וְאַמִּיץ לֵב, וְכַיּוֹצֵא בָּהֶן.

משנה תורה, הלכות דעות א,א

Individuals possess many different temperaments. These temperaments are different from each other, and at times, contrary to each other:

Some are fiery individuals who are always angry. Others are calm-minded and never angry: If they do get angry, their anger is mild and is aroused on rare occasions.

Some are excessively haughty. Others are excessively meek.

Some are lustful, never satiated in the quest for their desires. Others are exceptionally pure-hearted and do not lust even for those things that their bodies require.

Some are greedy and not satisfied by all the money in the world, as per the verse, "He who loves money is never satisfied by money" (Kohelet/Ecclesiastes 5:9). Others are frugal, making do with a minimum amount, and not even pursuing all that they need.

Some afflict themselves with starvation, hoard their money, and cannot spend even a penny on food without experiencing great pain. Others knowingly squander all their wealth.

The same dichotomy applies to other temperaments: the frivolously carefree and the mournfully depressed, the miserly and the openhanded, the cruel and the tenderhearted, the cowardly and the courageous, and so on.

Maimonides, *Mishneh Torah, Laws of Temperaments* 1:1

Text 2

Nature is strong and she is pitiless. She works in mysterious ways, and we are her victims. We have not much to do with it ourselves. Nature takes this job in hand, and we only play our parts. In the words of old Omar Khayyam, we are only impotent pieces in the game He plays upon this checkerboard of nights and days; Hither and thither moves, and checks, and slays, and one by one back in the closet lays. What had this boy had to do with it? He was not his own father; he was not his own mother. . . . All of this was handed to him. He did not surround himself with governesses and wealth. He did not make himself. And yet he is to be compelled to pay.

Clarence Darrow's defense of Leopold and Loeb, Illinois v. Nathan Leopold and Richard Loeb, August 22, 1924

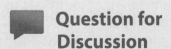

Question for Discussion

Do you think it is possible for a person to effectively alter their essential nature?

Text 3

מִדּוֹת הַטִּבְעִים הַנּוֹלָדִים בְּטֶבַע מִבֶּטֶן אִמּוֹ שֶׁלֹּא יוּכַל לְשַׁנּוֹתָם כְּלָל מֵהֵיפֶךְ לְהֵיפֶךְ, כְּמוֹ מֵרַחֲמָנוּת לְאַכְזָרִיּוּת, וּמִפַּזְרָנוּת לְקַמְצָנוּת, אוֹ לְהֵיפֶךְ כו' עַד שֶׁמַּגִּיעַ מִדּוֹת הַלָּלוּ בְּעֶצֶם הַנֶּפֶשׁ מַמָּשׁ כְּנִזְכַּר לְעֵיל שֶׁהוּא בִּלְתִּי שִׁינוּיִים כְּלָל.

תורת חיים, שמות ח"א רג,א

One cannot change natural inborn tendencies from one extreme to the other—for example, from a merciful nature to a cruel one, or from a squandering nature to a miserly one—because these traits are rooted in the essence of the soul, which is unchangeable.

Rabbi Dovber of Lubavitch, *Torat Chaim, Shemot* 1:203a

Text 4

אַל יַעֲבוֹר בְּמַחְשַׁבְתְּךָ דָּבָר זֶה . . . שֶׁהַקָּדוֹשׁ בָּרוּךְ הוּא גּוֹזֵר עַל הָאָדָם מִתְּחִלַּת בְּרִיָּתוֹ לִהְיוֹת
צַדִּיק אוֹ רָשָׁע. אֵין הַדָּבָר כֵּן, אֶלָּא כָּל אָדָם וְאָדָם רָאוּי לִהְיוֹת צַדִּיק כְּמשֶׁה רַבֵּנוּ אוֹ רָשָׁע
כְּיָרָבְעָם, אוֹ חָכָם אוֹ סָכָל, אוֹ רַחֲמָן אוֹ אַכְזָרִי, אוֹ כִּילַּי אוֹ שׁוֹעַ. וְכֵן שְׁאָר כָּל הַדֵּעוֹת. וְאֵין לוֹ מִי
שֶׁיִּכְפֵּהוּ וְלֹא גּוֹזֵר עָלָיו, וְלֹא מִי שֶׁמּוֹשְׁכוֹ לְאֶחָד מִשְּׁנֵי הַדְּרָכִים, אֶלָּא הוּא מֵעַצְמוֹ וּמִדַּעְתּוֹ נוֹטֶה
לְאֵיזֶה דֶּרֶךְ שֶׁיִּרְצֶה . . . וְדָבָר זֶה עִקָּר גָּדוֹל הוּא, וְהוּא עַמּוּד הַתּוֹרָה וְהַמִּצְוָה.

משנה תורה, הלכות תשובה ה,ב–ג

*Do not let the thought cross your mind . . . that God decrees whether a person will be
righteous or wicked from birth, for this is not so. Rather, each individual is fit to be as righteous
as our teacher Moshe/Moses or as wicked as Jeroboam, wise or foolish, merciful or cruel,
miserly or openhanded, and so forth. There is no one who compels, decrees, or pulls a person
in either direction. Rather, by his own initiative, he pursues whichever path he desires. . . .*

This concept is an essential principle, a pillar upon which stands the Torah and mitzvot.

Mishnah Torah, op. cit., Laws of Repentance 5:2–3

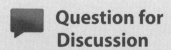 **Question for Discussion**

Why do you think Maimonides considers the principle of unqualified free choice so essential to Judaism?

Text 5

אֵין לְךָ אַהֲבָה בְּמָקוֹם יִרְאָה, וְיִרְאָה בְּמָקוֹם
אַהֲבָה.

ספרי, דברים לב

*Where there is awe there is no love, and
where there is love there is no awe.*

Sifrei, Devarim/Deuteronomy 32

Text 6

וְאַתָּה יִשְׂרָאֵל עַבְדִּי יַעֲקֹב אֲשֶׁר בְּחַרְתִּיךָ זֶרַע אַבְרָהָם אֹהֲבִי . . .

ישעיהו מא,ח

But you, Israel My servant, Ya'akov/Jacob whom I have chosen, the seed of Avraham, who loved Me . . . .

Yeshayahu/Isaiah 41:8

Text 7

וְהָאֱלֹקִים נִסָּה אֶת אַבְרָהָם . . . וַיֹּאמֶר קַח נָא אֶת בִּנְךָ אֶת יְחִידְךָ אֲשֶׁר אָהַבְתָּ אֶת יִצְחָק, וְלֶךְ לְךָ אֶל אֶרֶץ הַמֹּרִיָּה וְהַעֲלֵהוּ שָׁם לְעֹלָה עַל אַחַד הֶהָרִים אֲשֶׁר אֹמַר אֵלֶיךָ . . . וַיִּקַּח אַבְרָהָם אֶת עֲצֵי הָעֹלָה, וַיָּשֶׂם עַל יִצְחָק בְּנוֹ, וַיִּקַּח בְּיָדוֹ אֶת הָאֵשׁ וְאֶת הַמַּאֲכֶלֶת . . . וַיָּבֹאוּ אֶל הַמָּקוֹם אֲשֶׁר אָמַר לוֹ הָאֱלֹקִים, וַיִּבֶן שָׁם אַבְרָהָם אֶת הַמִּזְבֵּחַ, וַיַּעֲרֹךְ אֶת הָעֵצִים, וַיַּעֲקֹד אֶת יִצְחָק בְּנוֹ, וַיָּשֶׂם אֹתוֹ עַל הַמִּזְבֵּחַ מִמַּעַל לָעֵצִים. וַיִּשְׁלַח אַבְרָהָם אֶת יָדוֹ, וַיִּקַּח אֶת הַמַּאֲכֶלֶת לִשְׁחֹט אֶת בְּנוֹ. וַיִּקְרָא אֵלָיו מַלְאַךְ ה' מִן הַשָּׁמַיִם, וַיֹּאמֶר אַבְרָהָם אַבְרָהָם וַיֹּאמֶר הִנֵּנִי. וַיֹּאמֶר אַל תִּשְׁלַח יָדְךָ אֶל הַנַּעַר, וְאַל תַּעַשׂ לוֹ מְאוּמָה, כִּי עַתָּה יָדַעְתִּי כִּי יְרֵא אֱלֹקִים אַתָּה, וְלֹא חָשַׂכְתָּ אֶת בִּנְךָ אֶת יְחִידְךָ מִמֶּנִּי.

בראשית כב, א-יב

God tested Avraham. . . . He said, "Please take your son, your only one, whom you love, Yitzchak/Isaac, and go to the land of Moriah, and bring him up there as an offering upon one of the mountains which I shall tell you. . . .

Avraham took the wood for the offering and placed it on Yitzchak, his son. He took in his hand the fire and the knife. . . .

They arrived at the place of which God had spoken to him. Avraham built the altar and arranged the wood. He bound Yitzchak, his son, and he placed him on the altar atop the wood. Avraham stretched out his hand and took the knife to slaughter his son.

An angel of God called to him from Heaven, and said, "Avraham! Avraham!"

He replied, "Here I am."

He said, "Do not stretch out your hand against the lad nor do anything to him, for now I know that you stand in awe of God, since you have not withheld your son, your only one, from Me."

Bereishit/Genesis 22:1–12

Text 8

Do I contradict myself? Very well, then, I contradict myself; I am large—I contain multitudes."

Walt Whitman, *Leaves of Grass*, "Song of Myself," part 51

Text 9

Angels are beings in the world that is the domain of emotion and feeling; and since this is the case, the substantial quality of an angel may be an impulse or a drive—say, an inclination in the direction of love, or a seizure of fear, or pity, or the like. . . . Whereas among human beings emotions change and vary either as persons change or according to the circumstances of time and place, an angel is totally the manifestation of a single emotional essence. The essence of an angel, therefore, is defined by the limits of a particular emotion. . . .

The real difference between man and angel is not the fact that man has a body, because the essential comparison is between the human soul *and the angel. The soul of man is most complex and includes a whole world of different existential elements of all kinds,*

while the angel is a being of single essence and therefore in a sense one-dimensional. In addition, man—because of his many-sidedness, his capacity to contain contradictions, and his gift of an inner power of soul, that Divine spark that makes him man—has the capacity to distinguish between one thing and another, especially between good and evil. It is this capacity which makes it possible for him to rise to great heights, and by the same token creates the possibility for his failure and backsliding, neither of which is true for the angel. From the point of view of its essence, the angel is eternally the same; it is static, an unchanging existence, whether temporary or eternal, fixed within the rigid limits of quality given at its very creation.

Rabbi Adin Steinsaltz, *The Thirteen Petalled Rose* [Jerusalem: Koren Publishers, 2012], pp. 5–7

Text 10

כָּל הַמִּדּוֹת כְּלוּלוֹת זוֹ מִזּוֹ . . . וּכְדִכְתִיב בְּאַבְרָהָם שֶׁהוּא מִדַּת הַחֶסֶד וְהָאַהֲבָה, "עַתָּה יָדַעְתִּי
כִּי יְרֵא אֱלֹקִים אַתָּה" עַל יְדֵי שֶׁלָּבַשׁ מִדַּת הַגְּבוּרָה, "וַיַּעֲקֹד אֶת יִצְחָק בְּנוֹ" "וַיִּקַּח אֶת
הַמַּאֲכֶלֶת" כוּ'. וּמַה שֶּׁאָמַר הַכָּתוּב "אַבְרָהָם אוֹהֲבִי" "וּפַחַד יִצְחָק" הִנֵּה הַהֶפְרֵשׁ וְהַהֶבְדֵּל
הַזֶּה הוּא בִּבְחִינַת גִּילוּי וְהֶעֱלֵם, שֶׁבְּמִדַּת יִצְחָק הַפַּחַד הוּא בִּבְחִינַת גִּילוּי, וְהָאַהֲבָה מְסוּתֶּרֶת
בִּבְחִינַת הֶעֱלֵם וְהֶסְתֵּר. וְהַחֵיפֶךְ בְּמִדַּת אַבְרָהָם אָבִינוּ עָלָיו הַשָּׁלוֹם.

תניא, אגרת הקודש יג

All of a person's attributes incorporate one another.... Thus, it is written of Avraham, "[N]ow I know that you stand in awe of God," for, though he was characterized by love and kindness, he garbed himself in the attribute of awe when he bound his son Yitzchak and took the knife, etc.

[If all attributes incorporate one another,] why then does the verse characterize Avraham as one who personified love, and Yitzchak as one who personified awe?

The distinction exists [only] with regard to manifestation and concealment of the attribute in question. In Yitzchak's mode of Divine service, the awe was manifest while the love was concealed. For Avraham, the opposite was the case.

Rabbi Shne'ur Zalman of Liadi, *Tanya, Igeret Hakodesh* 13

Text 11

כְּשֶׁחָלָה רַבִּי יוֹסֵי בֶּן קִיסְמָא, הָלַךְ רַבִּי חֲנִינָא בֶּן תְּרַדְיוֹן לְבַקְּרוֹ. אָמַר לוֹ: "חֲנִינָא אָחִי, אִי אַתָּה יוֹדֵעַ שֶׁאוּמָה זוֹ מִן הַשָּׁמַיִם הִמְלִיכוּהָ, שֶׁהֶחֱרִיבָה אֶת בֵּיתוֹ וְשָׂרְפָה אֶת הֵיכָלוֹ, וְהָרְגָה אֶת חֲסִידָיו וְאִבְּדָה אֶת טוֹבָיו, וַעֲדַיִין הִיא קַיֶּמֶת, וַאֲנִי שָׁמַעְתִּי עָלֶיךָ שֶׁאַתָּה יוֹשֵׁב וְעוֹסֵק בַּתּוֹרָה וּמַקְהִיל קְהִלּוֹת בָּרַבִּים וְסֵפֶר מוּנָח לְךָ בְּחֵיקְךָ". אָמַר לוֹ: "מִן הַשָּׁמַיִם יְרַחֵמוּ". אָמַר לוֹ: "אֲנִי אוֹמֵר לְךָ דְּבָרִים שֶׁל טַעַם, וְאַתָּה אוֹמֵר לִי מִן הַשָּׁמַיִם יְרַחֵמוּ, תָּמֵהַּ אֲנִי אִם לֹא יִשְׂרְפוּ אוֹתְךָ וְאֶת סֵפֶר תּוֹרָה בָּאֵשׁ". אָמַר לוֹ: "רַבִּי, מָה אֲנִי לְחַיֵּי הָעוֹלָם הַבָּא?" אָמַר לוֹ: "כְּלוּם מַעֲשֶׂה בָּא לְיָדְךָ?" אָמַר לוֹ: "מָעוֹת שֶׁל פּוּרִים נִתְחַלְּפוּ לִי בְּמָעוֹת שֶׁל צְדָקָה וְחִלַּקְתִּים לַעֲנִיִּים". אָמַר לוֹ: "אִם כֵּן, מֵחֶלְקְךָ יְהִי חֶלְקִי, וּמִגּוֹרָלְךָ יְהִי גוֹרָלִי".

תלמוד בבלי, עבודה זרה יח,א

When Rabbi Yosei ben Kisma fell ill, Rabbi Chanina ben Teradyon went to visit him.

Rabbi Yosei said to him, "Chanina, my brother! Do you not know that Heaven has imposed [the Romans] as rulers [over the Jews]? They destroyed His house, burned His sanctuary, killed His pious ones, and caused His nobles to perish. The Roman rule still exists. And yet, I heard that you sit and engage in Torah study and convene gatherings in public [to teach Torah], and a scroll rests in your lap! [Why do you endanger yourself by publicly defying the Roman ban on Torah study?]"

Rabbi Chanina replied, "Heaven will have mercy [upon me]."

Rabbi Yosei rejoined, "I am telling you something sensible and you reply that Heaven will have mercy! Why, I would be amazed if the Romans do not burn you and the Torah scroll in fire!"

Rabbi Chanina asked, "My master, how do I stand with regard to the World to Come?"
Rabbi Yosei replied, "Have you performed any worthy deeds?"
Rabbi Chanina answered him, "[As custodian of the local charity,] I once inadvertently distributed my own funds to the poor instead of money from the charity fund. [Yet, I did not seek reimbursement.]"
Rabbi Yosei told him, "If that is so, let my portion be from your portion and let my lot be from your lot [in the World to Come]!"

Talmud, Avodah Zarah 18a

Text 12a

וּשַׁבְתֶּם וּרְאִיתֶם בֵּין צַדִּיק לְרָשָׁע, בֵּין עֹבֵד אֱלֹקִים
לַאֲשֶׁר לֹא עֲבָדוֹ.

מלאכי ג,יח

You will once again discern between the righteous and the wicked, between he who serves God and he who does not serve Him.

Malachi 3:18

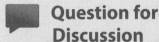

Question for Discussion

Rabbi Chanina risked his life to teach Torah in brave defiance of a Roman edict. With such a merit in hand, why did Rabbi Yosei still doubt whether he was deserving of the World to Come until notified about the charity incident?

Text 12b

אָמַר לֵיהּ בַּר הֵא הֵא לְהִלֵּל: "הַיְינוּ צַדִּיק הַיְינוּ עוֹבֵד אֱלֹקִים, הַיְינוּ רָשָׁע הַיְינוּ לֹא עֲבָדוֹ?" אָמַר לֵיהּ: "עוֹבֵד וְלֹא עֲבָדוֹ תַּרְוַויְיהוּ צַדִּיקֵי גְמִירֵי נִינְהוּ. אֶלָּא אֵינוֹ דּוֹמֶה שׁוֹנֶה פִּרְקוֹ מֵאָה פְּעָמִים לְמִי שֶׁשּׁוֹנֶה פִּרְקוֹ מֵאָה וְאֶחָד". אָמַר לֵיהּ: "וּמִשׁוּם חַד זִמְנָא קָרֵי לֵיהּ וְלֹא עֲבָדוֹ?" אָמַר לֵיהּ: "צֵא וּלְמַד מִשּׁוּק שֶׁל חַמָּרִים, עֲשָׂרָה פַּרְסֵי בְּזוּזָא, וְאַחַד עָשָׂר פַּרְסֵי בִּשְׁנֵי זוּזִים".

ילקוט שמעוני, מלאכי תקצא

Bar Hei Hei asked Hillel, "Is not 'a righteous person' the same as 'he who serves God,' and 'a wicked person' the same as 'he who does not serve Him'?"

Hillel replied, "'He who serves' and 'he who does not serve' both refer to completely righteous individuals. However, he who reviews his study one hundred times ('he who does not serve') cannot be compared to one who reviews his study 101 times ('he who serves')."

Bar Hei Hei asked, "'He who does not serve' is called so merely because of a difference of one time?"

To which Hillel replied, "Go and take a lesson from the marketplace of wagon drivers. For the distance of ten parsangs (Persian miles), they charge one zuz, whereas for eleven parsangs, they charge two zuzim."

Midrash, *Yalkut Shimoni*, Malachi 591, ad loc.

Questions for Discussion

1. Why should reviewing one's study one extra time make such a difference? After the first one hundred times, is an extra revision going to make it or break it?

2. Why would a journey of eleven miles cost the passenger double the fare of a journey of ten miles?

Text 12c

שֶׁבִּימֵיהֶם הָיָה הָרְגִילוּת לִשְׁנוֹת כָּל פֶּרֶק מֵאָה
פְּעָמִים, כִּדְאִיתָא הָתָם בִּגְמָרָא מָשָׁל מִשּׁוּק שֶׁל
חַמָּרִים שֶׁנִּשְׂכָּרִים לְעֶשֶׂר פַּרְסֵי בְּזוּזָא, וּלְאַחַד עָשָׂר
פַּרְסֵי בִּתְרֵי זוּזֵי, מִפְּנֵי שֶׁהוּא יוֹתֵר מֵרְגִילוּתָם.
וְלָכֵן זֹאת הַפַּעַם הַמֵּאָה וְאַחַת הַיְתֵרָה עַל הָרְגִילוּת
שֶׁהוּרְגַל מִנְּעוּרָיו שְׁקוּלָה כְּנֶגֶד כּוּלָן וְעוֹלָה עַל גַּבֵּיהֶן
בִּיֶתֶר שְׂאֵת וְיֶתֶר עָז, לִהְיוֹת נִקְרָא עוֹבֵד אֱלֹקִים.

תניא, פרק טו

In those days, it was customary to review each lesson one hundred times. The Talmud illustrates this with the analogy of the donkey drivers. The drivers would charge one zuz for ten parsangs (Persian miles), but demanded two zuz for driving eleven parsangs because it exceeded their customary practice.

Therefore, the 101st review, which was beyond the normal practice to which the student had been accustomed since childhood, was equivalent to the previous one hundred reviews combined. In fact, it surpassed them by far, to the extent that this student was subsequently called "he who serves God."

To which Hillel replied, "Go and take a lesson from the marketplace of wagon drivers. For the distance of ten parsangs (Persian miles), they charge one zuz, whereas for eleven parsangs, they charge two zuzim."

Tanya, op. cit., ch. 15, ad loc.

Text 13

רַבִּי חֲנִינָא בֶּן תְּרַדְיוֹן, הַגַם שֶׁמָּסַר נַפְשׁוֹ עַל הַתּוֹרָה, הָיָה מְפַקְפֵּק וּמִסְתַּפֵּק מְאֹד פֶּן יֵשׁ בִּמְסִירוּת נֶפֶשׁ זֹאת הָאֱלֹקִית תַּעֲרוֹבוֹת הֶסְפֵּם הַטִּבְעִי דְּנֶפֶשׁ הַבַּהֲמִית, שֶׁאֵינוֹ נִקְרָא עוֹבֵד אֱלֹקִים עֲדַיִין . . . וְעַל כֵּן שָׁאַל: מַהוּ לְעוֹלָם הַבָּא - שֶׁלֹּא יִזְכֶּה בּוֹ רַק הָעוֹבֵד אֱלֹקִים . . . וְהֵשִׁיבוֹ: כְּלוּם מַעֲשֶׂה בָּא לְיָדוֹ בְּהִיפוּךְ הַטֶּבַע לְגַמְרֵי? וְאָמַר לוֹ: מִמָּעוֹת שֶׁל פּוּרִים כו', לִהְיוֹת שֶׁטֶּבַע הַשְּׁקִידָה וְהַהַתְמָדָה בִּתְשׁוּקָה עַל דִּבְרֵי חָכְמָה שֹׁרֶשָׁהּ בָּאָה מִמִּדַּת הַשְּׁחוֹרָה שֶׁהִיא גוֹרֶמֶת עוֹצֶם בְּחִינַת הַכִּיוּוּץ בְּעַצְמוֹ, וְהִיא הַגּוֹרֶמֶת מִדַּת הַקַּמְצָנוּת בְּמָמוֹן . . . אַךְ מִדַּת הַפַּזְרָנוּת, שֶׁהוּא בְּחִינַת הַהִתְפַּשְׁטוּת הֵיפֶךְ הַכִּיוּוּץ, שֹׁרֶשָׁהּ מִמִּדַּת הַלְּבֵינָה, וְהוּא הֵיפֶךְ טֶבַע הַשְּׁקִידָה וְהַהַתְמָדָה לְצַמְצֵם וּלְכַווֵץ אֶת עַצְמוֹ כו'. וְכַאֲשֶׁר אָמַר לוֹ מִמַּעֲשֵׂה פִּיזוּר הַצְּדָקָה, הֵכִין בְּטִבְעוֹ הַגַּשְׁמִי שֶׁהוּא פַּזְרָן שֶׁהוּא מִנֶּגֶד גָּדוֹל לְטֶבַע הַשְּׁקִידָה וְהַהַתְמָדָה. וְאָז אָמַר לוֹ: אִם כֵּן, מֵחֶלְקְךָ יְהֵא חֶלְקִי כו'. דְּהַיְינוּ מִפְּנֵי שֶׁרָאָה שֶׁאֵין תַּעֲרוֹבוֹת הֶסְפֵּם טִבְעִי כְּלָל בִּמְסִירוּת נֶפֶשׁ שֶׁלּוֹ עַל הַתּוֹרָה, וְנִקְרָא עוֹבֵד אֱלֹקִים כְּנִזְכָּר לְעֵיל, וְרָאוּי הוּא לְעוֹלָם הַבָּא.

מַאֲמָרֵי אַדְמוֹ"ר הַזָּקֵן, תקס"ט, ע' כג

Although Rabbi Chanina ben Teradyon had risked his life for Torah, he was extremely doubtful and unsure [of the worthiness of his achievements]. Perhaps his self-sacrifice was a result of his natural proclivities—in which case he would not be considered to be one "who serves God."

He therefore asked, "How do I stand with regard to the World to Come?"—because only those who truly serve God merit it. . . .

Rabbi Yosei responded by asking whether he had gone completely against his nature to perform a worthy deed.

Rabbi Chanina replied by relating the incident of the charity fund.

A studious nature is rooted in introversion, which makes a person closed and withholding. This nature results in a miserly temperament. . . . Being spendthrift results from a temperament of extroversion . . . and runs contrary to the studious nature.

When Rabbi Chanina related to Rabbi Yosei the incident of the charity fund, the latter sensed that Rabbi Chanina's nature was that of a spendthrift, which is diametrically opposed to the nature of studiousness.

Thus, Rabbi Yosei said to him, "If that is so, let my portion be from your portion." Rabbi Yosei saw that there were no natural tendencies involved in Rabbi Chanina's self-sacrifice for Torah, and he should therefore be considered as "he who serves God," and deserving of the World to Come.

Rabbi Shne'ur Zalman of Liadi, *Ma'amarei Admur Hazaken* 5569, p. 23, ad loc.

II. Introducing Change

Text 14

מַה הָיָה תְּחִלָּתוֹ שֶׁל ר' עֲקִיבָא? אָמְרוּ: בֶּן אַרְבָּעִים שָׁנָה הָיָה וְלֹא שָׁנָה כְּלוּם. פַּעַם אַחַת הָיָה עוֹמֵד עַל פִּי הַבְּאֵר. אָמַר: מִי חָקַק אֶבֶן זוֹ? אָמְרוּ לוֹ: הַמַּיִם שֶׁתָּדִיר נוֹפְלִים עָלֶיהָ בְּכָל יוֹם. אָמְרוּ לוֹ: עֲקִיבָא! אִי אַתָּה קוֹרֵא אֲבָנִים שָׁחֲקוּ מָיִם **(איוב יד, יט)?** מִיָּד הָיָה רַבִּי עֲקִיבָא דָּן קַל וָחוֹמֶר בְּעַצְמוֹ: מַה רַךְ פָּסַל אֶת הַקָּשֶׁה, דִּבְרֵי תּוֹרָה שֶׁקָּשִׁין כַּבַּרְזֶל עַל אַחַת כַּמָּה וְכַמָּה שֶׁיַּחַקְקוּ אֶת לִבִּי שֶׁהוּא בָּשָׂר וָדָם. מִיָּד חָזַר לִלְמוֹד תּוֹרָה.

אבות דרבי נתן ו

What were Rabbi Akiva's [scholarly] origins? The sages recount that he was forty years old and had not studied anything at all. He was once standing near the mouth of a well. He asked [those nearby], "Who bore a hole in this stone?" They replied, "The water. It falls upon it constantly, each day. Why, Akiva, do you not know the verse 'Water erodes stones (Iyov/Job 14:19)'?"

Rabbi Akiva immediately made the following assessment: "If a soft substance can bore through hard material, certainly the words of Torah, which are as strong as steel, can penetrate my heart of but flesh and blood." He immediately went to study Torah.

Avot DeRabbi Natan, ch. 6

Text 15

Old habits can't be thrown out the upstairs window. They have to be coaxed down the stairs one step at a time.

Mark Twain

Text 16

תָּפַסְתָּ מְרוּבָּה - לֹא תָּפַסְתָּ, תָּפַסְתָּ מוּעָט – תָּפַסְתָּ.

תלמוד בבלי, ראש השנה ד,ב

If you take a lot, you have taken nothing at all; if you take a little, you at least have that.

Talmud, Rosh Hashanah 4b

Text 17

אֲפִילוּ רָשָׁע גָּמוּר בְּלְבָבוֹ, וְכָל יֵצֶר מַחְשְׁבוֹת לִבּוֹ רַק רַע כָּל הַיּוֹם, אִם יְעוֹרֵר רוּחוֹ וְיָשִׂים הִשְׁתַּדְּלוּתוֹ וְעִסְקוֹ בְּהַתְמָדָה בַּתּוֹרָה וּבַמִּצְוֹות, וַאֲפִילוּ שֶׁלֹּא לְשֵׁם שָׁמַיִם, מִיָּד יִנְטֶה אֶל הַטּוֹב, וּבְכֹחַ מַעֲשָׂיו יָמִית הַיֵּצֶר הָרַע, כִּי אַחֲרֵי הַפְּעוּלוֹת נִמְשָׁכִים הַלְּבָבוֹת.

ספר החינוך, מצוה טז

If a wicked individual whose inclination is devoted entirely to evil persistently invests effort in the performance of Torah and mitzvot—even for an ulterior motive—he will immediately be pulled toward goodness, and with the power of his deeds he will slay his evil inclination. Rabbi Akiva immediately made the following assessment: "If a soft substance can bore through hard material, certainly the words of Torah, which are as strong as steel, can penetrate my heart of but flesh and blood." He immediately went to study Torah.

The heart is drawn after the deed.

Sefer Hachinuch, Commandment 16

Text 18

הַדְּבָרִים שֶׁהִרְגִּיל הָאָדָם בָּהֶם נַעֲשֶׂה אֶצְלוֹ טֶבַע שֵׁנִי.

שבילי אמונה

Things that a person does regularly become second nature.

Rabbi Meir Eldabi, *Shevilei Emunah*, p. 33b (Warsaw 1874)

FIGURE 7.1

Four stages of competence

	Incompetence	Competence
unconscious	1	4
conscious	2	3

III. Harnessing Our Inner Infinity

Text 19a

וְהָלַכְתָּ בִּדְרָכָיו.

דברים כח,ט

You shall walk in His paths.

Devarim 28:9

Text 19b

וְהַמִּצְוָה הַשְּׁמִינִית הִיא שֶׁצִּוָּנוּ לְהִדַּמּוֹת בּוֹ יִתְעַלֶּה לְפִי יְכָלְתֵּנוּ.

ספר המצוות לרמב"ם, מצות עשה ח

The eighth mitzvah commands us to emulate God to the extent of our ability.

Maimonides, *Sefer Hamitzvot*, Positive Commandment 8

Key Points

1   While Judaism recognizes that we have unchangeable, deep-rooted tendencies, Judaism does not believe that our actions are predetermined.

2   We have the ability to decide our own future because, while one trait may be more dominant than another, we contain the capacity for all traits. It is just that the less dominant traits will require more effort to bring to the fore.

3   The truest accomplishments in life are a product of working to overcome our natural tendencies and to reveal our dormant traits.

4   Change can be achieved by:

   • Understanding why we want to change

   • Visualizing the change

   • Breaking it down into small steps

   • Anticipating backsliding

   • Acting on a positive resolution immediately

   • Monitoring progress to determine whether the change has become habitual

5   By transcending our personal limitations and exercising the Godliness contained in our souls, we emulate God's infinity.

Bibliography

Text 1 – Rabbi Moshe ben Maimon (1135–1204). Better known as Maimonides or by the acronym Rambam; born in Cordoba, Spain. After the conquest of Cordoba by the Almohads, he fled Spain and eventually settled in Cairo, Egypt. There, he became the leader of the Jewish community and served as court physician to the vizier of Egypt. His rulings on Jewish law are considered integral to the formation of halachic consensus. He is most noted for authoring the *Mishneh Torah,* an encyclopedic arrangement of Jewish law, and for his philosophical work, *Guide for the Perplexed.*

Text 3 – Rabbi Dovber of Lubavitch (1773–1827). The eldest son of and successor to Rabbi Shne'ur Zalman of Liadi, also known as "the Miteler Rebbe"; he greatly expanded upon and developed his father's groundbreaking teachings. He was the first Chabad rebbe to live in the village of Lubavitch. Dedicated to the welfare of Russian Jewry, at that time confined to the "pale of settlement," he established Jewish agricultural colonies. He was arrested on libelous charges in 1826; however, he was released shortly thereafter. His most notable works on chasidic thought include *Sha'ar Hayichud, Torat Chayim,* and *Imrei Binah.*

Text 9 – Rabbi Adin Steinsaltz (Even-Yisrael) (1937–). Born in Jerusalem, Steinsaltz is considered one of the foremost Jewish thinkers of the 20th century. Praised by *Time Magazine* as a "once-in-a-millennium scholar," he has been awarded the Israel Prize for his contributions to Jewish study. He is the founder of the Israel Institute for Talmudic Publications, a society dedicated to the translation and elucidation of the Talmud.

Text 10 - Rabbi Shne'ur Zalman of Liadi (1745–1812). Chasidic rebbe and founder of the Chabad movement, also known as "the Alter Rebbe" and "the Rav." Born in Liozna, Belarus, he was among the principal students of the Magid of Mezeritch. His numerous works include the *Tanya,* an early classic containing the fundamentals of Chasidism; *Torah Or; Likutei Torah;* and *Shulchan Aruch HaRav,* a reworked and expanded code of Jewish law. He is interred in Hadiach, Ukraine, and was succeeded by his son, Rabbi Dovber of Lubavitch.

Course Conclusion

Throughout the seven months of this course, we have explored seven distinct areas of personal development. It has been quite a journey. We plumbed the world of sleep and left reenergized. We overcame anger and mastered our emotions. We turned our food struggles into mindful eating. We examined happiness and came away happier. We sanctified the gift of verbal communication. We understood faith and embraced knowledge. Finally, we introduced change that did not seem possible, laying the groundwork for future growth and personal advancement.

In doing so, we have fulfilled a directive of the Ba'al Shem Tov: to derive a lesson in our relationship with G-d from everything that we see or experience. As we have seen, our pillows have a life-changing message for us, as do our dinner plates. This is something that the Rebbe would emphasize at the conclusion of each of his many public addresses. He always looked for and demanded a lesson—a bottom line that can take any experience or concept and apply it to

our daily lives with concrete action. "*Hama'aseh hu ha'ikar,*" the Rebbe would never tire of repeating—"Action is the main thing."

After coming together for seven classes in order to explore fresh concepts in Torah, we naturally come away with at least a meaningful morsel or two—messages that resonate deep within, which we can turn into practical enhancements to our personal lives.

If you have no time to do this in class, you may wish to ask your students to do this at home.

Ask the class to take a minute to revisit the Key Points that are found at the conclusion of each lesson. Ask them to glide through the lists and to circle the point from each lesson that resonated most with them. Then help them suggest ways in which those points in particular might be used to introduce a positive element to their lives. Remind them of the theme of the seventh lesson—that every inspiring concept needs grounding by way of a practical resolution.

Take a look at the Key Points of each lesson. Circle one concept in each lesson that resonates the most for you. How can these concepts be translated into a practical improvement in your life?

_____

_____

_____

It's about time that I _____.

(fill in resolution here)

Additional Readings

Lessons From a Hummingbird - Learning to Love Your Life

By Catherine Roozman Weigensberg

Where were you ten, twenty years ago? I don't mean geographically - I'm talking about your inner presence, your mindset, your core being…

I've passed the half-century milestone now and I reflect: How have I grown? Have I achieved all that I could thus far? Can I be a better Jew? A more productive citizen? And the answer to these questions is in the affirmative - yet I now love where I'm at…because I can appreciate the journey thus far and the paths yet untraversed.

A relatively new and very dear friend of mine is awaiting a double lung transplant; she is presently focusing on staying on an even plane - meditating, appreciating the lessons of the Torah and miraculously performing good deeds in every imaginable way as she continues on through the next stage of her significant journey. She is my inspiration, the reason for my awakened reflection and introspection.

Have you ever had the privilege of watching a tiny hummingbird, seemingly floating from flower to flower while effortlessly sipping its precious nectar? Its wings are barely visible as they beat as much as 70 times per second. This exceptional creature can fly backwards and forwards, maintaining its position while feeding. A remarkable bird, it is, and my friend is equally impressive in her ability to nourish herself and others while struggling to live, to breathe.

She puts the rest of us to shame. Her determination, courage, remarkable talents and intelligence have transported me to a new level of understanding of where I need to be in this world and why I should love who I am. She is that rare, exquisite flower in the heart of a barren desert - and she loves where she's at spiritually.

Can we accomplish this sense of peace without an existing threatening medical condition or impending life changing surgery?

Our society has become increasingly focused on youth and external beauty. We have forgotten the value of wrinkles earned through life experiences, and instead reward and worship those with the most artificial appearances, the tautest skin and most comical expressions created by pulling, lifting, and injecting. We have virtually ignored the sacrifices and immeasurable value of the aged population who laid a solid foundation for all of us. Yet in Judaism, there is great emphasis and importance on the need to honor our elders.

I'll tell you who I think was a stunning woman. Golda Meir. Aesthetically, she may not have qualified as a beauty, but her face portrayed her fierce devotion to Israel, her undeniable intelligence and a unique ability to astound others with her majestic presence and inner radiance - a glow which would certainly outshine any Hollywood "beauty" by my standards. Her face was not smooth and unmarred, but rather well-defined by lines and chiseled with furrows earned through hard work and devotion to her family, friends, her people, and the world.

I'm tired of the countless accolades and attention showered upon celebrities at entertainment award ceremonies for their various achievements in the industry. I'm sure that they have done a fine job, but let us also applaud and recognize the true heroes: the single parents who struggle to provide food and shelter for their kids, the health-challenged individuals who surmount incredible obstacles each day in order to survive in a so-called 'able' world, the healthcare workers who compassionately nurse the ill and the dying, the children who emerge from underpriviledged situations to become productive citizens…the list goes on and on…

Loving where you're at involves much more than accepting yourself. It implores attention to the needs of others, less focus on oneself, appreciation for acts of kindness and true friendship. It's about holding the door open for the person behind you without stressing over the consequences of its political correctness. It is being aware of the power of humanity and decent behavior. It means performing good deeds on a daily basis.

Like the skillful hummingbird, loving where you're at means hovering from journey to journey while dexterously maintaining your position in this world.

This piece is dedicated to my very dear friend Melody Masha Pierson. May she be blessed with strength and renewed health!

The True You -
Who You Are and How You Express Yourself

-- Samech Vov 100 Years – Part Four --

What is the driving force of all human behavior? What lies at the core of the psyche? What is the Kabbalistic/Chassidic view on the unconscious? Which is stronger –

willpower or pleasure? How powerful are these two forces in our lives?

This week's essay, as part of our continuing series discussing central themes of the Rebbe Rashab's magnum opus, Hemshech Samech Vov, attempts to tackle an incredibly complex discussion on the psychology of the soul. 100 years ago this week, in one of the most profound analyses ever written on the nature of the psyche, the discourses of Lech Lecho and Vayeira 5666/1905 take us on a journey into the innermost recesses of our souls.

Most of us most of the time are immersed into the minutiae of our lives. Our struggle for survival, whatever shape it takes on, requires that we dedicate a disproportionate amount of our time and energy to the means rather than the ends: We work hard to earn money so that we can buy the things that make us happy. We eat, exercise and visit the doctor to maintain our health.

Just take your average day and count how many hours you spend commuting, preparing, cooking, shopping, traveling, socializing, sleeping – all to hopefully achieve certain goals, some immediate, most long term.

The process to achieve our goals so consumes our lives that for many of us it *becomes* our lives: We live to work instead of the other way around. To the extent that we can even forget what our goals are in the first place – so distracted we become by our plans. In a take-of of a famous cliché: Life is what happens to you while you are busy making other plans. We make elaborate plans to achieve certain objectives, and at the end of the day the process wears us down to the point that we no longer have the strength and time to remember the objectives, let alone benefit or enjoy them.

It therefore should be no surprise that we don't have much time to focus on our souls – on our inner lives, the lives of our loved ones and the pursuit of our higher values. To temporarily relieve our existential desperation and enjoy a quick fix of transcendence many us compartmentalize: We carve out moments – weekends, vacations, holidays – which we dedicate to prayer, reading, meditation, music, arts, romance and religion – which help us reconnect. But these are fleeting moments in comparison to the hours that we spend on the means.

The plot thickens. Perhaps the most devastating effect of our being inundated by the mundane means of life, preparing, preparing and preparing, is that it distorts our perception of reality.

What is real: The tangible deluge of the daily grind of our quotidian lives which utterly consumes our time and focus, or the invisible world of our souls and the inner dimensions of existence?

Who has the time and energy to even focus on this question? So, by default our immediate preoccupations dictate our reality and our priorities. The means of our lives first conceal our end goals, and then replace them, like an imposter masquerading as the real thing.

How refreshing is it then when we hear someone uncover the mask and describe for us in intimate detail the nature of our true selves, the nature of reality and the purpose of our existence?

This is precisely what the Rebbe Rashab does in his classic Hemshech Samech Vov. He takes us on a trip into the inner workings of the universe, and you return a different person.

In the first part of this series, we discussed that the purpose of existence is to introduce into the world a dimension that is beyond the world; to transform the material universe into a Divine home.

Samech Vov breaks down the anatomy of existence into three dimensions: 1) The inner force of existence (*memaleh kol almin*). 2) The force that transcends existence (*sovev kol almin*). 3) The force that transcends both existence and non-existence, which has the power to integrate existence with transcendence.

In order to achieve this on the macrocosmic level, we have to generate this process within our microcosmic selves, which also consist of these three dimensions:

1) Our personal, specific intelligent and emotional faculties (ten faculties in all, corresponding to the ten sefirot: three intellectual ones – chochma, binah, daat, and seven emotions – chesed, gevurah, tiferet, netzach, hod, yesod and malchut.). The spectrum of human conscious experience is defined by our intellect and emotions, as they are expressed through (the three "garments") thought, speech and action.

2) Our transcendent faculties (corresponding with the level of *Keter*), sometimes referred to "all encompassing faculties", because they but reflect and affect the entire person, not like the ten individual self contained faculties (in the first category) which express only one part of the individual.

3) The essence of the soul (*etzem ha'neshomo*), which transcends and therefore has the power to integrate the previous two dimensions.

One distinction between the personal faculties (category one) and the transcendent ones (category two) can be understood as the difference between the conscious psyche and the unconscious one.

A disclaimer should be made that this "unconscious" state should not be confused by the one described by Freud, Jung and other contemporary psychologists. The Kabbalistic/Chassidic "unconscious" is actually more like "supra-conscious", in the sense that it reflect the person's inner identity and vision, while the specific faculties express limited and particular aspects of life, which is what we call "conscious" life.

For instance, you can use your intelligence to analyze football statistics (in case you were wondering: this is my own example, not one used in Samech Vov), or to build your business, or you get emotional over a moving scene in a film — and it may be completely fictional or tangential, with no connection at all with your soul's identity or purpose. In other words, your conscious life can be disconnected (or milder: unaligned) from your "supra-conscious" being. Essentially, this is what happens when we live our days consumed with the means and neglecting our higher goals – a psychological dissonance, what Marx called "alienation" when there is a dichotomy between who you are (your identity) and what you do (your activities).

A good analogy to explain this is the creative process of any given production. Whether it is a new business venture, a book, a film, a composition of music or the construction of a building every effective creation begins with a vision, which reflects the identity of the creator, and then the vision is translated into a specific plan which is then implemented piece by piece, until its conclusion, when the initial vision comes to fruition.

If you were to enter a construction zone you can see the plumbers laying pipes and the electricians wiring the joint, with no clue as to the vision, let alone the identity, of the architect. The same

with a book or another production: If you read the first draft of one chapter of a new book, you may not have inkling as to the greater objective of the author. "Never show a fool half a job" is a Yiddish euphemism ("a naar veizt men nit kayn halbe arbet"). Even after the conclusion of the project, it is no small feat to understand the bigger picture, and not be distracted by the obvious details, especially if it is a complex and comprehensive creation.

Every business needs a mission statement to begin with. The mission is usually an expression of the creator's vision and dream, which goes back into his/her supra-consciousness.

For conscious life (our conscious faculties) to be lived to its fullest, it needs to be informed and directed by the supra-conscious, transcendental faculties.

Just imagine the said plumbers and electricians deciding mid-course to follow their own instincts instead of the blueprint created by the architect! No matter how skilled they are, their specific strengths are only as good as the direction they receive from the vision of the project. Indeed, the more skilled they are the greater damage they can cause should they choose to wander off their own way.

So what does the transcendental "supra-conscious" look like? What faculties does it contain?

A centennial ago this week, the Rebbe Rashab explains this "supra-conscious" state in the discourses beginning with verses in these weekly chapters about Avraham's journey and commitment – perhaps because in history Avraham reflects the transcendental roots of spiritual life in a material world. Avraham set into motion the _vision_, becoming, as it were, the historical "supra-conscious" state which informs the rest of history to follow.

The vision, mission, goals, end – as opposed to the means (the ten conscious faculties) – consist of two components: _Taanug_ and _Rotzon_. The literal translation of these two Hebrew words, respectively, is pleasure and will. But these English words/concepts hardly convey the true meaning of the original, which requires a short introduction.

The soul, before it expresses itself through any of its faculties, has a personality – a unique identity. When you say, for example, that a melody touched your soul or that you feel loved, you in effect are describing your soul's experience as opposed to one of its faculties (e.g. plumbers, electricians) at work. This is not to say that the soul cannot express its inner identity via its faculties; however the faculties can have a "life of their own" if they are not being directed by the "supra-conscious" identity of the soul.

The most natural state of the soul, when it is at its deepest peace, is a state of pleasure (_taanug atzmi_). Not objectified pleasure, not pleasure as an experience, focused on some specific goal – but simply a state of being, a state of utter calm and belonging.

In addition to the essential state pleasure, the second dimension of the supra-conscious state is will (_rotzon_), which is the soul extending and expressing itself. Will, in effect, reveals the interests of the inner pleasure (which always remains hidden in its essential form) and reaches outside of itself seeking something on the outside to fulfill its inner self.

Both supra-conscious pleasure and will stem from the same source in the essence of the soul. They are not two distinct faculties, but one. The only difference between them is that pleasure is the internal dimension and will the external one, which expresses the inner pleasure.

Supra-conscious pleasure is who you are – your essential identity; Will is how your identity expresses itself, seeking to fulfill and realize your inner self (pleasure).

It's critical to distinguish this supra-conscious pleasure from conscious "pleasure" as we know it. Conscious pleasure – regardless of its cause, healthy or unhealthy – is object oriented: You have pleasure in a certain feeling, activity or experience. You therefore desire the things that bring you pleasure.

The same with will: Conscious will reflects the different things we want, whether they are informed, healthy and productive or not. Supra-conscious will reflects the soul in search of its destiny – the "will of all wills", the "essence will" or the "will to will", which precedes all attributes and faculties.

This also explains the apparent contradiction about pleasure or will – which is more dominant? On one hand we find that pleasure is the root of all. If you have no pleasure in something you won't want. Clearly, will is a product of desire. On the other hand we also see that if you set your mind that you don't want something you won't have any pleasure in it, even if it's a natural pleasure.

Samech Vov explains that this interplay between pleasure and will is only on the conscious level. Because both pleasure and will are two sides of the soul's essence, that's why they are interchangeable: In certain instances pleasure affects the will, in others willpower can affect pleasure. But even when it does, it only affects the conscious level of pleasure, not its essential state, which always remains more intimate and fundamental than will; even when will overrules conscious pleasure it has within it the essential supra-conscious pleasure (which remains concealed).

No doubt that this subject matter requires much more elaboration. But even on an ostensible level it gives us a fascinating insight what we are capable and the infinite possibilities we have before us.

It is an absolute breath of fresh air (to say the least) to hear that we all have at the heart of our soul a deep calm and profound pleasure.

In today's society we have been programmed to think that we are all dysfunctional "damaged goods". And then our self-fulfilling prophesy of doom is fulfilled. Looking around we see a cruel world, greed and corruption the norm, with the occasional glimpses into human nobility, but only occasional. The wicked prosper and good suffer, people hurting each other all the time, even those they presumably love, children scarred by parents, long term committed relationships the exception, inhumane behavior of senseless murders around the globe – all this feeds our fears and insecurities that we will never attain lasting, meaningful pleasure, only bouts of escape.

Comes Samech Vov, written one hundred years ago, in most difficult times with bloody progroms and more, and tells us that we each have within a deep-seated state of pleasure – an innate knowledge that we belong and have an indispensable role to play.

The only way to free ourselves from the inbred psyche of our desperate universe and its regurgitated message is to access the supra-conscious dimension within ourselves, a force that transcends the common laws of society and the lim-

ited resources of our conscious faculties. And then align our conscious lives with our supra-conscious identity, so that our daily activities are infused with the vision and clarity of our inner selves.

How do you align your inner and outer life?

Through a multi-fold plan:

1)   Free yourself of some of the trappings that hold you hostage and keep you from seeing the end from the means. Transcend your conscious wills and pleasures that offer superficial satisfaction.

2)   Recognize the "peace at the center" that lies at the core of your being – the pleasure in the essence of your soul.

3)   Actualize the supra-conscious pleasure of your soul with your willpower: To want and desire to realize your soul's mission in this world, and then act upon it.

4)   Practically this means, as the Rebbe Rashab eloquently concludes, that by living a virtuous life filled with mitzvot we have the power to uncover the essence of Divine will and pleasure and actually reveal it in this universe.

That is the ultimate achievement: The ability to defy paradoxes and consciously experience the supra-conscious, to reveal the unrevealable and express the inexpressible – in a total fusion of that which is beyond, and beyond beyond, with the here and now.

Reprinted with permission from meaningfullife.com

Ten Steps to Greatness

Avraham, "father of all nations", was the first true pioneer. He stood up to an entire selfish world and trail blazed a spiritual path to life, forever changing history. It was Avraham's embrace of a higher set of values of love, generosity and service that forged the standard for the basic human rights that we take today for granted.

What was Avraham's secret? What shaped this man? From where did he derive the power and courage to defy the tide of his times? How can we emulate Avraham and acquire his courage in our own lives?

This week's Torah portion tells the story of Avraham. And it can be summed up in the concise words of the Mishne: "Our father Avraham was tested with ten challenges, and he withstood them all – to indicate how great was our father Avraham's love" (Ethics of the Fathers 5:3).

[The standard translation of "nisyonos" in this statement is "tests" or "trials". But perhaps "challenges" is a more accurate and appropriate translation. Linguists of the world: Please weigh in].

Why did Avraham need to be tested? G-d must have known that Avraham had unique qualities and that he would withstand the trials; why was it necessary to actually put Avraham through the difficulties he endured? Does every man of faith need to be challenged?

The Hebrew word for "test" (or "challenge") – "nisayon" – shares the same root with the word "ness", which means miracle and also banner. A miracle reveals the extraordinary within the ordinary; the Divine within the natural. The same is with a "nisayon", a challenge: Every person has innate qualities. By virtue of being created in the "Image of G-d" every soul contains enormous reservoirs of extraordinary potential. However, these powers remain dormant when unactualized. A "nisayon" – the true test of one's character – is a challenge that actualizes our potential

and brings the best out of us by revealing the powerful forces we carry within. Like a banner the challenge spiritually elevates us and allows us to fly high.

When we pass a difficult test in life, two things happen at once: A deeper part of our soul is revealed, to the point that it can actually bring on true transformation of the human being. And, as a result, a deeper, transformative dimension of Divine light manifests in existence.

Thus, the Mishne can be read: "Our father Avraham was *exalted* with ten challenges, and he withstood them all – to indicate how great was our father Avraham's love".

That was Avraham. What about us?

Note the Mishne's emphasis (twice) on "*our father Avraham*", indicating that we all, as his children, inherit the features of our father. Both Avraham's profound virtues and his tremendous fortitude is our birthright as children of "our father Avraham".

Each of us in our own lives will be tested, or rather, challenged. [Tested has negative connotations with condescending implications, feeding into the nursery school stereotype that "an angry, long-bearded man in heaven is out to get us". Challenged is much more appropriate]. Each challenge is actually an opportunity to grow – to draw out great strengths from within. Each triumph over a challenge lifts us to unprecedented heights.

Everything that happened to the patriarchs is an indication for their children (Midrash Tanchuma Lech Lecho 9. Bereishis Rabba 40:6). *All the events that happened with the Patriarchs [Avraham, Isaac and Jacob] come to teach us about the future…they were shown what would happen to their descendants* (Ramban Lech Lecho 12:6).

Just as Avraham endured ten challenges, one more difficult than the previous, we, his children, too undergo in our lifetimes ten similar challenges. With one important qualification: Once Avraham proved himself, his children do not need to be challenged with quite the same intensity. And especially today, after all that we have endured throughout history, we no longer need, thank G-d, to go through "fire" and face life threatening challenges of pain, suffering and death.

Sadly, some of us are still faced with awful challenges. But collectively, we are blessed to live in freedom, without the persecution of old, unlike Avraham who faced the threat of death for his beliefs. And individually as well, after all that we have suffered, at this point we can expect and hope, and pray to G-d that enough is enough: Our challenges today should only be positive ones, focused on eliciting our inner potential.

Here are Avraham's ten challenges and one way that they can be applied to our lives today:[1]

1. Avraham's early childhood, when he had to be hidden for a number of years.

2. Avraham being thrust into a fiery furnace for his refusal to acknowledge the arch-idol of his native Ur Kasdim, the emperor Nimrod, and his continued commitment to teaching the world the truth of a one, non-corporeal and omnipotent G-d.

3. *Lech Lecho* – the upheaval and change of leaving his home and building a new life.

4. Famine – despite G-d's blessings of prosperity.

5. Pharaoh's abduction of Sarah.

6. War.

7. The Covenant, when Avraham hears about the future subjugation and suffering of his children at the hands of different nations.

8. Circumcision.

9. Banishing Ishmael for his home.

10. The Akeidah (binding of Isaac).

To achieve greatness, every one of us needs to experience, in one form or another, these ten challenges. If you study your life and the life and history of your family you will find glimpses of ten different trials and tribulations, what we call "nisyonot". (They may or may not be in the same order as they occurred in Avraham's life).

1. The challenge of childhood

---

1 Opinions vary as to the exact nature of Avraham's ten challenges (as to what Avraham's ten challenges actually entailed consisted of). Here we followed the interpretation of the Pirkei D'rebbi Eliezer (chapter 26-31).

All opinions agree on seven of these challenges (not in chronoligical order): 1) Lech Lecho; 2) Hunger; 3) Pharaoh's abduction of Sarah; 4) War; 5) Circumcision; 6) Banishing Ishmael; 7) Akeidah. All the opinions (except for Maimonides) also include: 8) Avraham being thrust into the fire; 9) The Covenant, when Avraham hears about the future suffering of his children at the hands of different nations (Pirkei D'rebbi Eliezer ch. 26. Avot D'rebbi Natan ch. 33. Midrash Tehillim 95. Bartenura. Rabbeinu Yonah). Regarding the tenth challenge – some consider 10) Avimelech's abduction of Sarah (Bartenura), or Avraham hiding for 13 years (Pirkei D'rebbi Eliezer ch. 26).

Maimonides does not include #8 and #9, and instead separates into two challenges the banishment of Hagar and Yishmael, and includes Avimelech's abduction of Sarah (which the others consider as part of #3) and Avraham's taking Hagar as concubine. (Some explain

that Maimonides enumerates only the challenges that are specifically stated in Biblical verse). Rabbeinu Yonah considers the banishment of mother and son as one, and instead adds the purchase of Sarah's burial plot (Meorat haMachpeilah).

The early formative years of a child are the most precious. They define the strengths the child will accumulate and the challenges the child will face throughout his or her entire life. It is therefore absolutely vital to create a spiritually nurturing environment for your child and protect your child, in these impressionable years, from narcissistic and corrupting influences.

2. The challenge of commitment

Sometime in life, often early on, and perhaps more than once in a lifetime, you will be asked (with or without words) to make a choice: Either conform or "burn". Today, thankfully, "burn" isn't literal. But the price of choosing the "road less traveled", the path of virtue and faith, will be threatened by material pressures that consume us like "fire". Will you choose to bow and worship an "idol" – money, fame, superstars, whatever – or do you commit to a higher cause?

3. The challenge of change

As you mature into an adult the time comes to "cut the (psychological) umbilical cord", and leave your home and comfort zones to discover yourself and what you are capable of. This can be a formidable challenge. More specifically, the journey consists of freeing yourself from the subjective forces that shape our lives: Our natural, biased, tendencies; parental influences; and social programming. "Lech Lecho" commands us to leave our inertia-based environments and experience the "real you" – who *you* are and what original contribution do *you* make, as opposed to being a product of others.

4. The challenge of deprivation

Then there will be those times when you may experience deep hunger and wonder whether your choices was all worth it. You committed to G-d and yet you have no "food on your table". You may need to wander to strange, hostile places to acquire some nourishment. Will you give up or see it through?

5. The challenge of sexuality

And then your most intimate needs may be compromised or abducted. Your heart challenged and your love denied. Will this break you?

6. The challenge of confrontation

No matter who you are and what your life space is like, you will be faced with confrontations. Even when you are not looking for adversary, enemy forces will assault you. They may take on the shape of people – so-called friends, co-workers, neighbors, surrounding nations, or they may be inner fears, psychological phobias, haunting ghosts of the past. But whatever form it takes you can rest assured that you will have to fight a battle or two in your life. These battles will either demoralize you or strengthen you.

7. The challenge of suffering

No one is immune to loss and some form of pain in our lifetimes. Even when G-d is merciful, we will, in our current condition, experience the loss of a loved one, the break of a promise or the dissolution of a dream. We are mortals and fragile creatures. Health issues will crop up. Here too, the challenge is whether we can discover deeper resources to help us through the harder times.

8. The challenge of transformation

Avraham's circumcision at age 99 marked his metamorphosis to become spiritually complete, as G-d says to him: through circumcision you will "walk before Me and become complete". The covenant "in you flesh" will bond you with me forever (a covenant stated thirteen times in the Torah). For Avraham the challenge was compounded by the fact that he as 99 years old at the time. Today the challenge is to ensure that our children (8 day year old boys, and girls are considered circumcised upon birth) have engraved in their very flesh Avraham's' Divine covenant. The challenge of transformation is not just a partial, limited commitment to a higher cause, but one that is complete and permeates every aspect of our lives, including the material and physical.

9. The challenge of discipline

Often, in the name of deep love and spiritual conviction, we can overwhelm ourselves and those around us. Avraham, the epitome of love (chesed), found it difficult to send away his son Ishmael. But this discipline (gevurah) was necessary for the welfare of Avraham's own home as well as of Ishmael and Hagar. We too will have the challenge in our lives, where we will need to exercise profound discipline lest we become consumed by spiritual and sensual passions.

10. The challenge of becoming Divine

Finally, the ultimate challenge will be when you are asked to be ready to give up the single thing you love most for G-d. Not with the intention of actually having to relinquish it – but you cannot be privy to that at the time or it will defeat the entire purpose; you will feel as though you actually will be sacrificing your most precious possession. Only to discover, that when you are

sincerely ready for such a sacrifice, you not only lose nothing; in return you gain immortality and an eternal connection to the very thing you love so much).

These are the ten general challenges that we will all face in our lifetimes (obviously, with many subsets within each). How we will rise to these ten challenges will define our lives.

The key thing to always remember, with every fiber of our being, is that these are all challenges that you have the power to withstand, and when you do they will help catapult you to greatness.

Avraham was not just a man of distant history. His story is our story. His travels paved the way for our own. His endurance demonstrates – and empowers us, his children, with the ability to not just survive, but to thrive and reach immortality.

Over 3600 years of difficult history is a living testimony to a man's absolute dedication to a higher cause. Through all these millennia, and all of history's upheavals, Avraham remains the pioneering spirit that changed the world forever, and is admired today perhaps even more than in his own time. If that does not instill in us confidence and inspiration that we too (with far less difficulties than Avraham's) can see it through, what will?

Reprinted with permission from meaningfullife.com

Which woman is not eager to be more fulfilled, more effective, happier, healthier, self actualized to a greater degree?

It's about time we test-drive the wisdom of the ages with a balance of practical and insightful spiritual self-help... And so, through the vision of many, this course was born.

I am grateful to my authors, **Rabbi Zalman Moshe** and **Mrs. Leah Abraham** for the exemplary dedication they have displayed on many levels during their involvement with this curriculum. From the earliest moments of planting the seeds for the course ideas, through their excellent research and skilled writing, they have proven to be a most valuable asset to the *Rosh Chodesh Society*.

Tremendous gratitude goes to our experienced and seasoned curriculum development team, **Rabbi Naftali Silberberg** and **Rabbi Mordechai Dinerman**, who have brought the actual course to fruition through their expert curricular knowledge. Special appreciation goes out to **Rabbi Mordechai Dinerman** for his selfless and untiring work as the lead editor on this project.

Rabbi Yakov Paley and **Mrs. Chava Shapiro** have done a superb job editing the individual lessons, each with their own unique blend of skill and understanding.

Rabbi Shmuel Kaplan, chairman, has been instrumental in formulating the vision of the *Rosh Chodesh Society* since its inception and continues to be a source of guidance as we are blessed to experience tremendous growth within our sisterhood.

Mrs. Shula Bryski, Mrs. Michal Carlbach, Mrs. Rochel Holzkenner, Mrs. Devorah Kornfeld, Mrs. Chana Lipskar, Mrs. Ahuva New, Mrs. Binie Tenenbaum have graciously agreed to lend their years of expertise and experience, review curricula, assist in revisions, and aide in general course development by serving as our steering committee for existing and future projects.

Our talented production teams have expended numerous hours to bring our instructional materials to production. **Mrs. Ya'akovah Weber** meticulously copy edited and proofread the texts with a great measure of attention and dedication. **Rabbi Zalman Moshe Abraham** created the beautiful, artistic cover of this book with fantastic talent, heart and soul. **Chazak Publishing House** designed the book together with a keen, creative eye and generosity of character. I am deeply thankful to all of you. You always rise to the occasion.

We extend great appreciation to Chabad.org and The Meaningful Life Center and meaningfullife.com, for allowing us to reprint articles and book excerpts as Additional readings for our course's seven lessons.

We laud **Rabbi Zalman Abraham**, our marketing director, for his creative vision, innovative marketing skills, attentiveness to the finest of detail and for producing all our beautiful marketing materials. **Rabbi Mendel Bell**, who heads our online division, not only oversees and ensures the integrity of our cyberspace field, but brings new meaning to the "user-friendly" definition.

Special mention must be made regarding our very gifted multi-media team. **Nechama Rivkah Dubov** has not only dreamed up and produced the videos and PowerPoint presentations, she has also done so with the greatest of spirit and an unwavering smile. **Mrs. Chava Shapiro** and **Mushka Groner** have assisted in both of these undertakings and their input has proven to be invaluable. Having the ability to work with **Getzy Raskin**, heading the filming crew, and **Moshe Raskin**, who is simply so good at all things video, is certainly a blessing I'm sure many would wish for. We make note of our good fortune.

Thank you **Spotlight Design**, for the **JLI** Multiplex pages. Many thanks to **Mr. Shimon Leib Jacobs**, who prints our books, and to **Mary Stevens**, for distribution. We owe much gratitude to **Rabbi Mendel Sirota**, who oversees production, shipping and handling, and always goes the extra mile to turn the impossible, possible. I acknowledge your efforts.

Kudos to **Mrs. Fraydee Kessler**, an administrator and single-handed project manager *par excellence*. She is much more than her title and job description can ever tell you and my appreciation for her knows no bounds. Allow me an additional shout-out to **Chana'le Dechter** who multi-tasks with such grace, integrity and sensitivity. And has never said no.

As well, I extend my gratitude to **Rabbi Dubi Rabinowitz**, Chief Operating Officer, for managing and leading multiple teams and projects while paying close attention to the needs and wants of the *Rosh Chodesh Society*.

There are no words with which to acknowledge **Rabbi Levi Kaplan**, a master at everything he does - too many things to enumerate - but each one completed to perfection. Your efforts do not go unnoticed.

The *Rosh Chodesh Society* is enormously grateful for the encouragement of **JLI**'s chairman, and vice chairman of *Merkos L'Inyonei Chinuch* - Lubavitch World headquarters, **Rabbi Moshe Kotlarsky**. We are fortuitously blessed with the unwavering support of **JLI**'s principal benefactors, **Mr. and Mrs. George and Pamela Rohr**, who have staunchly spearheaded and invested in the growth of the organization with an unparalleled commitment. Their dedication is evident and alive within the thousands of Jewish students studying Torah around the globe. May your merit stand us all in good stead and may you reap unbridled kindness all the days of your long and auspicious lives.

JLI's devoted executive board - **Rabbi Chaim Block, Rabbi Hesh Epstein, Rabbi Yosef Gansbourg, Rabbi Shmuel Kaplan, Rabbi Avrohom Sternberg**, and **Rabbi Yisrael Rice** - give countless hours to the development of **JLI**. Their dedication, commitment, and sage advice have helped the organization grow and flourish.

The constant progress of **JLI** is a testament to the visionary leadership of our director, **Rabbi Efraim Mintz**, who is never content to rest on his laurels, and who boldly encourages continued innovation and change. On a personal note, I must thank you, once again, for this benevolent, outstanding and truly beneficent opportunity. You have endowed me with the vehicle to fulfill a lifelong passion and dream. Your merit is great. Thank you for sharing it with me.

The *Rosh Chodesh Society*, **JLI**'s woman's division, was launched on the anniversary of the first *yahrtzeit* of **Rabbi Gavriel Noach Holtzberg** and his wife, **Rebbetzin Rivkah ZHotzberg, H"YD**. The Holtzbergs were devoted Chabad emissaries in Mumbai, India. There, far from their families, friends, and comforts of home, they lovingly served the local community as well as the many tourists who visited the area, until they were slain in an unspeakably horrific terrorist attack. May the merit of the countless Jewish women who are engaged in these Torah studies serve as a testament to the heroic life they led, and continue to perpetuate their noble deeds.

On behalf of all the individuals who play a role in the *Rosh Chodesh Society*, particularly our affiliates out there on the front lines fulfilling their positions, I offer up a prayer to Almighty G-d: May He actualize the hopes of the Lubavitcher Rebbe of righteous memory, and may we experience the world as it will be, when filled with the knowledge of G-d as the waters cover the sea. Amen.

Shluchos! Each and every day the world becomes a far better place thanks to you. Indeed, this is the ultimate acknowledgment.

Shaindy Jacobson

Director, *Rosh Chodesh Society*

Brooklyn, New York

6 Tishrei, 5773

JEWISH LEARNING INSTITUTE

The **Rohr Jewish Learning Institute**

An affiliate of
Merkos L Inyonei Chinuch
The Educational Arm of
The Chabad Lubavitch Movement
822 Eastern Parkway, Brooklyn, NY 11213

Chairman
Rabbi Moshe Kotlarsky
Lubavitch World Headquarters
Brooklyn, NY

Principal Benefactor
Mr. George Rohr
New York, NY

Executive Director
Rabbi Efraim Mintz
Brooklyn, NY

Executive Committee
Rabbi Chaim Block
S. Antonio, TX

Rabbi Hesh Epstein
Columbia, SC

Rabbi Yosef Gansburg
Toronto, ON

Rabbi Shmuel Kaplan
Potomac, MD

Rabbi Yisrael Rice
S. Rafael, CA

Rabbi Avrohom Sternberg
New London, CT

Rabbinic Consultant
Rabbi Dr. J. Immanuel Schochet
Toronto, ON

Advisory Board
Rabbi Shmuel Kaplan
Chairman
Potomac, MD

Rabbi Dovid Eliezrie
Yorba Linda, CA

Rabbi Yosef Gopin
West Hartford, CT

Rabbi Mendel Kotlarsky
Brooklyn, NY

Rabbi Shalom D. Lipskar
Bal Harbour, FL

Dr. Stephen F. Serbin
Columbia, SC

Director of Operations
Rabbi Levi Kaplan
Brooklyn, NY

Strategic Developments
Rabbi Dubi Rabinowitz
Brooklyn, NY

Rosh Chodesh Society

Rabbi Shmuel Kaplan
Chair

Mrs. Shaindy Jacobson
Director

Mrs. Fraydee Kessler
Administrator

Rabbi Mendy Elishevitz
Web Design

Rabbi Mendel Bell
Web Administrator

Steering Committee

Mrs. Shula Bryski

Mrs. Michal Carlebach

Mrs. Rochel Holzkenner

Mrs. Devorah Kornfeld

Mrs. Chana Lipskar

Mrs. Ahuva New

Mrs. Binie Tenenbaum

IT'S ABOUT TIME:
Kabbalistic Insights for Taking Charge of Your Life

Author
**Rabbi and Mrs Zalman
Moshe & Leah Abraham**

Editors
Rabbi Mordechai Dinerman
Rabbi Yakov Paley
Mrs. Chava Shapiro

Copy Editor
Mrs. Ya'akovah Weber

Multimedia
Development
Nechama Rivkah Dubov
Mushka Groner
Mrs. Chava Shapiro
Mr. Moshe Raskin
Getzy Raskin

Affiliate Support
Mrs. Fraydee Kessler
Mrs. Chana'le Dechter

Production
Rabbi Mendel Sirota

Online Division
Rabbi Mendel Bell
Rabbi Mendel Sirota

Marketing
Rabbi Zalman Abraham

Publication Design
Rabbi Eliyahu Wilhelm
Rabbi Yakov Gopin
Chazak Publishing House
Israel

Printing
Mr. Shimon Leib Jacobs
Point One Communications
Montreal, QC

Accounting
Ms. Musie Karp
Mrs. Shaina B. Mintz

ROSH CHODESH SOCIETY

UNITED STATES

ARIZONA
Fountain Hills, AZ
Chabad of Fountain Hills
Mrs. Tzipi Lipskier
480-776-4763
tzipi@jewishfountainhills.com

CALIFORNIA
Calabasas, CA
Chabad of Calabasas
Mrs. Shaina Friedman
818-222-3838
shaini@jewishcalabasas.com

Folsom, CA
Chabad Folsom
Mrs. Goldie Grossbaum
916 608 9811
info@jewishfolsom.org

Fresno, CA
Chabad of Fresno
Mrs. Chanie Zirkind
559-432-2770
chabadfresno@sbcglobal.net

Irvine, CA
Chabad of Irvine
Rebbetzin Binie Tenenbaum
949 786 5000
binie@chabadirvine.org

Laguna Niguel, CA
Chabad of Laguna Niguel
Mrs. Kreinie Paltiel
9498317701
Kreinie@ChabadLagunaNiguel.com

Los Altos, CA
Chabad Los Altos
Mrs. Nechama Schusterman
6508586990
nechama@bayareafc.org

Malibu, CA
Chabad of Malibu
Mrs. Sarah Cunin
3204566588
sarah@jewishmalibu.com

Newbury Park, CA
Chabad of Newbury Park
Mrs. Tzippy Schneerson
805-499-7051
sschneerson@gmail.com

Oakland, CA
Chabad of Oakland
Mrs. Shulamis Labkowski
(510) 545-6770
info@jewishoakland.org

Pacific Palisades, CA
Chabad of Pacific Palisades
Mrs. Zisi Cunin
310-454-7783
info@chabadpalisades.com

Pleasanton, CA
Chabad of the Tri-Valley
Mrs. Fruma Resnick
925-846-0700
Fruma@JewishTriValley.com

Rancho Mirage, CA
Chabad of Rancho Mirage
Mrs. Chaya Posner
7607707785
info@chabadrm.com

Redwood City, CA
Chabad of Redwood City
Mrs. Ella Potash
6502320995
ella@jewishredwoodcity.com

S Francisco, CA
RTC-Chabad
Rebbetzin Sara Hecht
4153868123
office@rtchabad.org

S. Diego, CA
Chabad of Downtown
Mrs. Nechama Dina Carlebach
6197028518
Info@chabaddowntown.com

Santa Monica, CA
Chabad Living Torah Center
Mrs. Rivka Rabinowitz
310-394-5699
rabbi@livingtorahcenter.com

Temecula, CA
Chabad Jewish Center
Temecula Valley
Mrs. Dina Hurwitz
9518131401
jewishtemecula@gmail.com

Thousand Oaks, CA
Chabad of Thousand Oaks
Mrs. Shula Bryski
805 493 7776
shula@jewishto.org

Toluca Lake, CA
Chabad of Toluca Lake
Mrs. Michal Carlebach
818-308-4118
chabadtl@gmail.com

Ventura, CA
Chabad of Ventura
Mrs. Sarah Miriam Latowicz
805-658-7441
chabadventura@aol.com

COLORADO
Denver, CO
Chabad/Lubavitch of Colorado
Mrs. Elka Popack
303 780 0537
elkapopack@gmail.com

CONNECTICUT
Milford, CT
Chabad Jewish Center of Milford
Mrs. Chanie Wilhelm
203-878-4569
chanie@jewishmilford.com

DLAWARE
Wilmington, DE
Chabad of Delaware
Mrs. Rochel Flikshtein
3025299900
Office@ChabadDE.com

FLORIDA
Boca Raton, FL
Chabad of East Boca Raton
Mrs. Ahuva New
561-417-7797
Office@chabadbocabeaches.com

Bradenton, FL
Chabad of Bradenton & Lakewood
Ranch
Mrs. Chanie Bukiet
9417523030
Chanie@chabadofbradenton.com

Ft. Lauderdale, FL
Chabad of Las Olas
Mrs. Rochel Holzkenner
954-224-7162
rochelholzkenner@gmail.com

Miami, FL
Chabad at Midtown
Mrs. Chana Gopin
305-573-9995
info@maormiami.org

Palmetto Bay, FL
Chabad of Palmetto Bay
Mrs. Chani Gansburg
786-282-0413
chabadpalmettobay@gmail.com

Sarasota, FL
Chabad of Sarasota
Mrs. Sara Steinmetz
9419250770
steinmetz.sara@gmail.com

Sunny Isles Beach, FL
Chabad Russian Center
Mrs. Chanie Kaller
3058035315
Rabbi@chabadrc.org

Surfside, FL
The Shul of Bal Harbour
Rebbetzin Chani Lipskar
3058681411
info@theshul.org

Tampa, FL
Chabad of Tampa Bay
Mrs. Sulha Dubrowski
813 963 2317
lamplightersd@gmail.com

GEORGIA
Atlanta, GA
Chabad Intown
Mrs. Leah Sollish
4048980434
leah@chabadintown.org

Atlanta, GA
Chabad of Georgia
Mrs. Dassie New
404-843-2464 x102
office@chabadga.com

Kennesaw, GA
Chabad Jewish Center
Mrs. Nechami Charytan
6784607702
info@jewishwestcobb.com

ILLINOIS
Chicago, IL
Jewish Women's Group
Mrs. Dinie Cohen
773-262-1381
ndcohen@sbcglobal.net

Glenview, IL
Rohr Chabad Center of Glenview
Mrs. Sara Benjaminson
8479980770
Chabad@ChabadofGlenview.com

Highland Park, IL
North Suburban Chabad
Mrs. Michla Schanowitz
847 433-1567
yschanow@sbcglobal.net

Northbrook, IL
Lubavitch Chabad of Northbrook
Mrs. Esther Rochel Moscowitz
847-564-8770
info@chabadnorthbrook.com

IOWA
Davenport, IA
Chabad Lubavitch of the Quad Cities
Mrs. Chana Cadaner
563-355-1065
Chana@Chabadquadcities.com

Iowa City, IA
Chabad Lubavitch of Iowa City
Mrs. Chaya Blesofsky
319-358-1323
chabadiowa@msn.com

KANSAS
Overland Park, KS
Neshei Chabad of KC
Mrs. Blumah Wineberg
913 649 4852
nesheichabad@gmail.com

LOUISIANA
Metairie, LA
Chabad Jewish Center
Mrs. Chanie Nemes
504-454-2910
rabbi@jewishlouisiana.com

MARYLAND
Annapolis, MD
Chabad of Anne Arundel County
Mrs. Hindy Light
443-321-9859
hindy@chabadaac.com

Baltimore, MD
Aleph Learning Institute
Mrs. Rochelle Kaplan
4104862666 x 2
alephjli@gmail.com

Bel Air, MD
Chabad of Harford County
Mrs. Fraida Malka Schusterman
443-353-9718
Chabad@HarfordJewish.com

Potomac, MD
Chabad of the Village
Mrs. Chana Kaplan
301-433-4524
villagechabad@gmail.com

MASSACHUSETTS
Chestnut Hill, MA
Chabad at Chestnut Hill
Rebbetzin Grunie Uminer
6177389770
grunie@chabadch.com

Peabody, MA
Chabad of Peabody
Mrs. Raizel Schusterman
978 977 9111
raizel@jewishpeabody.com

Stoughton, MA
Shaloh House
Mrs. Chana Gurkow
781-344-6334
rabbi@shalohhouse.com

Sudbury, MA
Chabad Center of Sudbury
Mrs. Shayna Freeman
978-443-0110
info@chabadsudbury.com

MICHIGAN
Southfield, MI
FREE of Michigan
Mrs. Tzippy Misholovin
248 569 8514
free.michigan@yahoo.com

West Bloomfield, MI
The Shul
Mrs. Itty Shemtov
2487884000
itty@theshul.net

MINNESOTA
Minnetonka, MN
Chabad Minneapolis
Ms. Rivkie Grossbaum
952-929-9922
rivka@ChabadMinneapolis.com

MISSOURI
Saint Louis, MO
Chabad of Greater St. Louis
Rebbetzin Shiffy Landa
3147250400
chaim@showmechabad.com

NEW JERSEY
Cherry hill, NJ
Chabad Lubavitch in Cherry Hill
Mrs. Dinie Mangel
8568841500
Chabadccnj@gmail.com

Clinton, NJ
Chabad of Hunterdon County
Mrs. Rachel Kornfeld
908-238-9002
rachel@jewishhunterdon.com

Freehold, NJ
Chabad of Freehold
Mrs. Zisi Bernstein
732-972-3687
zisinj@gmail.com

Hoboken, NJ
Chabad Hoboken
Mrs. Shaindel Schapiro
201 386 5222
chabadhoboken@gmail.com

Morristown, NJ
Morristown RCA
Mrs. Gani Goodman
917-860-0146
jdomber@gmail.com

NEW YORK
Bronx, NY
Chabad Lubavitch of Riverdale
Rebbetzin Sorah Shemtov
718-549-1100 ext. 15
sorahshmtv@gmail.com

Brooklyn, NY
Chabad of Midwood
Mrs. Devorah Marosov
718 338 3324
dmarsow@gmail.com

Brooklyn, NY
Chabad Neshama
Rebbetzin Esther Winner
718 946-9833 ext.104
estherwinner@gmail.com

Brooklyn, NY
Chabad of Ditmas Park
Mrs. Chana'le Levin
(347) 850-2255
ChabadofDitmasPark@gmail.com

Forest Hills, NY
Congregation Machane Chodosh
Rebbetzin Mushky Mendelson
347-867-8672
rabbi@machanechodosh.org

ROSH CHODESH SOCIETY

New York, NY
Upper Midtown Chabad
Mrs. Raizy Metzger
2127583770
raizymetzger@yahoo.com

New York, NY
Chabad Young Professionals UES
Mrs. Devora Wilhelm
3474515420
chabadyp@gmail.com

New York, NY
Aleph Learning
Rebbetzin Rachel Benchimol
646-827-9181
rachel@alephlearning.org

Suffern, NY
Chabad of Suffern
Mrs. Devorah Gancz
845-368-1889
info@jewishsuffern.com

OHIO
Cincinnati, OH
Chabad Jewish Center
Mrs. Chana Mangel
513-793-5200
office@chabadba.com

Dayton, OH
Chabad of Greater Dayton
Mrs. Devorah Leah Mangel
937-643-0770
chabad@chabaddayton.com

New Albany, OH
Chabad of Columbus
Mrs. Esther Kaltmann
614-610-4293
esther.kaltmann@sbcglobal.net

PENNSYLVANIA
Allentown, PA
Chabad of the Lehigh Valley
Mrs. Devorah Halperin
610-351-6511
Rabbi@chabadlehighvalley.com

Newtown, PA
Lubavitch of Bucks County
Mrs. Rosie Weinstein
215-497-9925
rosie@jewishcenter.info

TEXAS
Arlington, TX
Chabad of Arlington
Mrs. Risha Gurevitch
817 451 1171
rishi@arlingtonchabad.org

Dallas, TX
Chabad of Dallas
Mrs. Michal Shapiro
972-818-0770
moshenaparstek@gmal.com

Fort worth, TX
Chabad of Fort Worth
Mrs. Chana Tovah Mandel
817-263-7701
Cgi@chabadfortworth.com

Houston, TX
Chabad at Rice
Mrs. Rochel Lazaroff
713 522 2004
Rochel@aishelhouse.org

Houston, TX
Chabad Lubavitch
Mrs. Leah Marinovsky
713 5411774
leahfeige2@aim.com

Plano, TX
chabad of plano
Mrs. rivkie block
972 596-8270
connect@chabadplano.org

S. Antonio, TX
Chabad Lubavitch
Mrs. Rivkie Block
210-492-1085
chabadsa@sbcglobal.net

VIRGINIA
Norfolk, VA
Chabad of Tidewater
Mrs. Rashi Brashevitzky
757-616-0770
Rabbilevi@chabdoftidewater.com

WASHINGTON
Mercer Island, WA
Chabad of Mercer Island
Mrs. Devorah Kornfeld
2066799117
y-kornfeld2@yahoo.com

OLYMPIA, WA
Chabad of Olympia
Mrs. Chava Edelman
360-584-4306
info@jewisholympia.com

Spokane, WA
Chabad of Spokane
Mrs. Chaya Sarah Hahn
509-443-0770
rabbihahn@gmail.com

WISCONSIN
Mequon, WI
Center for Jewish Life
Mrs. Dinie Rapoport
262.242.2235
dinie73@gmail.com

AUSTRALIA

St Kilda East, Victoria
Beis Chabad Ohel Devorah
Mrs. Sara Rosenfeld
+61395259014
rivkahgroner@gmail.com

BELGIUM
Brussels
ejcc
Mrs. Nehama Tawil
(32)22311770
ntawil@ejcc.eu

Bruxelles, Belgium
Ohel Menachem
Mrs. Shulamit Pinson
32 476 217 445
info@ganihai.com

BRAZIL
S. Paulo, SP
Beit Chabad
Mrs. Sarah Steinmetz
55 11 3081-3081
sarah@chabad.org.br

CANADA
Richmond, BC
Chabad of Richmond
Mrs. Chanie Baitelman
604-277-6427
admin@chabadrichmond.com

Vancouver, BC
Chabad of Downtown
Mrs. Malky Bitton
778-688-1273
malky@chabadcitycentre.com

Thornhill, ONT
Chabad @ flamingo
Mrs. Faygie Kaplan
905-763-4040
faygie@chabadflamingo.com

Toronto, ONT
Chabad on the Avenue
Mrs. Chana Gansburg
41.546.8770
chana@chabadavenue.com

Montreal, QC
Chabad Queen Mary
Mrs. Simcha Fine
(514) 738-3434
simchafine@gmail.com

Ville s Laurent, QC
Chabad Ville s Laurent
Mrs. Leah Silberstein
514-747-1199
info@chabadvsl.com

DENMARK
Copenhagen
ChabaDanmark
Mrs. Rochel Loewenthal
4533161850
Info@chabad.dk

FRANCE
Marseille, Marseille
Beth Habad Marseille 8ème
Mrs. Vivi (Rivka) Altabé
336 11 600 305
loubavitch13008@gmail.com

GUATEMALA
Guatemala City
Chabad of Guatemala
Mrs. Yael Pelman
7185047344
yaell@hotmail.com

ISRAEL
Jerusalem
Chabad Center of Talbiya
Mrs. Chana Canterman
054-682-3737
chabadtalbiya@gmail.com

RUSSIAN FEDERATION
Moscow, Russia
Chabad of Moscow
Mrs. Rivky Wilansky
7-495-645-50-00
doamitzvah@gmail.com

SWEDEN
Malmö
Chabad Malmo
Mrs. Reizel Kesselman
4640979358
chabadmalmo@gmail.com

SWITZERLAND
Lugano
Chabad Lugano
Rebbetzin Yuti Kantor
+41 91 921 3720
Yuti@jewishlugano.com

Luzern
Chabad of Central Switzerland
Mrs. Rivky Drukman
+41 41 361 1770
Info@ChabadLuzern.com

UNITED KINGDOM
Middx, England
Lubavich foundation
Mrs. Shterna Sudak
02088000022
Shternasudak@yahoo.com

London, London
Brondesbury Park Synagogue
Mrs. Kezi Levin
0208 4510091
kezi@bark.org

Westminster, London
Chabad of Belgravia
Mrs. Chana Kalmenson
+44 758 592 0195
jewishbelgravia@gmail.com

Edgware, Middlesex
Lubavitch of Edgware
Mrs. Sarah Jacobs
0208-905-4141
sarahjacobs@loe.org.uk

URUGUAY
Montevideo, MV
Beit Jabad Uruguay
Rebbetzin Rochel Shemtov
+59827093444
rabino.shemtov@jabad.org.uy

US VIRGIN ISLANDS
S. Thomas
Chabad Lubavitch of the Virgin Islands
Mrs. Henya Federman
3407142770
henya@jewishvirginislands.com

VENEZUELA
Caracas
Hogar Jabad Lubavitch
Mrs. Chani Rosenblum
58-212-2647011
chaniros1@gmail.com

THE JEWISH LEARNING MULTIPLEX

Brought to you by the Rohr Jewish Learning Institute

In fulfillment of the mandate of the Lubavitcher Rebbe, of blessed memory,
whose leadership guides every step of our work,
the mission of the Rohr Jewish Learning Institute is to transform
Jewish life and the greater community through the study of Torah,
connecting each Jew to our shared heritage of Jewish learning.

While our flagship program remains the cornerstone of our organization,
JLI is proud to feature additional divisions catering to specific populations,
in order to meet a wide array of educational needs.

THE ROHR JEWISH LEARNING INSTITUTE,
a subsidiary of *Merkos L'Inyonei Chinuch,*
is the adult education arm of the Chabad-Lubavitch Movement.

TORAH STUDIES

Torah Studies provides a rich and nuanced encounter with the weekly Torah reading.

MYSHIUR
TALMUD LEARNING INITIATIVE

MyShiur courses are designed to assist students in developing the skills needed to study Talmud independently.

SINAI SCHOLARS SOCIETY
IN PARTNERSHIP WITH CHABAD ON CAMPUS

This rigorous fellowship program invites select college students to explore the fundamentals of Judaism.

JLI TEENS
YOUNG SMART JEWISH
IN PARTNERSHIP WITH CTEEN: CHABAD TEEN NETWORK

Jewish teens forge their identity as they engage in Torah study, social interaction, and serious fun.

TORAH
IN PARTNERSHIP WITH CHABAD ON CAMPUS

The rigor and excellence of JLI courses, adapted to the campus environment.

TORAHCafé

TorahCafe.com provides an exclusive selection of top-rated Jewish educational videos.

BRILLIANT LEARNING. NATURALLY.
National JEWISH RETREAT

This yearly event rejuvenates mind, body, and spirit with a powerful synthesis of Jewish learning and community.

ROSHCHODESH
society

The Rosh Chodesh Society gathers Jewish women together once a month for intensive textual study.

JLI ACADEMY
PEDAGOGY · CURRICULUM · MARKETING

Select af[X]liates are invited to partner with peers and noted professionals, as leaders of innovation and excellence.

the LAND & the SPIRIT
Mission to Israel

Mission participants delve into our nation[X] rich past while exploring the Holy Land[X] relevance and meaning today.

NOTES

NOTES

NOTES